THE POLITICS OF ABORTION IN THE UNITED STATES AND CANADA

■ Comparative Politics Series

Gregory S. Mahler, Editor

COMPARATIVE
POLITICS
SERIES

T199

THE POLITICS OF ABORTION IN THE UNITED STATES AND CANADA

A Comparative Study

Raymond Tatalovich

M.E. Sharpe
Armonk, New York
London, England

Library of Congress Cataloging-in-Publication Data

Tatalovich, Raymond.
The politics of abortion in the United States and Canada :
a comparative study / by Raymond Tatalovich.
p.   cm. — (Comparative politics)
Includes bibliographical references and index.
ISBN 1-56324-417-9 (c). — ISBN 1-56324-418-7 (p)
1. Abortion—Political aspects—United States.
2. Abortion—Political aspects—Canada.
3. Abortion—Government policy—United States.
4. Abortion—Government policy—Canada.
5. Pro-choice movement—United States.
6. Pro-choice movement—Canada.
7. Pro-life movement—United States.
8. Pro-life movement—Canada.
I. Title.
II. Series: Comparative politics (Armonk, N.Y.)
HQ767.5.U5T38
1996
363.4′6′0973—dc20
96–23923
CIP

Printed in the United States of America

The paper used in this publication meets the minimum requirements of
American National Standard for Information Sciences—
Permanence of Paper for Printed Library Materials,
ANSI Z 39.48-1984.

∞

BM (c)   10   9   8   7   6   5   4   3   2   1
BM (p)   10   9   8   7   6   5   4   3   2   1

To Mother,
Her Compassion, Her Honor, Her Love

Ray

Contents

List of Tables

Acknowledgments

Friends and colleagues, some current and some past, from both sides of the forty-ninth parallel were instrumental in my ability to produce this study. Foremost I acknowledge one of the premier scholars of Canadian abortion politics, Professor F.L. Morton, of the University of Calgary, who provided an extraordinarily detailed review of my manuscript for M.E. Sharpe. An intellectual debt also is owed to Professor T. Alexander Smith, of the University of Tennessee. Not only do I rely heavily on his important work *The Comparative Policy Process* (1975) in laying out the process hypotheses I test, but Alex also agreed to review my introductory and concluding chapters. My meeting Professor Sharon L. Sutherland, of Carleton University, at a conference in Mexico City was fortuitous indeed, because she has the reputation of being a keen observer of Canadian bureaucratic politics. She graciously offered me her interpretations over the course of this project and in addition referred me to her personal contacts within the Canadian government. Thanks, Sharon, and you too, Warren. In Mexico City I also met Professor Robert J. Jackson and his wife and coauthor, Doreen; their major textbook on Canadian government and politics was a ready reference by my side.

I integrated into this work research on abortion in Canada that I coauthored elsewhere with Byron W. Daynes, of Brigham Young University, E. Marvin Overby, of the University of Mississippi, and Donley T. Studlar, of West Virginia University. Allow me to extend a special thank-you to Routledge for giving me permission to reprint tables 7.1 and 7.2, which appeared in Donley T. Studlar and Raymond Tatalovich, "Abortion Policy in the United States and Canada: Do Institutions Matter?" in Marianne Githens and Dorothy McBride Stetson, eds., *Abortion Politics: Public*

Policy in Cross Cultural Perspective (New York: Routledge, 1996). I was also the sole author or a coauthor of conference papers based upon my preliminary research for various chapters: "Judicial Activism, Legal Abortion, and Policy Outcomes: Comparing the U.S. and Canadian Experiences" was presented at the 1992 annual meeting of the American Political Science Association; "Federalism and the Delivery of Abortion Services: Comparing the U.S. and Canada" was presented at the 1993 annual meeting of the Western Political Science Association; "Patterns of Abortion Voting in the Canadian House of Commons" was presented at the 1993 annual meeting of the Canadian Political Science Association; "Moral Conflict, Post-Materialism, and the Mobilization of Interests: Abortion Politics in Canada and the United States" was presented at the 1995 annual meeting of the Canadian Political Science Association; and "Church and Abortion in the United States and Canada: Patterns of Rhetoric and Mobilization" was presented at the 1995 annual meeting of the Society for the Scientific Study of Religion.

What started this book was a focused research project on abortion implementation in Canada, supported under the 1991–1992 Faculty Research Grant Program of the Government of Canada, and which stimulated me to think about doing a more comprehensive and comparative case study. What enabled me to finish the project, without further delays, was a grant of academic leave with pay from Loyola University of Chicago during the fall 1995 semester. Loyola University of Chicago also awarded me a Small Research Grant to subsidize a third research trip to Ottawa in August 1995, when I visited the Canadian Bar Association, the Canadian Medical Association, and the National Library of Canada and collected other research odds and ends.

Two more individuals were significant others for me because they "kept the faith" despite my slowed progress on this manuscript. In 1992 Professor Gregory Mahler, of the University of Mississippi, invited me to include this cross-cultural analysis in his Comparative Politics Series for M.E. Sharpe. And my former classmate at the University of Chicago, Patricia A. Kolb, editor extraordinaire at M.E. Sharpe, saw this project through to a successful completion. Thanks, Greg and Pat, for being there when I needed you.

Finally, Sir Frederic and Lady Beatrice, our basset hounds, deserve some gratitude of sorts. It's not easy petting two bassets while typing at your personal computer, which partly may explain my missed deadlines, but they insisted, so I had to learn that technique. And my love to you, Anne, the one constant in my life.

THE POLITICS OF
ABORTION IN THE
UNITED STATES
AND CANADA

Introduction

Cross-Cultural Research on Abortion

The development of abortion policy in Canada and the United States offers a unique opportunity for cross-cultural research. Though Canada is a constitutional monarchy and the United States is a democratic republic, both were originally founded as English colonies. The Americans openly rebelled against British authority in the late eighteenth century, created a constitution with great potential for a national government, but later added the Bill of Rights, which circumscribed national authority and reflected the strength of libertarian values. Canada did not formally separate from the English Commonwealth until the mid-twentieth century, though the queen of England "continues to be Canada's monarch" (Jackson and Jackson 1994, 186), and only recently—in 1982—did the Constitution Act establish the Charter of Rights and Freedoms as part of Canada's fundamental law.

Both governments are federal systems, and the recent narrow defeat of a separatist referendum in Quebec recalls to mind the bloody civil war that erupted when southern states seceded from the United States. Indeed, the linguistic rivalries between francophone Quebec and the rest of English-speaking Canada overlie more fundamental sovereignty issues about provincial self-government, notably a "special status" for Quebec, which may become more volatile than the racial animosities between whites and African-Americans in the United States. So quite different political consequences may result from the fractures in the Canadian polity.

The end of the Civil War saw a sustained nationalization of American politics as the federal government gained power at the expense of states' rights and, moreover, when the Supreme Court came to exercise a policy-making role over states through its "incorporation" of the Bill of Rights. In Canada, however, the provinces always have enjoyed substantial autonomy from the central government, but today the Supreme Court of Canada may be especially reluctant to raise legal objections against Quebec legislation in order to avoid a constitutional confrontation. Prior to 1982 the Supreme Court of Canada took a restrained approach to judicial review, though after the Charter of Rights and Freedoms was established, the Canadian Supreme Court began to imitate the U.S. Supreme Court by rendering decisions that defended unpopular minorities and alternative lifestyles (Morton and Knopff 1992).

On the other hand, Canada is a parliamentary government, which allows for greater decision-making capacity than the U.S. system of "separated institutions sharing power," as the U.S. separation-of-powers arrangement is commonly characterized. Further bolstering the governing potential of its parliamentary arrangement is Canada's multiparty system, in which the Social Democratic, Liberal, Progressive Conservative, and now Reform parties are more ideological and cohesive than their weak counterparts—Democrats and Republicans—in the United States.

Abortion Studies

In both countries changes in abortion policy were achieved at the national level, but implementation rests with subnational authorities—the states and provinces. There are excellent studies of abortion politics—and policy—by political scientists in Canada and the United States, but none offers a *comparative* analysis of both countries from common vantage points. While I will draw from existing literature, this discussion wherever possible will be driven by empirical data, case studies, and statistical analysis. The fundamental question underlying this comparative analysis of abortion politics, therefore, is whether the policy-making dynamics in Canada are similar to those in the United States, and if not, then how specifically they differ. While Canada is culturally and economically close to the United States, its parliamentary system is more analogous to similar regimes on the Continent.

In this volume, I compare the policy-making process in the United States and Canada, focusing on the period that followed a major policy change toward liberalized access to abortion as well as the subsequent period, which promises even greater access in Canada but more restrictive policies in the United States. The first phase began in Canada in 1969, when the availability of abortion was liberalized as part of an omnibus bill on health services passed by the House of Commons. In the United States it was demarcated by the *Roe v. Wade* decision of 1973. The second phase came one year apart in both countries during the late 1980s. In Canada, it was the Supreme Court ruling in *Morgentaler v. The Queen* (1988), which proclaimed the 1969 law unconstitutional, leaving Canada without a statute governing abortion. In the United States it was triggered by another Supreme Court case, *Webster v. Reproductive Health Services* (1989), which gave states more latitude to regulate abortions.

While research on abortion policy in the United States emphasizes national governing institutions, especially the courts (Craig and O'Brien 1993; Rubin 1987), there has been comparative research on the making and implementation of state abortion policy (Wetstein 1996; Segers and Byrnes 1995; Goggin 1993). In Canada, to the contrary, almost all case studies of the abortion controversy have focused on the courts and central governmental authorities (Brodie, Gavigan, and Jenson 1992; Morton 1992). Moreover, to date there has been only a limited number of comparative, cross-cultural abortion studies (Githens and Stetson 1996; Jelen and Chandler 1994; Henshaw 1994; Glendon 1987; Lovenduski and Outshoorn 1986; Schwartz 1981; Field 1979), and most give scant if any attention to Canada, so there is need for more comparative research on abortion policy. To guide this analysis, and ultimately to offer some meaningful conclusions, the empirical data and case studies are organized so that three types of hypotheses—systemic, process-oriented, and abortion-specific—may be addressed.

Research Hypotheses

Systemic

The systemic hypotheses focus on regime attributes as they are impacted by the abortion controversy. The first systemic hypothesis is that a legislative policy (Canada) would facilitate consensus building and generate more compliance than a judicial decree (United States). Jelen (1994, 188) drew that distinction in his study of public opinion in both these countries: "Legislatures are thought to be more responsive to public opinion and are permitted to fashion compromises not available to courts." Decision making by a legislature is likely to reflect the prevailing political climate of the country and to seek some kind of policy consensus among contending interests, and thus would arouse less controversy than a decision rendered by an unelected judiciary. This is the crux of Glendon's (1987) complaint that the focus on abortion "rights" as enforced by a judicial decree is more likely to lead to a political backlash. She claims that a widely held but "erroneous" belief "is that the present legal situation in the United States with respect to abortion is not particularly unusual" because "the experience of other societies that have been just as deeply divided as ours, if not more so, on the abortion question, shows that when the legislative process is allowed to operate, *political* compromise is not only possible but typical" (Glendon 1987, 40). Thus:

> *Hypothesis S1:* An abortion policy enacted by an elected parliament will more quickly and fully generate political consensus than one promulgated by an unelected Supreme Court.

Schwartz (1981) included abortion as well as Prohibition and marijuana as three case studies of "politicized moral causes" in her comparative study of the United States and Canada. She noted that "a striking characteristic of American life is the ease with which moral causes are translated into political issues" (p. 65) and thus hypothesized that "in other countries, even when the same moral issues arise, they will be treated more cooly, with less emotional fervor. There will be less polarization among affected interests, and the issues will not play a prominent role in the political sphere" (p. 67). She also observed that "Canadians were reluctant to present their case through the medium of party politics, in contrast to American actions" and, furthermore, "the relation between a parliamentary system and party discipline plays a role in how moral causes are treated" (p. 84). As she elaborated:

> These properties of government mean that there is less to fear in Canada from single-issue moral campaigns. This is not to suggest that some legislators may not suffer electoral defeat because of concerted efforts to overcome them, but it is probably less likely than in the United States, and in general, less disruptive. More to lose also means more to win: The attraction of individual legislators to single issues that will bring them attention is more of an American phenomenon. (Schwartz 1981, 84)

Looking back on the post-1969 period, the time frame for Schwartz's observations, her diagnosis begs the question of why the abortion controversy "burned out" in Canada and did not escalate to higher levels of political conflict. Part of the answer may be that the Canadian public is more deferential to political elites, whereas a populist strain among Americans is strong enough to allow attacks on the political establishment, as was illustrated by McCarthyism during the 1950s (Shils 1956). Says Lipset (1990, 15): "The greater sense of restraint in Canada and other elitist democracies is seen as inhibiting the kind of mass conformist outbursts that have occurred south of the border."

Likely a stronger explanation is institutional rather than cultural. In essence, the Canadian parliamentary system, with its disciplined single-party majority, was better able to control agenda setting and policy formation than was the case in the United States. The U.S. separation-of-powers system and bicameral legislature (the Canadian Senate is not an equal of the House of Commons) coupled with a weak two-party system means that there are many more access points to the policy-making process in the United States as compared to Canada. To influence policy under a parliamentary regime, interest groups normally must work *with* the government and its governing party. But in the United States interest groups may try to influence the White House, either legislative chamber, or the majority and minority parties, and may even pressure agencies of the executive branch. Indeed, one can speculate that single-issue groups are more than a match for the Republicans and Democrats, so much so that our major political parties may be subject to "capture" by pro-life or pro-choice forces. "As the United States entered the decade of the 1990s," observed Goggin (1993, 1), "battles over abortion were raging in all branches and at all levels of government." Therefore:

> *Hypothesis S2:* Given the structural differences between a separation-of-powers system of government and a parliamentary one, the institutional scope of conflict over moral conflict will be greater in the United States than in Canada.

Another systemic hypothesis pertains to federalism. While both countries are federal systems, the division of authority between central government and subnational governments is expected to have greater impact in Canada, since its federation has moved toward greater decentralization, whereas federalism in the United States has, if anything, been going in the opposite direction, toward centralization (Riker 1964; Gibbins 1982; Brown-John 1989). There is considerable variation in availability of abortion services among the U.S. states and the Canadian provinces, though the provinces of Canada are generally considered more autonomous vis-à-vis the central government than are the states in the United States. It is also noteworthy that the U.S. Supreme Court in 1973 effectively "nationalized" policy on abortion and subsequently disallowed much policy discretion by the states, whereas not until 1988 did the Supreme Court of Canada begin to mandate national standards for abortion services.

Observations made almost thirty years ago about the fragile nature of the Canadian federation seem even more relevant today. In his classic work on federalism, Riker (1964, 112) argued that "Canadian federalism is considerably less centralized in tone than is federalism in the United States and the basic reason for this difference is doubtless the existence of a variety of non-federal loyalties." Nearly two decades later another observer, a Canadian (Gibbins 1982), confirmed that its federalism was becoming more decentralized while the opposite movement was occurring in the United States. Indeed, even after several years of Republican administrations, federalism in the United States is not nearly as decentralized as its Canadian counterpart (Brown-John 1989).

Garreau's (1981) contention that there are several "nations" in North America is not without some foundation, particularly with respect to religious subcultures. Both countries have sizable populations of religious groups who would be expected to be less supportive of abortion: Catholics in Quebec and Ontario, fundamentalist Protestants in the western provinces of Canada, and southern fundamentalists and northern Catholics in the United States. Thus, I anticipate that the differential effects of federalism on abortion policy making and implementation would be greater in Canada.

> *Hypothesis S3:* Federalism allows greater provincial and regional differences in the implementation of abortion policy in Canada as compared to state and regional variations in the United States.

The final systemic hypothesis focuses on the thorny question of whether political culture exists, and if so, what its impact will be. Canada, like the United States, was an English colony, in which the development of legal structures was influenced by the English common-law tradition. Yet observers (Merelman 1991; Gans 1988) point out key differences in the political cultures of these two nations. According to Lipset (1990, 212), "America reflects the influence of its classically liberal, Whig, individualistic, antistatist, populist, ideological origins," whereas Canadians "can still be seen as Tory-mercantilist, group-oriented, statist, deferential to authority—a 'socialist monarchy,' to use Robertson Davies' phrase." One manifestation, often cited, of marked differences in political ethos is the Canadian universal health care system (Marmor 1991), which is fundamentally unlike the American system of privately insured fee-for-service medicine. Even the Clinton health care reforms of 1993 had rejected the single-payer concept that underlies the Canadian system. In short, if citizens in the United States are more suspicious of governmental authority and adhere more closely to nineteenth-century liberalism than Canada, then:

> *Hypothesis S4:* The more collectivist political ethos of Canada suggests more support for legalized abortion and more deference to political elites than would be the case in the United States.

Despite the claims of Gans, Merelman, and Lipset that the political cultures of the United States and Canada are quite different, solid evidence to support that interpretation is scarce. Thus this investigation will continue a line of research that attempts to conceptualize, operationalize, and validate empirically the argument that the political ethos of the United States is dissimilar to Canada's (see Pierce, Steger, Steel, and Lovrich 1992).

Process

The hypotheses about the policy-making process are extrapolated from the literature on moral conflict, specifically two volumes. One is *Social Regulatory Policy: Moral Conflicts in American Politics* (Tatalovich and Daynes 1988). Its conclusion offers fourteen propositions about which variables are most important to how and why such conflicts are processed in our separation-of-powers system of government. The second, an earlier work by T. Alexander Smith entitled *The Comparative Policy Process* (1975), modified the framework of analysis used by Theodore J. Lowi (1964) to include the new category of emotive-symbolic policy. As the Smith case studies were based on parliamentary systems, his hypotheses consider how those kinds of regime process issues involving intense conflict over divergent values and morality.

Smith (1975, 90) defined emotive-symbolic policies as those that "generate emotional support for deeply held values . . . [and] the values sought are essentially noneconomic." His concept was extended to abortion in the United States by Tatalovich and Daynes (1981a) and in Europe by Lovenduski and Outshoorn (1986). Analysis of case studies across North America and Europe suggested to Smith that emotive-symbolic policy making is characterized by (1) government refusal to take a stand, (2) breakdowns in party discipline, (3) backbench leadership, and (4) procedural unorthodoxy (Smith 1975, 92). Close examination of six episodes of moral conflict in the United States (Tatalovich and Daynes 1988) indicates, as Smith assumed, that they are disputes not over economic interests but over social norms and moral values. Beyond that, the American policy process is distinguished by single-issue groups that politicize moral conflicts as zero-sum games and judicial activism whereby a national policy is mandated by "incorporation" doctrine. These six propositions can be reconciled as five hypotheses that ought to be applicable to both Canada and the United States.

First, the failure of government leadership means that the time-honored tradition of collective responsibility in parliamentary regimes is avoided. One method that has been used to displace conflict over abortion is a call for a national referendum in which a plebiscite can decide the issue (Millns and Thompson 1994; Girvin 1994). Popular referenda have been used in a number of states to resolve such questions as whether to fully legalize abortion, as in Washington State (Hanna 1995) and Maryland (Carney 1995), or to restrict its funding. As to why governments avoid such issues, Smith (1975, 92) gives three reasons, namely "that groups of relatively equal strength within the government orbit are threatening the cohesiveness of the coalition; that the government is almost bound to alienate a significant portion of the public by making its views known; or that constituency pressures are so powerful upon backbenchers as to override leadership or party caucus pressures."

There are two other ways of abdicating responsibility over moral conflicts at the national level. In federal systems, such as the United States and Canada, the government might urge that a policy be established allowing the states or provinces to retain jurisdiction over the issue. In the United States, in fact, for nearly two centuries the states controlled abortion policy through their "police powers" to regulate public order, health, and morality. Returning a controversial policy to subnational political elites not only removes it from the national political agenda but also allows policy diversity reflecting majority opinion within each province or state.

The other method of avoiding responsibility is to defer the issue to the courts, and many observers argued that the U.S. Supreme Court became involved with a host of moral conflicts, beginning with its school desegregation decision in *Brown v. Board of Education* (1954), precisely because the president and Congress were not inclined to take a firm stand. Indeed, liberal constitutional scholars have developed a rationale to defend the judiciary's taking a "principled" stand on moral conflicts when the popular branches of government, fearing electoral reprisals, have refused to act.

In the United States abortion was legalized by the landmark *Roe v. Wade* decision of the Supreme Court in 1973, but in virtually all parliamentary regimes the method of enacting liberalized abortion policies was by statute (Glendon 1987). That was also true for Canada's reformed abortion law of 1969, though the adoption in 1982 of the Canadian Charter of Rights and Freedoms ultimately led to its nullification by the Supreme Court of Canada in its 1988 *Morgentaler* ruling. Another instance was Germany, whose constitutional court can invalidate legislation; there the abortion dispute found its way to the highest court in 1975 (Mezey 1983) and again in 1993 (Czarnowski 1994).

A national referendum or plebiscite may be the preferred way for the government in a parliamentary and unified (nonfederal) system to escape policy responsibility, but appeals to states' rights and especially abdication to judicial authority are other techniques available to the prime minister of Canada or the president of the United States. In sum, Tatalovich and Daynes (1988) find judicial activism on a range of moral conflicts, not simply because advocates seek redress before the courts but because the elected branches do not relish having those issues on the legislative agenda. From this perspective, Smith's (1975) conception of emotive-symbolic policy making can accommodate judicial activism as an antidote to political inertia.

In the U.S. separation-of-powers system, the legislative and executive branches are not bound together by a similar kind of collective responsibility; to the contrary, "divided government" has most often characterized the U.S. political system in the postwar era. To apply Smith's logic to the American regime suggests that during periods of "unified government," when the same party holds the majority in Congress as well as the White House, there would be resistance by the White House to promoting a legislative agenda that might arouse constituency groups or serve to fracture its political coalition. On the other hand, under the "normal" conditions of divided government, which have characterized the United States in recent decades, there are political incentives to exploit moral conflicts for electoral advantages. Thus:

> *Hypothesis P1:* In a parliamentary regime, such as that of Canada, or under conditions of unified government in the United States, there is a tendency for the government to equivocate and not promote moral causes in its formal legislative agenda.

Second, says Smith (1975, 92) a "refusal by backbenchers to accept the whip obviously implies strong dissension" within majority party ranks, which explains why the government failed to take a stand in the first place. In parliamentary regimes where the governing party sustains cohesion at 90 percent and above, a serious threat to party unity when the government's program is under consideration is effectively a vote of no confidence and, as such, can force the leadership to schedule new elections. To avoid that political embarrassment, the government would be well advised not to promote such measures as its legislative program.

In the Congress, the Democratic caucus can designate a roll call as a so-called party vote and thus force more accountability from the rank-and-file membership, but that occurs relatively infrequently. Normally a party vote occurs when 51 percent of Democrats oppose 51 percent of Republicans, meaning that sizable numbers of partisans regularly dissent from the party position on a host of issues. To extend Smith's thinking to the congressional arena, we anticipate that party leaders in Congress, when dealing with moral conflicts, would not attempt to whip the vote by having the caucus designate a particular roll call to be a party vote or by publicly defining an upcoming vote as a litmus test of party loyalty. Thus:

> *Hypothesis P2:* On moral conflicts such as abortion, the legislative leadership will not attempt to whip the vote by defining roll calls as a test of membership loyalty to their political party.

Third, given the failure of governments to tackle moral conflicts head-on and the reluctance of legislative leaders to muster party discipline, the consequence is that "backbench leadership arises when ordinary legislators become de facto leaders attempting to resolve such conflicts" (Smith 1975, 92). From time to time "mavericks" are elected to Congress who promote socially divisive issues that their colleagues ignore. Some members of Congress have regularly championed moral causes, one being Senator Jesse Helms (R-North Carolina), who supports school prayer and rails against homosexuality, pornography, and abortion. And nobody personifies pro-life militancy like Representative Henry Hyde (R-Illinois). In parliamentary regimes the "Private Members' Bill" is a device to allow backbenchers to sponsor legislation without the endorsement of the government. In Canada, says Thorne (1990, 21–22), "members of the Opposition and back-benchers of the majority party have found in these Bills one of the few available means of self-expression." As expected, they deal with

> moral or contentious issues which governments wish to avoid. Capital punishment, the rights of the unborn, and making Canada a nuclear-free zone were each the subject of at least one Bill in the eighties. Human rights, as in Pat Carney's 1980 Act to Prohibit Discrimination on the Grounds of Sexual Orientation, and freedom of information, such as Bill C-254, which sought access to certain records concerning Defence, are other frequent concerns. (Thorne, 1990, 22)

It is anticipated that members of Parliament or Congress who introduce legislation on moral conflicts, who floor-manage those bills, and who lead the legislative debate on the floor will be legislators who are not (floor) leaders of the majority party. Thus:

> *Hypothesis P3:* On moral conflicts, legislators who propose legislation, floor-manage the bills, and carry the parliamentary debate will be rank-and-file members of the majority party or members of the minority party, but not leaders of the majority party in the legislature.

Fourth, by "procedural unorthodoxy" Smith (1975, 92) means a parliamentary maneuver that "violates procedural norms," such as the discharge petition to force a committee of the House of Representatives to release a bill for consideration, or a filibuster in the Senate to prevent action, or the guillotine and Early Day Motion (EDM) in Great Britain and closure in Canada to prevent lengthy debate. The free vote also can be viewed in this manner. In Great Britain, government "neutrality" on questions regarding abortion, capital punishment, homosexuality, Sunday entertainment, and divorce effectively made those free votes (Moyser 1979). Hibbing and Marsh (1987), Marsh and Read (1988), and Read, Marsh, and Richards (1994) analyzed unwhipped or free votes on abortion, capital punishment, and homosexuality precisely because these rare occasions, when MPs are not subject to party discipline, permit researchers to determine what personal and constituency factors most strongly affect the decision-making process.

Unwhipped voting on moral conflicts exposes the fault lines in the majority party because questions such as abortion, gay rights, and the death penalty are crosscutting issues that do not reflect economic class. If anything, there is a reverse class cleavage to moral conflict in many instances, because elites or upper socioeconomic status (SES) groups are more tolerant than the masses or lower SES groups. This tendency, not limited to the United States, is what Seymour Lipset (1963, 92) labeled "working class authoritarianism"; Skerry (1978) also observed that less affluent people opposed government funding of abortions more than the affluent. In Canada, Morton and Knopff (1992) contend that a "Court Party" has emerged within the intelligentsia (academics, members of the media, people in the legal profession) to promote a postmaterialist agenda that legitimizes a variety of lifestyles, and they have utilized a litigation strategy precisely because such controversial issues would be troublesome for politicians. Thus:

> *Hypothesis P4:* Moral conflicts fracture the unity of the majority party in the legislature because such issues are crosscutting and do not reinforce economic class cleavages that normally divided political parties of the left from the right.

A caveat to hypothesis P4 is required because, on occasion, economic cleavages that divide major parties can overlap the fault lines that divide population groups on social regulatory or emotive-symbolic issues. The debate over redesigning the Canadian flag is one instance that Smith (1975, 112–22) calls to mind. In trying to fashion a flag that accommodated both French-speaking Quebec and the English-speaking provinces, the dispute divided the majority Liberal Party (dominant in Quebec Province) from the Progressive Conservatives, whose strength was located across the rest of Canada. However, these episodes—when economic and "moral" disputes reflect similar socioeconomic cleavages—are the exceptions that prove the rule.

A final proposition from Tatalovich and Daynes (1988, 211), that "grassroots activism is linked to single-issue groups where moral conflict is involved," was based on case studies of school prayer, pornography, crime, affirmative action, gun control, and abortion. Elsewhere, after an exhaustive review of group mobilization over abortion, Tatalovich and Daynes (1993, 62) concluded that "the unique attribute of moral conflict is the highly visible role played by single-issue groups, particularly by those who defend traditional norms," and moreover, "coalition-building will be more extensive among groups advocating social change." Animal rights activists also are organized as single-issue groups that span the ideological spectrum (Jasper and Nelkin 1992, 178). The logic of pluralism implies that moral conflicts cannot envelop the organizational life of a country—meaning that there are boundaries to the scope of social conflict—because the greatest number of organizations are founded to defend the economic interests of their members. Olson (1969, 160–61) says that the exceptions are philanthropic organizations, religious lobbies, and people committed to "lost causes." Umbrella ("peak") associations, such as the AFL-CIO, the United States Chamber of Commerce, and trade associations, which represent sectors of the economy, would not embrace moral causes that might fracture their internal unity and jeopardize their political effectiveness on other issues. Therefore:

> *Hypothesis P5:* Single-issue groups are the dominant form of political mobilization on moral conflicts, especially among defenders of the status quo, whereas coalition building is more extensive among advocates of social change, though it generally will not extend to economic interests.

Abortion-Specific

The final four hypotheses are gleaned from specific observations about why abortion specifically might impact the United States and Canada in different ways. The doctrine of parliamentary supremacy, which Jackson and Jackson (1994, 179) call "a basic premise of parliamentary democracy," means that legislatures "in theory, repeal or modify any principle set out in common law that applies to their jurisdiction." Mildred Schwartz subscribed to that commonly held view and argued that a "fundamental difference" between the two regimes was that the legislative branch was dominant in Canada whereas the federal judiciary was a greater force in the United

States. Therefore, "when moral interests are successful in taking their case to the Constitution (as they were with prohibition and threaten to do again with abortion), they have the means of incorporating their view of conduct into the core of political values. The drama of this symbolism is absent from Canada" (Schwartz 1981, 85). However, that scenario may be less applicable today, following adoption of the Charter of Rights and Freedoms, since the Supreme Court of Canada has adopted a more activist approach to defend individuals from the state (Morton and Knopff 1992).

Rights rhetoric can polarize a society, just like political ideology or religious dogma, and moral conflicts, by definition, are zero-sum games. Ted Jelen claims that for Canada (but more so for the United States, because abortion couples religious truths with the rhetoric of legal rights), "both of these forces carry the implicit threat of democratic incivility" (Jelen 1994, 193). While some observers believe that Canadian constitutional law is becoming more like that of the United States, there seems little doubt that rights-based jurisprudence has dominated public law in the United States for a long time. Thus:

> *Hypothesis A1:* The predominance of a rights-based jurisprudence in the United States means that the abortion controversy will be more politicized there compared to Canada.

We might also expect a difference between the United States and Canada in the scope of *social* conflict, given the assumption that voluntary associations are more deeply embedded in the American social fabric, with the result that a greater potential for political mobilization exists in the United States. Others have observed (Merelman 1991; Presthus 1973) that Canadian politics is less pluralistic than political combat in the United States. And the more collectivist and deferential political culture of Canada would militate against factionalism. A study of environmental activists led Pierce, Steger, Steel, and Lovrich (1992, 187) to conclude that "while Canadians may well have a more positive view of interest groups than Americans do generally, the American institutional setting produces a higher level of policy process participation by interest groups." If so, then:

> *Hypothesis A2:* The scope of social conflict—meaning the number, variety, and type of interest groups mobilized for political combat— will be greater in the United States than in Canada.

But political activism spans a continuum between conventional acts, such as voting or writing one's representative, and unconventional means, including demonstrations, boycotts, and direct-action tactics—even violence. Those who become involved in moral conflicts are motivated by principle, morality, or the well-being of others, and rarely by profits. Social scientists are reconsidering altruism as a motivator for political behavior, one grounded not in self-interest but in a shared "perception of themselves as one with all humankind" (Monroe, Barton, and Klingemann 1991, 335). Apparently unconventional political activities are "both more approved and more common" in the United States than in Britain and elsewhere on the Continent (Merelman 1991, 178); for Canada, Lipset (1990, 96) reports only 73 protest demonstrations during the 1948–1982 period as compared to 3,350 in the United States. Since individualist forms of political activism are qualitatively different from social conflict among organized interests, and given the rise of extremist tactics by segments of the pro-life movement in recent years, the following proposition seems warranted:

> *Hypothesis A3:* Direct-action tactics and unconventional political behavior will be more common among pro-life activists in the United States than in Canada, whereas pro-choice activists are less likely to engage in such activities in both countries.

Finally, as a related dimension, a consideration may be the strength of a postmaterialist ethic in postindustrial societies. It has been argued (Inglehart 1990) that a "culture shift" from materialistic values to such values as belonging and self-actualization will occur. In this social milieu, economic conflicts are displaced by issues such as civil rights, environmental protection, alternative lifestyles, and peace. That scenario of the postindustrial era has been criticized by those who argue that a new division of opinion will emerge, between "the New Left issue agenda, including liberalizing abortion, women's lib[eration], gay rights and other new morality issues" and "the New Right issue agenda, which includes right-to-life, anti–women's lib[eration], creationism, antipornography, and support for traditional moral and religious values" (Flanagan 1987, 1306). All these examples are moral conflicts, but the question is whether conflicts associated with postmaterialism will be greater in the United States or in Canada.

On overall "human development indicators" collected by the United Nations Development Programme (1994, 104, 185, 194–95) Canada ranks first and the United States eighth, but these include a variety of social indices such as crime rates, where the American experience is worse than that of every other Western industrialized nation. On some purely economic measures, however, the United States is generally ahead of Canada—higher per capita gross national product, lower unemployment (particularly chronic unemployment)—and in a statistic that may be particularly relevant, *twice* as many Canadians belong to unions (35 percent) as compared to Americans (17 percent). With regard to the environment—probably the purest example of a postmaterialist issue—Canada has much higher levels of sulfur and nitrogen emissions per capita compared to the United States. While it seems counterintuitive to believe that postmaterialist attitudes can flow from objective conditions that reflect a less secure economic base, nonetheless Pierce, Steger, Steel, and Lovrich (1992, 44) reported that more environmental activists in Ontario held postmaterialist values than those living in the state of Michigan. So it is a close call based on the objective measures. If we assume that the United States is arguably more affluent and economically advanced—even marginally—than Canada, then:

> *Hypothesis A4:* The debate over abortion should be moralistic and reflect a clash of cultures more in the United States than in Canada, because the United States is a more postindustrial society and manifests stronger postmaterial values.

Organization of This Book

Chapter 1 previews the abortion politics in both nations, recalling 1950s and 1960s writings on abortion, identifying the cast of characters who were involved in reforming antiabortion laws, and explaining how ultimately "therapeutic" abortions became codified as the law of Canada and the United States. Case studies will highlight the role of organized medicine and the legal establishment in each country. This background information offers a beginning assessment for hypothesis S1, on consensus building, and Hypothesis A1, on how rights-based rhetoric transformed the abortion debate.

Chapter 2 discusses the reasoning in *Roe v. Wade* (1973) and its progeny of Supreme Court cases, showing how the decision in *Webster v. Reproductive Health Services* (1989) marked a major departure in abortion jurisprudence. No Western nation, including Canada, so fully constitutionalized abortion rights as did *Roe*, and even the Canadian Supreme Court's rulings in its trilogy of abortion cases in 1988–1989 reflected more judicial restraint than full-blown activism. The material in this chapter will be used to assess directly hypothesis A1, on rights-based constitutionalism, as well as hypothesis S2, on the degree of institutional conflict in the Canadian and American political regimes.

Chapter 3 describes various efforts by Congress to limit the impact of *Roe* and the failed attempt of Parliament to recriminalize abortion in Canada following the Supreme Court ruling in *Morgentaler v. The Queen* (1988), which invalidated the existing 1969 Criminal Code. Who are the pro-life and pro-choice leaders in Parliament and Congress? What factors influence how members of the House of Representatives or Senate and the House of Commons vote on abortion legislation? The bulk of this material is directed to answering four of the process hypotheses, P1 on sponsorship of abortion bills, P2 on legislative leadership, P3 on backbencher activism, and P4 on disunity within the governing party.

Chapter 4 gives the parameters of public opinion on abortion in Canada and the United States and proceeds to delineate the scope of conflict on abortion by examining the kinds of interest groups that compose the pro-life lobby and the pro-choice coalition. Similarities and differences are pointed out and key organizational actors are identified, with particular attention given to the role of feminism and organized religion. Then the degree of unconventional political activism by pro-lifers is assessed. Ultimately I draw on this extensive discussion to evaluate hypothesis P5, on single-issue groups, hypothesis A2, with respect to social conflict, and hypothesis A3, related to direct-action tactics.

Chapter 5 assesses whether polarization on abortion is a top-down or bottom-up agitation by looking at electoral constraints on policy making. The coverage is asymmetrical because the 1973 *Roe* decision catapulted the abortion issue into the U.S. political arena, making it a potential influence on six presidential elections, the Republican and Democratic platforms, the views of the parties' nominees, and presidential campaign rhetoric. In contrast, only the 1988 and 1993 Canadian elections could have been influenced by the (then pending) judicial proceedings on abortion, so a less richly developed portrait of abortion politics in Canada must be presented. Since the electoral process reflects upheavals in society, these dynamics have bearing on hypothesis S1, regarding legislative consensus building, on S2 to the degree that elections may heighten institutional conflict between branches of government, and generally on A2 as an indication of how extensive the scope of social conflict over abortion is.

Chapter 6 focuses on the executive branch and the activities of national agencies that deal with abortion policy. Departments and ministries with responsibility for abortion policies are examined. Have the executive and legislative branches sought to micromanage abortion policy implementation? And have pro-life or pro-choice lobbyists tried to influence appointees to abortion-sensitive positions in the permanent government? Here again there is abundant testimony that abortion has politicized the workings of the permanent government in the United States, but has the reputation of the Canadian central bureaucracy for "neutral competence" been similarly compromised? As a reality check, the abortion-related activities of the quasi-governmental National Action Committee on the Status of Women will be evaluated because it operated during the periods of Liberal, then Progressive Conservative, and then Liberal rule.

The pro-life agenda of the Reagan administration was sustained by the Bush administration, but the Clinton administration reversed many of those antiabortion policies. Abortion policy in Canada involved both sides of the political spectrum. The 1969 reform law was passed under Liberal prime minister Pierre Elliot Trudeau while the 1988 *Morgentaler* case, which nullified that statute, occurred under Conservative prime minister Brian Mulroney. Did the Trudeau government or Mulroney government seek to politicize abortion policy? The findings of this analysis have direct bearing on hypothesis P1, which questions the degree to which moral causes are politicized by the government, and are relevant to the scope of institutional conflict (S2) between popularly elected and nonelected policymakers.

Chapter 7 examines abortion implementation and the roles played by subnational public authorities and private health care decision makers to assess how fully abortion services have been provided. In both countries access to abortion providers may be related to region, urbanism, and type of hospital, and to the presence of clinic facilities. Since the Canadian reformed abortion law was enacted in 1969 and *Roe v. Wade* was decided four years later, we can measure the degree of compliance or noncompliance with the law over two decades. These statistical data permit a direct test of hypothesis S3, which implies policy variability due to federalism, and hypothesis S4, which assumes that the Canadian collectivist ethos will yield consequences different from those of the individualistic political culture of the United States.

The findings of each chapter are summarized in the conclusion, explaining which hypotheses have been validated, which have been rejected, and why. An overall sense of whether abortion has been more conflictual in the United States or in Canada will lead to a discussion of how the advent of a postmaterialist society (hypothesis A4) impacts moral conflicts and, more important, why social forces apparently converge but institutional forces diverge regarding abortion politics and policymaking in the United States and Canada.

1

Background to Controversy

Origins of American and Canadian Abortion Policy

In both the United States and Canada, the origins of the abortion controversy date back to the mid-1960s, though the first agitations for reform in the United States can be traced to the 1950s. The similarities between these countries are more revealing than any differences, and indicate that the period of abortion reform was more an elitist phenomenon than a mass movement. At the margins, however, one could argue that public opinion was more instrumental in the United States than north of the border. The powerful normative lesson of this early period is that the way a controversial issue is defined for purposes of public debate can affect in large measure the ability of elites to manage the scope of conflict and, therefore, engender consensus building. In both cultures, abortion reform was tied to health care and thus was not polarized in moral terms. This is especially important for the United States to the extent that its Catholic population—even though smaller than Canada's—had not been mobilized into a pro-life counteroffensive. In the United States, the abortion question had also undergone a longer incubation period before it gained a place on the policy agenda, unlike the relatively quick pace by which the abortion issue was transformed into public policy in Canada. Differences between the U.S. separation-of-powers system and the parliamentary regime of Canada largely explain that situation.

Agenda Setting in Two Nations

What motivated the 1960s abortion reformers in the United States and Canada was medical need, not feminist theory or rights jurisprudence. In the United States, it took some time for that need to be publicized. Early writing on abortion "during the first half of this century was aimed at professional audiences, not the general public. These books surveyed the range of abortion problems and called for remedial action, but no coordinated effort was made to effect social reforms" (Tatalovich and Daynes 1981a, 40). In the mid-1960s Bates and Zawadski observed (1964, 115): "It is a relatively recent event to have physicians of national reputation speaking and writing on the social repercussions of our abortion laws." Those who did, moreover, acted as prominent individuals and not as representatives of organized medicine.

Only one article on abortion was recorded in the *Readers' Guide to Periodic Literature* prior to 1930, and during the 1930s and 1940s a total of fifty-one were indexed (Sarvis and Rodman 1973, 7). Analysis of the *New York Times* (Buutap 1979, 96) found 117 items on the topic of abortion between 1947 and 1961, after which that coverage increased threefold (to 392 items) during the period from 1962 to 1969.

My analysis of American periodical indexes shows a steady rise in the number of articles devoted to abortion over the period 1953–1992 (table 1.1), and the ratio of articles to publications in three American indexes shows a similar increase until 1978–1982, when it increased by approximately one-third. It stabilized during 1983–1987, then rose by 50 percent during 1988–1992. If these trend data in citations are an indication of general issue saliency and not simply agenda setting by media elites, then nearly twenty years after *Roe v. Wade* (1973), the Supreme Court decision that constitutionalized a right to abortion, the beginning of the end of the abortion controversy is *not* at hand.

The situation in Canada following the *Morgentaler v. The Queen* ruling (1988), which left the country with no criminal code on abortion, seems even more intense when compared to the earlier period. The data indicate that abortion received almost no press coverage in Canada during the period before the 1969 Criminal Code was reformed. No articles appeared during the 1953–1957 period, and thereafter the ratio of articles to publications was one-third to one-half the ratio for the United States through 1982. The gap in coverage narrowed somewhat between 1983 and 1987, a time when Dr. Henry Morgentaler began locating abortion clinics outside his Quebec base, thus provoking demonstrations by pro-lifers and legal battles with local authorities. A review of the *Canadian News Index* for 1980–1984 led McDaniel (1985, 83) to conclude that abortion "has become a major social issue in Canada," given that some 1,100 articles on that topic appeared in Canadian newspapers and magazines. For the most recent period (1988–1992), the ratio of articles to publications jumped threefold in Canada to *exceed* the coverage given to abortion in the United States. There was intense media coverage of the trilogy of abortion cases—*Morgentaler, Borowski,* and *Daigle*—which has not yet subsided. So one can conclude that those rulings by the Canadian Supreme Court served to publicize the abortion issue, though it remains to be seen whether they provoked a political backlash akin to what happened here following the decision in *Roe.*

For the period of the 1960s that led to the enactment of abortion reforms by the Canadian Parliament and various American states, the implication from these comparisons is that although both reform movements were more elitist than mass agitations, that characterization is especially apt for Canada. Relatively little publicity encouraged the political leadership of Canada to deal with abortion reforms, whereas a sympathetic press facilitated those efforts in the United States.

A decade before the Criminal Code was reformed, an article in *Chatelaine* campaigned for abortion liberalization in Canada, but apparently its crusade was not adopted by other news organizations, with one exception. The 1959 article, say Brodie, Gavigan, and Jenson (1992, 23), "was a quite classic version of an internationally familiar genre. It began with an example of an uncomplicated case, that of a fourteen-year-old pregnant as the result of a gang-rape who could not abort even after such an awful experience." Beginning in 1961, the *Globe and Mail* of Toronto "mounted an editorial crusade for abortion law reform. Abortion-related news was routinely accorded front-page coverage, while scores of editorials were used to cheer reformers, chide the timid, and castigate the opposition" (Morton 1992, 20).

In the United States, though the numbers were small, there was a notable increase in articles on abortion during the early and mid-1960s (see table 1.1), and many were published in popular magazines: *Time, Newsweek, Look, Life, Atlantic Monthly, Cosmopolitan, The Nation, Reader's Digest, Redbook, Saturday Evening Post, Saturday Review, Mademoiselle, Parents' Magazine, Playboy,* and the *New York Times Magazine.* As Tatalovich and Daynes summarized their content:

> In many instances, these forums did not explicitly advocate abortion liberalization, but their mere recitation of facts and acknowledgment of an abortion problem suggested the need for remedial action. The impact of these publications was to aid the cause of abortion reform, less from a moral posture than from a problem-solving perspective. Common to these discussions was the recitation of a litany of problems affecting abortion. (Tatalovich and Daynes 1981a, 86)

The popular literature of that day defined six aspects of the abortion problem (Tatalovich and Daynes 1981a, 86–94). First, the claim was fully accepted that illegal abortions were widespread and that while some were

Table 1.1

Citations to Abortion Articles in Indexes to Periodical Literature in the United States and Canada, 1953–1992

Period	United States[*]		Canada[†]		Legal Developments Chronology
	N	Journal Ratio[‡]	N	Journal Ratio	
1953–57	44	0.100	0	0.000	
1958–62	59	0.134	3	0.042	ALI Model Penal Code (1959), United States Thalidomide scare (1962), United States
1963–67	163	0.270	9	0.115	State reforms begin (1966–67), United States
1968–72	372	0.617	24	0.308	State reforms continue (1968–72), United States Criminal Code reformed (1969), Canada
1973–77	501	0.633	31	0.287	Roe v. Wade (1973), United States R. v. Morgentaler (1975), Canada Badgley Report (1977), Canada

1978–82	660	0.833	43	0.398
1983–87	712	0.899	149	0.578
1988–92	1,315	1.352	460	1.782

*Citations to U.S. articles tabulated from *Readers' Guide to Periodic Literature* (1953–87); *Index of Legal Periodicals* (1953–87); *International Index: A Guide to Periodical Literature in the Social Sciences and Humanities* (1953–66); *Social Sciences and Humanities Index* (1967–74); and *Social Science Index* (1975–87).

†Citations to Canadian articles tabulated from *Canadian Index to Periodicals and Documentary Films* (1953–1964), updated as the *Canadian Periodical Index* (1965–1987).

‡Journal ratio is the number of articles divided by the average number of journals indexed in three U.S. sources and one Canadian source. As the number of indexed publications grew over three decades, averages are based on two decades spanning each time frame: 1950 and 1960 for 1953–57 and 1958–62; 1960 and 1970 for 1963–67 and 1968–72; 1970 and 1980 for 1973–77 and 1978–82; 1980 and 1990 for 1983–87 and 1988–92.

Morgentaler v. The Queen (1988), Canada
Borowski v. Canada (1989), Canada
Tremblay v. Daigle (1989), Canada
Webster v. Reproductive Health Services (1989) United States
Bill C-43 (1989–90), Canada

performed by legitimate physicians illicitly, too many were bungled attempts by amateurs or self-abortionists. In a law review article, for example, two researchers estimated that there were a million illegal abortions in the United States each year and that five thousand ended in death (Leavy and Kummer 1962, 126). But statistics did not carry as powerful a message as accounts of human tragedy. Especially poignant was an article by Jack Star (1965, 150) for *Look* magazine that recounted a case observed by a gynecologist at Mount Sinai Hospital in New York City: The patient had a friend "use a catheter while she lay on a kitchen table," and then, after unknowingly piercing the wall of the uterus, her friend "emptied an entire 10-ounce bottle of a strong disinfectant," which subsequently "entered the bloodstream at the perforation and carried poison throughout her body. The liver was damaged. Red-blood cells were destroyed. The kidneys were so damaged that waste products piled up in the body. Despite massive doses of antibiotics, intravenous fluids and blood, her condition worsened. We had to take out her uterus, Fallopian tubes and ovaries, drain pelvic abscesses and tie off the main vein to the heart, the vena cava, to prevent infected particles in the bloodstream from getting back to the heart. This poor woman was in the hospital for a month."

Second, the popular press stressed that existing abortion laws were commonly violated by prevailing medical practices, so the objective of reformers was to make the law compatible with medicine. An editorial in *The Nation* (1968) entitled "Humane Doctors, Inhumane Law" focused on charges of unprofessional conduct by the California State Board of Medical Examiners against physicians who had performed therapeutic abortions in hospitals. Of course, this problem had been dramatized by the publicity surrounding Sherri Finkbine in the early 1960s (see pages 35–36).

Third, other stories detailed gross fetal abnormalities, pregnancies that resulted from sexual attacks, and imminent threats to the mother's health. The *New York Times* editorialized:

> As for aborting an unborn child who may have a grave physical or mental defect, there can be nothing in moral law to require that monstrously deformed fetuses, such as the thalidomide victims of three years ago, must be allowed to struggle through birth in order to lead a short, pitiful institutionalized existence that can hardly be called life. (*New York Times* 1965, 20)

Similarly, an article in *The New Republic* (Ridgeway 1963, 14) alleged that then-current laws allowed hospitals to refuse an abortion to "a 14-year-old girl impregnated by her father, a woman raped on the street by a man she had never seen, a mentally defective girl coerced into intercourse and in no position to take care of a child."

Fourth, the periodical literature used case histories and statistics to argue that a class bias existed. Wealthier clients seemed able to obtain abortions at private hospitals, or they traveled abroad, while poor women who relied on public hospitals had less access to abortions. Fifth, the columnists and editorial writers made reference to opinion polls and surveys of doctors to argue that public attitudes supported more-liberal abortion laws. As *Time* (1967, 33) put it: "All the polls show that Americans heavily favor reform."

Finally, Tatalovich and Daynes took note of "what the pro-abortion arguments failed to mention as well as what they emphasized," namely:

> To the extent that the explicit goal was therapeutic abortion reform, the intellectual debate tended to focus on those narrow issues relevant to that objective. Thus very little notice was given to abortion in terms of a woman's right though the question of elective abortion lay beneath the surface of the abortion dialogue, particularly in the late 1960s and early 1970s. (Tatalovich and Daynes 1981a, 92)

Legal Developments in Abortion Policy

In the United States

In the United States abortion was not prohibited or regulated before 1821, when Connecticut banned any abortion after quickening, although no death penalty was prescribed. Then followed New York in 1829, which made abortions before quickening illegal, though a lesser crime, and stipulated the first therapeutic exception: legalizing abortions "necessary to preserve the life of such mother, or shall have been advised by two physicians to be necessary for such purpose" (Lader 1966, 87). This law became a model for legislation by other states, but before that precedent was established, the woman retained substantial autonomy over the decision to abort prior to quickening. Mohr's definitive study of nineteenth-century abortion laws concluded:

> The common law did not formally recognize the existence of a fetus in criminal cases until it had quickened. After quickening, the expulsion and destruction of a fetus without due cause was considered a crime, because the fetus itself had manifested some semblance of a separate existence: the ability to move. The crime was qualitatively different from the destruction of a human being, however, and punished less harshly. Before quickening, actions that had the effect of terminating what turned out to have been an early pregnancy were not considered criminal under the common law in effect in England and the United States in 1800. (Mohr 1978, 3)

From 1830 to 1849, sixteen more states adopted antiabortion laws; twenty-five more acted between 1850 and the turn of this century; and the last seven laws were enacted between 1900 and 1965 (Tatalovich and Daynes 1981a, 18). By the late 1880s antiabortion policy was fully established in state law, though as Mohr (1978, 245) shows, nobody took decisive action against abortion where it existed. Abortion thus was ignored until the problem of criminal abortions was publicized widely during the decade of the 1960s.

The original antiabortion laws prohibited terminations of pregnancy except when the life of the woman was endangered. The statutes of Alabama and Oregon (and the federal law governing the District of Columbia) included risks to the mother's life and health as exceptions; those of Colorado and New Mexico cited risks to the mother's life and serious or permanent bodily injury; and Maryland's stated that an exception could be made when "no other method will secure the safety of the mother." But the laws of Massachusetts, New Jersey, Louisiana, and Pennsylvania made no explicit mention of therapeutic exceptions (Tatalovich and Daynes 1981a, 24).

Beginning in 1966, when Mississippi added rape as another therapeutic exception, over the next seven years thirteen more states "reformed" their criminal codes to allow a range of therapeutic abortions. Going beyond therapeutics, Alaska, Hawaii, New York, and Washington repealed their antiabortion laws in 1970, thereby legalizing abortion as an elective procedure (table 1.2). A diffusion study of those pre-1973 liberalized abortion laws (Mooney and Lee 1995) found that the odds of state action increased where "demand" for abortion reform was manifested in terms of women making up a larger share of the state's workforce, a strong medical establishment, and regions where neighboring states already had approved more permissive laws on abortion. On the other hand, constraints against liberalization occurred in states with larger concentrations of Catholics or fundamentalist Protestants, where political parties were highly competitive, or during election years—which would cause electoral anxieties for politicians confronting a policy issue such as abortion. An important caveat by researchers Mooney and Lee, which comports fully with the argument of this book and with that of Tatalovich and Daynes 1981a, is that "the influence of the medical establishment waned on this issue as the morality-based debate became predominant" (Mooney and Lee 1995, 620).

The American Law Institute (ALI) had been urging abortion reforms that would take into account the physical or mental health of the mother, a physical or mental defect in the child, and pregnancy from rape, incest, or felonious intercourse. The fourteen reformed laws showed "how substantial the influence of the (ALI) Model Penal Code has been, particularly in terms of the grounds stated to authorize abortions" (George 1973, 23). If the four decriminalization statutes are also considered, then all eighteen state laws au-

Table 1.2

States with Liberalized Abortion Laws, 1966–1972

Mississippi (1966)	New Mexico (1969)
California (1967)	Oregon (1969)
Colorado (1967)	Alaska (1970)*
North Carolina (1967)	Hawaii (1970)*
Georgia (1968)	New York (1970)*
Maryland (1968)	South Carolina (1970)
Arkansas (1969)	Virginia (1970)
Delaware (1969)	Washington (1970)*
Kansas (1969)	Florida (1972)

Note: Asterisk indicates a state that repealed its original antiabortion law, thereby making abortion an elective procedure.

thorized abortions to save the mother's life and in cases of forcible rape; all but Mississippi's included reference to the mother's physical or mental health, and all except for Mississippi's and California's (which then-governor Ronald Reagan signed into law) permitted abortions where fetal abnormalities were indicated. Oregon went well beyond the ALI guidelines by adding a socioeconomic criterion similar to the wording of the British Abortion Act of 1967: "In determining whether or not there is substantial risk (to the woman's physical or mental health) account may be taken of the mother's total environment, actual or reasonably foreseeable" (Roemer 1971, 40).

In Canada

Canadian abortion law followed English legal precedents. Until the nineteenth century, abortion was a common-law offense in England only after the woman was "quick with child," though Lord Ellenborough's Act of 1803 was the first to codify abortion as a crime. Abortion after quickening became a capital (death penalty) offense, while abortion before quickening was a lesser crime. In 1837 the English law dropped this distinction as well as the death penalty, and in 1861 Section 58 of the Offences Against the Person Act mandated that a woman who procured her own abortion also was guilty of a crime (Dunsmuir 1991, 3). Section 58, which remained in force in Britain until 1967 and which was the basis for Canadian law until 1953, stated that the offense was an unlawful administering of poison or an unlawful use of instruments to procure a miscarriage, implying that some abortions might be lawful (Walls 1982, 6). In 1896 the Royal College of

Physicians was advised that efforts to save a mother's life would be a good defense against a charge of illegal abortion (Potts, Diggory, and Peel 1977, 283, n. 7).

In Canada, the first criminal law on abortion was enacted in 1869, providing a penalty of life imprisonment for the person who procured a miscarriage. Dunsmuir notes: "While such statutes reflected societal and religious objectives of protecting the fetus, they were also influenced by concerns about the mother's health. Nineteenth century abortions were medically dangerous and . . . often performed by non-physicians" (Dunsmuir 1991, 4). This point—the purpose behind the original antiabortion laws—has been debated at length in the United States; clearly the same complex of reasons was advanced in Canada and England.

The pre-1969 Criminal Code of Canada had three sections on abortion. Section 237 made abortion an offense for the persons who procured it and performed it. Section 209 made the killing of an unborn child a crime but did not extend to the person who, in good faith, considered it necessary to "preserve the life of the mother." And Section 45 stipulated that anyone who performed a surgical operation to benefit that person, given the state of health and other circumstances of the case, was protected from criminal liability if the operation was done with reasonable care and skill (Hebert and Dunsmuir 1989, 2). Prior to 1969 those laws were never reviewed by the judiciary. Only the *McCready* case (1909) had relevance, but the suggestion by a superior-court judge that abortions to save the life of a pregnant woman were probably legal was a comment from the bench *(obiter dictum)* and thus did not create a legal precedent in Canada.

In England, the Offences Against the Person Act of 1861 allowed no therapeutic exceptions for the life or health of the mother and for that reason was challenged by the medical and legal professions. In 1935 the British Medical Association (BMA) created a special Committee on Abortion whose report the following year recommended that the law be revised to permit some therapeutic abortions (Hindell and Simms 1971, 68). In 1936 the Abortion Law Reform Association (ALRA) was founded with a more ambitious policy agenda (Hindell and Simms 1971, 57). What really dramatized the issue was the famous case involving Dr. Aleck Bourne, who had been a member of the BMA Committee on Abortion and later of the ALRA Medico-Legal Council (Hindell and Simms 1971, 69–72). During 1938 this prominent English obstetrician notified the attorney general that, with consent from her parents and for no fee, he had performed an abortion on a fourteen-year-old who had been gang-raped by four soldiers. He invited the Crown to prosecute him, as a test case, but the jury acquitted him after forty minutes of deliberation.

In *R. v. Bourne* (1939), a provision much like that found in the Criminal Code of Canada was interpreted by Justice Macnaghten to incorporate

> the substance of the [1929] Infant Life (Preservation) Act, (which did not apply to abortion), and directed the jury that an abortion might be lawful if it was done in good faith to preserve the life of the mother. Furthermore he denied that this provision required the threat of immediate death: if the doctor, on reasonable grounds, thought that the continuation of the pregnancy would make the woman a physical or mental wreck, the jury was entitled to take the view that the doctor had operated for the purpose of preserving the life of the mother. (Walls 1982, 7)

Twenty years later Macnaghten's interpretation was broadened in *R. v. Newton and Stungo* (1958) to mean that an abortion "was unlawful unless [it was] made in good faith for the purpose of preserving the life or health of the woman. When I say health, I mean not only her physical health but also her mental health" (Walls 1982, 7).

Thus the so-called Bourne Defense became the standard in English common law, and likely so in Canada as well, but legal questions persisted. Section 45 of the Canadian Criminal Code essentially codified the common-law "defence of necessity," which "exonerates from all criminal responsibility a person who, in a given situation, has no other choice but to transgress the law in order to avoid graver consequences if it were obeyed." However, for abortions "there were some doubts before 1969 whether the defence of necessity was applicable since no judicial precedent could be invoked" (Hebert and Dunsmuir 1989, 3). An amendment to the Canadian Criminal Code in 1953 had revised the language of Section 45 to omit the word *unlawful* (de Valk 1974, 38). Says Walls (1982, 10–11): "There was some doubt therefore as to whether the common law definition of therapeutic abortion and its expanded version given in *Bourne* were any longer applicable." It was this legal ambiguity that gave rise to reform efforts, first in Great Britain and then in Canada.

1960s Reform Agitation

Canadian Agitation

The Bourne Defense did not extend to eugenic reasons for abortion, such as in the case of birth defects from the drug thalidomide, nor were socioeconomic conditions justification for abortion, but according to Walls (1982, 9), the "most pressing reason for reform of the abortion law, however, was that criminal abortion continued to exist." In 1964 about 1,500 therapeutic abortions were done under the National Health Service, and another 300,000 were done in private clinics, but the estimates of illegal abortions ranged between 50,000 and 100,000 (Dickens 1979, 81).

In England during the period between 1952 and 1967 (when abortion reforms were finally enacted), there were several attempts to reform the abortion law through Private Members' Bills. It was during this time that the Abortion Law Reform Association was revived, after the 1962 thalidomide scare, and five years later the Society for Protection of Unborn Children was founded to rally the opposition forces (Potts, Diggory, and Peel 1977, 294). The enactment of abortion reforms by a Labour government came after two years of parliamentary and public debate. Grounds for abortion included a serious risk to the life or health of the mother, a substantial risk of congenital abnormality, and serious risk to existing children due to the burden on the mother from having additional children. The "total environment" could be considered in assessing the risks to her health (Potts, Diggory, and Peel 1977, 294).

Abortion reform in Great Britain had to have ramifications in Canada, according to Morton:

> Just as Canada's original abortion law was based on British precedent, so, too, was the movement during the 1960s to reform the law. British influence was still strong in Canadian society during the sixties, especially in legal circles. The Canadian Criminal Code, including its abortion provisions, was adapted from British criminal law in 1892 and tended to follow the latter. The Judicial Committee of the Privy Council had served as Canada's final court of appeal for constitutional questions until 1949, and British legal precedents were authoritatively cited in most fields of Canadian law. (Morton 1992, 18).

Not until the early 1960s was there any indication of public concern in Canada about abortion (de Valk 1974, xx), though reform came quickly after Great Britain acted. Three Private Members' Bills to legalize abortion were introduced in early 1966 and 1967 (Campbell and Pal 1989, 174), and each was referred to the Standing Committee on Health and Welfare, which received public testimony from October 1967 to March 1968. C-122 was submitted by New Democratic Party (NDP) MP Grace MacInnis and resembled the resolution of the Canadian Medical Association (CMA) in allowing therapeutic abortions in cases of grave danger to the woman's physical or mental health, where pregnancy resulted from a sex crime, or if a substantial risk existed that the fetus would be disabled. Another NDP member of Parliament, H.W. Herridge, introduced C-136 to incorporate the philosophy behind the British Abortion Act of 1967 into Canadian law, by allowing abortions when the woman's health and well-being or the health and well-being of other children would be threatened. Two physicians were to evaluate the woman's "total environment, actual or reasonably foreseeable" in making that determination. And C-136, from Liberal MP Ian Wahn, would have authorized therapeutic abortion committees (TACs) in hospitals to determine when a woman's life or health was threatened by the continuation of a pregnancy.

An interim report by the Standing Committee on Health and Welfare on December 19, 1967, stated that the existing law was unclear and that the Criminal Code should be amended to "allow therapeutic abortion under appropriate medical safeguards where a pregnancy will seriously endanger the life or health of the mother" (de Valk 1974, 55). The Herridge measure has been termed a "nonstarter" because its linking of "reproductive decisions to social needs . . . was far too radical and too 'social' for Canadian political discourse at that time" (Brodie, Gavigan, and Jenson 1992, 33). What troubled the MPs about C-122 was that "the provision for aborting 'defective' foetuses would involve too much risk for healthy ones . . . [and] since German measles was the major cause of deformities discussed at that time, some MPs were reluctant to accept that the possibility of deafness or blindness was sufficient reason for terminating a pregnancy" (Brodie, Gavigan, and Jenson 1992, 33).

On December 21, 1967, Bill C-195 was introduced into the House of Commons by Justice Minister Pierre Trudeau. It was an omnibus bill dealing with several moral questions: lotteries, passports, firearms, bail reform, homosexuality, and abortion. This bill authorized abortions when the pregnancy would or was likely to endanger the life or health of the mother. The Standing Committee proceeded with its hearings before issuing a final report on March 13, 1968, which criticized the government bill, particularly on how health was defined for purposes of abortion. The recommendation from the Standing Committee that the legislation read "where the pregnancy will endanger the life or seriously and directly impair the health of the mother" was ignored by the Liberal government (de Valk 1974, 80). The MPs were opposed to such wide-ranging meanings as the one used by the World Health Organization—"Health is a state of complete physical, mental and social well-being and not merely the absence of disease or infirmity" (see Committee on the Operation of the Abortion Law 1977, 255).

Bill C-195 was never enacted; the national election of 1968 returned the Liberals to power (now under Prime Minister Pierre Trudeau); and identical legislation was reintroduced by Justice Minister John Turner as Omnibus Bill C-150. Following its second reading on January 23, 1969, there was rancorous debate in the House of Commons for eleven days. Only one important amendment was accepted by the government, to permit abortions in hospitals that were not "accredited" but which had received specific approval from a provincial minister of health (de Valk 1974, 118). A motion to delete abortion from the omnibus bill lost by a 107–36 margin on May 9; five days later C-150 obtained a third reading, and final enactment came on August 26 (de Valk 1974, 125).

The packaging of abortion reform with so many other changes in the Criminal Code was viewed as a deliberate strategy by the Liberal government. Unlike in the United States, abortion reform was related to a new governmental philosophy toward public morality, as Justice Minister Turner told the House of Commons: "In a pluralist society there may be different standards, differing attitudes and the law cannot reflect them all. Public order, in this situation of a pluralistic society, cannot substitute for private conduct. We believe that morality is a matter for private conscience. Criminal law should reflect the public order only" (quoted in de Valk 1974, 104).

Walls (1982, 15) says that, compared to the 1967 reforms in Britain, C-150 "merely formalized what was already the practice in many Canadian hospitals. Its definition of therapeutic abortion was as restrictive as the definition in the *Bourne* decision in England in 1938." While many of the procedural hurdles could be simply pro forma, by not defining *health* within the statute, Parliament essentially said that abortion was legal so long as a hospital therapeutic abortion committee said it was legal. This loophole was a substantial one, and had a permissive environment developed after 1969, it could have evolved into a situation of legalized abortion for virtually any reason. In Canada, as in the United States, the vagueness of statutory language coupled with the fact that the abortion decision was left in the hands of physicians and women potentially could have depoliticized this issue and yielded a policy consensus. This is especially true given the more aggressive advocacy of liberalized abortion laws by the legal and medical communities in that country.

American Agitation

Oftentimes a pressing social problem is ignored until it is dramatized by a cause célèbre, which was the case with abortion agitation in the United States. It has already been noted that the American Law Institute (1959) recommended wholesale reforms in its Model Penal code, including legalizing abortion where "(a) the abortion is medically advisable because continuance of the pregnancy involves substantial risk that mother or child will suffer grave and irremediable impairment of physical or mental health; (b) the pregnancy resulted from forcible rape." But the ALI code had no immediate impact until the issue was highly publicized by Sherri Finkbine (1967) and coupled with the thalidomide scare of 1962. By now the story is legend among abortion proponents. The drug thalidomide was obtained by Finkbine's husband while he traveled in Europe, and Finkbine took between thirty and forty pills in mid-1962 to ease nervousness from her pregnancy. Through a UPI news story published in the *Arizona Republic,* she learned that the FDA head, Dr. Frances Kelsey, refused to permit distribution of the drug in the United States because four thousand to six thousand deformed infants in West Germany and another thousand in Great Britain were linked to thalidomide. It damaged the embryo and produced a malformation called phocomelia, with children born with flaps instead of arms, or no arms at all, and frequently with shortened thigh bones and twisted legs.

Thereupon Finkbine petitioned Good Samaritan Hospital for a legal abortion, and though state law permitted hospital abortions only to save the mother's life, many physicians loosely interpreted the law to include also cases in which childbirth would be psychologically destructive to the mother. The hospital's three-physician board approved her request and she was admitted, but then a local newspaper ran a front-page, black-bordered story that declared "Baby-deforming Drug May Cost Woman Her Child Here" (Finkbine 1967, 18). Within hours the story was on the wire services, and subsequently the county attorney stated that, regardless of the humanitarian motives, he would have to prosecute the attending physician if anyone brought a complaint. The Finkbines and the hospital filed suit, at which time her identity became known; Finkbine was Sherri Chessen, who hosted a television program for preschoolers called "Romper Room." Even though a judge dismissed the case, the hospital became overly cautious and canceled the operation, whereupon Finkbine boarded a plane for Sweden, where she aborted an infant found to be grossly deformed.

President Kennedy issued a plea that citizens dispose of any thalidomide tablets, and he announced that the FDA staff would be augmented. The Vatican issued a statement saying that a murder had been committed at Caroline Hospital, but here the episode fueled demands for reform. The momentum was sustained when a German measles epidemic hit the country, and due to that rubella outbreak thousands of congenitally abnormal babies were born. Once more physicians faced a legal dilemma, and a test case resulted in California.

Reputable physicians in California had discreetly done abortions where fetal abnormality, rape, or incest was indicated, but the attorney general and the state board of medical examiners brought charges of unprofessional conduct against two doctors who performed abortions on women who had contracted German measles during their pregnancies (*Newsweek* 1966a,

58). The movement for reform gained momentum as a result these kinds of highly publicized cases of respected physicians being prosecuted for following accepted medical practice on abortion (*Newsweek* 1966b, 92).

Early medical activists were located in California and New York, where involved groups included the Association for the Study of Abortion (New York), the Society for Humane Abortion (San Francisco), and the California Committee on Therapeutic Abortion (Los Angeles). In a relatively short period of time professional (*Medical Tribune* 1964; *Modern Medicine* 1967) and public opinion had galvanized behind reforms explicitly allowing therapeutic abortion, but there was less support for abortions performed for purely socioeconomic reasons or on demand. A 1962 Gallup Poll prompted by the *Finkbine* case asked respondents to evaluate this question:

> As you may have heard or read, an Arizona woman recently had a legal abortion in Sweden after having taken the drug thalidomide, which has been linked to birth defects. Do you think this woman did the right thing or the wrong thing in having this abortion operation? (quoted in Tatalovich and Daynes 1981a, 116)

A bare majority (52 percent) agreed with Sherri Finkbine, and afterward questions on abortion became standard on most national opinion polls. The results from polls taken during the 1960s are quite conclusive (Tatalovich and Daynes 1981a, 118). A consensus emerged very quickly behind the ALI abortion reforms, which featured "hard" or medical reasons—permitting the procedure in order to safeguard maternal health and where fetal deformity or rape was indicated. When the public was queried on "soft" justifications, however, the data suggested to Blake (1971, 542) that "disapproval for economic reasons characterizes about two-thirds of all respondents. Disapproval has declined somewhat during the decade [of the 1960s], but it is clear that Americans generally are predominantly negative toward economically practical reasons for abortion." That "legalized abortion is supported most strongly by the non-Catholic, male, well-educated 'establishment' " led Blake to underscore the class implications of the abortion debate:

> We may conclude, therefore, that changes in abortion laws, like most social changes, will not come about by agitation at the grass roots, or by the activity of righteously indignant individuals who cannot currently circumvent existing statutes. Rather, it is to the educated and influential that we must look for effecting rapid legislative change in spite of conservative opinions among important subgroups such as the lower classes and women. (Blake 1971, 548)

Medicine and Law in Two Countries

Given the fact that existing antiabortion statutes forced a collision between changing medical practice and the legal status quo, one would think that the

American Medical Association (AMA) and the American Bar Association (ABA) as well as the Canadian Medical Association (CMA) and the Canadian Bar Association (CBA) would be at the forefront of change. But the story is not that simple. While the AMA accommodated changing state laws and new attitudes among its membership, the proabortion activists were largely outside of organized medicine. The restrained advocacy of the medical establishment, and especially that of the legal establishment, in the United States stands in sharp contrast with what occurred in Canada.

The AMA and ABA

It has been said that the American Medical Association, founded in 1847, joined the battle against abortion after quickening as a way to distinguish "regular" physicians from the "quack" or "irregular" practitioners of that era. Mohr (1978, 34–35) claims that the antiabortion views of physicians were "partly ideological, partly scientific, partly moral, and partly practical." More certain is the fact that a Boston specialist in obstetrics and gynecology, Horatio Robinson Storer, mobilized the energies of the profession to outlaw most abortions. By the time of the AMA's 1857 annual convention, Storer was asked to chair a Committee on Criminal Abortion, but his committee did not make a formal recommendation until 1871. Its lengthy report, which laid the groundwork for an AMA abortion policy that survived until 1967, recommended that

> it be unlawful and unprofessional for any physician to induce abortion or premature labor, without the concurrent opinion of at least one respectable consulting physician, and then always with a view to the safety of the child— if that be possible. (Tatalovich and Daynes 1981a, 22)

As early as 1962 and 1963, and again in 1966, the California Medical Association reaffirmed "the concept of medically justifiable abortion" and voted to "express to the State Legislature its belief in the broadening of the therapeutic abortion law, taking into consideration the health of both the mother and the product of conception" (*Medical Tribune* 1966, 1). The Medical Society of the State of New York formally adopted the ALI recommendations in 1966, one year before the American Medical Association similarly acted. But the first time the AMA House of Delegates revisited the abortion question was in 1965, the same year that the National Association for Humane Abortion was organized. At its November meeting the AMA Board of Trustees submitted for the consideration of the House of Delegates a report from its Committee on Human Reproduction, which recognized "that disparities exist between state laws and indicated medical practices regarding contraception, abortion, and sterilization" and therefore recommended amending state laws "so as to reflect medical conscience and public opinion." It proposed reforms based on the ALI code, but a reference committee (which studies resolutions prior to their deliberation by all the delegates) was confused about what the committee had intended and, instead, concluded that the AMA ought not go beyond existing medical law and that the abortion problem seemed to be "essentially one for resolution by each state through action of its own legislature" (quoted in Tatalovich 1971, 177–79).

At the June 1967 AMA convention the Board of Trustees submitted another lengthy report from its Committee on Human Reproduction; changing strategy, the committee now advised that "rather than recommending changes in state law, the American Medical Association should adopt its own statement of position which can be used as a guide for component and constituent societies in states contemplating legislative reform." The ALI reforms were proposed, but now the reference committee reported "voluminous testimony" on the subject, "with the preponderance" favoring adoption of the reforms. And it agreed. But the reference committee said that the AMA should *update* its own policy and not endorse legislation, although it declared that it was ethically proper "for physicians to provide medical information to State Legislatures in their consideration of revision and/or the development of new legislation regarding therapeutic abortion" (quoted in Tatalovich 1971, 179). This change of policy by the AMA lent a prestigious voice to the cause of abortion reform.

By September 1967 seventeen state medical societies had adopted policies on abortion reform, ten similar to the AMA position, so how instrumental were they in getting abortion reforms enacted by state government? Even before the AMA changed its policy, Colorado, California, and North Carolina had enacted therapeutic abortion laws, but organized medicine in Colorado and North Carolina took no "official" action, California being the exception. Then in 1968 and 1969 seven more states adopted ALI-type abortion laws (see table 1.2); the state medical associations of Maryland and Georgia supported this liberalization in 1968, but in 1969 only two of five state medical association (those of Delaware and Oregon) did so (Tatalovich and Daynes 1981a, 54). This is not to say that medical professionals were not influential, even if the record of organized medicine was mixed. Case studies of California (Jain and Hughes 1968) as well as North Carolina (Jain and Sinding 1972) and Georgia (Jain and Gooch 1972) showed a decisive role by the medical establishment, even though in North Carolina and Georgia organized medicine had no formal policy on abortion reform.

Dr. Robert Ross, president-elect of the Medical Society of the State of North Carolina, testified that many physicians there had performed "therapeutic" abortions which were "technically in violation of the old [pre-1967] law" (Jain and Sinding 1972, 13). But the key to promoting legislative reform was a freshman member of the lower house, Democrat Arthur H. Jones, who had long been interested in family planning issues. Jones and his allies consulted with physicians, specifically with Dr. Edgar T. Beddingfield Jr., chairman of the medical society's Committee on Legislation, who urged that they follow the ALI model and offered technical and legal assistance from medical society staffers. Jones wanted to avoid the impression that his measure was a "doctor's bill" (because so many members of the legislature were lawyers), but in reality physicians dominated the testimony given before the upper and lower houses, and they made contact with their own representatives in the legislature. While the bill liberalized the abortion law, "proponents emphasized that the bill would make the abortion law not liberal but modern, providing doctors with legal backing to do in good conscience what many had already done in uncertainty" (Jain and Sinding 1972, 50–51). In sum, physicians with close ties to organized medicine in North Carolina played a crucial role by shaping the legislation to conform to the ALI guidelines and by mobilizing their expertise and their medical constituency to influence the lawmaking process.

Having endorsed the ALI reforms, however, the AMA resisted going much further. At the December 1969 convention, one delegate offered a resolution stating that the AMA policy was "unduly restrictive" and proposed its rescission so that the AMA could "go on record as recommending the repeal of all state abortion laws (except those restricting abortion to qualified physicians) so that all women, for whatever reason, can have abortions performed under safe, healthful conditions by qualified practitioners of medicine." But the reference committee studying this proposal reported that "by a ratio of approximately 12–1" testimony was opposed to the change, and the delegates upheld its recommendation (quoted in Tatalovich 1971, 188).

The last policy correction, for the moment, came in June 1970, when the AMA's Board of Trustees surveyed the fast-changing legal situation. Because some states authorized abortion for reasons other than therapeutic need, physicians in those jurisdictions would be violating their professional ethics should they choose to perform abortion in accordance with the new statutes. So the trustees recommended that the delegates "establish a policy on abortion that would permit the decision to interrupt pregnancy to be made by the woman and her physician. However, no physician should be required to perform an abortion and no hospital should be required to admit a patient for abortion." At the same time the delegates had to consider five resolutions on abortion, some splitting the AMA bureaucracy on this question, but ultimately a reference committee refused to endorse the repeal of all abortion laws, although it

> was impressed by the remarkable shift in testimony on abortion at this meeting as contrasted to the opposition to liberalization expressed by the testimony . . . only six months ago. . . . This shift in attitude has, no doubt, been influenced by the rapid changes in state laws and by the judicial decisions which tend to make abortions more freely available. (Tatalovich 1971, 189)

The delegates debated this matter for an hour, as a caucus of the National Federation of Catholic Physicians' Guilds met to issue a statement threatening resignations if "such a divisive policy is pursued" (quoted in Tatalovich 1971, 190). A motion to defer the report back to the trustees handily lost, 126–68, while an amendment calling for consultation with two other physicians prior to the decision to abort was approved, 103–73, with the result that the AMA established a new policy stating that "abortion is a medical procedure and should be performed only by a duly licensed physician and surgeon in an accredited hospital acting only after consultation with two other physicians" but that "no physician or other professional personnel shall be compelled to perform any act which violates his good medical judgment" or "be required to perform any act violative of personally-held moral principles" (quoted in Tatalovich 1971, 190–91). Since this statement did not explicitly endorse elective abortion, either as state law or as AMA policy, there was some further debate over how much it liberalized the old policy. At the November 1970 convention the New Jersey delegation submitted a resolution to rescind this policy and return to the 1967 policy statement. Not only was it disapproved, but an attempt by the reference committee to forge a compromise between the wording of the 1967 and 1970 policies was voted down (Tatalovich 1971, 191).

Pro-choice advocates regularly cite the AMA as being within their coalition, but clearly the American Medical Association at that time never explicitly endorsed abortion on demand. On the other hand, reforms permitting therapeutic abortion reforms did not inspire much opposition by the Catholic minority within organized medicine; its effort to defeat AMA policy changes came when attempts were made to endorse abortion as an elective procedure. In sum, while the AMA quickly joined the forces urging reform of the state abortion laws during this period, there is a sense that organized medicine treaded cautiously despite the widespread support among rank-and-file physicians across the country and, moreover, that the 1970 policy correction was forced by legal developments in certain states.

Certainly one cannot characterize the AMA as representing the vanguard of the agitation for abortion reform in the United States—unless, that is, its role is contrasted against the passivity of the U.S. legal establishment, the American Bar Association.

The ABA was long viewed as a stodgy and tradition-bound organization, but no more, since there is now a lively debate over whether America's legal establishment has come to embrace the activist social agenda of the left (Federalist Society for Law and Public Policy Studies 1994). However, the nonrole played by the ABA in the 1960s abortion reform agitation cannot be doubted. Indeed, the ABA never acknowledged the abortion problem of the 1960s despite heightened media coverage and new state laws, which did have an effect on organized medicine. Its first action came in 1972, when the ABA's House of Delegates approved the Uniform Abortion Act, which had been promulgated by the National Conference of Commissioners on Uniform State Laws because of the variety of state laws on abortion; two years later the ABA approved a Revised Uniform Abortion Act, rewritten to reflect changes from the landmark *Roe v. Wade* ruling.

In August 1976 the ABA refused to consider one resolution urging a constitutional amendment banning abortion as well as a counterresolution opposing any such action. The counterresolution, from the Law Student Division, called upon the House of Delegates to oppose "restrictions on the availability of abortion beyond the guidelines of *Roe v. Wade* . . . all attempts to amend the Constitution of the United States to restrict or prohibit abortion . . . attempts to restrict abortion through the withholding of federal funds for such purpose . . . [and] state and local attempts to circumvent the decision of *Roe v. Wade*" (American Bar Association 1976a, 2). However, the chair of the House of Delegates ruled, on a point of order, "that the recommendation was not within the purposes of the Association" and, on appeal, the floor sustained that ruling by a vote of 198 to 70 (American Bar Association 1976b, 32). Two years later, though, the delegates voted 170–57 to resolve "that the American Bar Association supports legislation on the federal and state level to finance abortion services for indigent women" (American Bar Association 1978, 591). Given that the Supreme Court in 1977 had upheld state prohibitions on the use of Medicaid monies for abortion, this action was intended by the Section of Individual Rights and Responsibilities to urge legislative action because "the ability to pay for an abortion is, in a real way, the equivalent of having a right to choose to have an abortion." Thus far, however, no action by the ABA had officially and explicitly endorsed a privacy-based right to abortion.

What finally got the attention of activists was the Supreme Court ruling in *Webster v. Reproductive Health Services* (1989). Declaring that "in light of the *Webster* decision, the recent attempts to enact ever more intrusive state restrictions on the availability of abortion procedures, and the continued efforts to have *Roe* v. *Wade* overturned, the ABA can no longer afford to be silent on this important public policy issue. The ABA should lend its strong voice in recognition of the constitutional right of all women to decide whether to have an abortion, free from governmental interference" (American Bar Association 1990a, 18). Originally the ABA's Section on Individual Rights and Responsibilities, the ABA's Section of Criminal Justice, the Commission on Women in the Profession (which was chaired by Hillary Rodham Clinton), the Beverly Hills Bar Association, and the National Association of Women Lawyers coauthored this resolution that subsequently garnered support at the February 1990 annual convention from four other ABA sections and several local bar associations (Dade County, Los Angeles County, San Francisco) as well as the Young Lawyers Division and the Law Student Division.

> The American Bar Association recognizes the fundamental rights of privacy and equality guaranteed by the United States Constitution, and opposes legislation or other governmental action that interferes with the confidential relationship between a pregnant woman and her physician, or with the decision to terminate the pregnancy at any time before the fetus is capable of independent life, as determined by her physician, or thereafter when termination of the pregnancy is necessary to protect the woman's life or health. (American Bar Association 1990b, 19)

This resolution easily passed by a 238–106 margin, but that action only spurred further controversy within the profession. Six months later, the State Bar of Texas (1990) brought forth a resolution that the ABA House of Delegates "declare that it recognizes and respects the right of individual ABA members to hold and express personal views on the profound issues presented by abortion, without being bound by an ABA policy supportive of a particular viewpoint." Ultimately it was withdrawn in favor of an alternative that narrowly passed the Assembly (885–837) and the House of Delegates (200–188). It resolved that the ABA, "without adopting a policy supportive of a particular viewpoint, recognizes and respects the right of individual ABA members to hold and express personal convictions, beliefs, and views on the profound issues presented by a decision to terminate pregnancy" and, furthermore, that the ABA "recognizes that the questions presented by a decision to terminate pregnancy are extremely divisive, and that the ABA, for the good of the Association, will not adopt a policy supportive of a particular viewpoint with respect to constitutional, moral, medical or other questions involved in a decision to terminate pregnancy"

(American Bar Association 1990c, 43). But this policy of "neutrality" did not go unchallenged.

Two years later the ABA flip-flopped yet again on abortion when the Assembly (voting 659–340) and the House of Delegates (by a 276–186 margin) adopted this two-paragraph resolution:

> BE IT RESOLVED, That the American Bar Association opposes state or federal legislation which restricts the right of a woman to choose to terminate a pregnancy (i) before fetal viability; or (ii) thereafter, if such termination is necessary to protect the life or health of the woman.
> BE IT FURTHER RESOLVED, That the American Bar Association supports state and federal legislation which protects the right of a woman to choose to terminate a pregnancy (i) before fetal viability; or (ii) thereafter, if such termination is necessary to protect the life or health of the woman. (American Bar Association 1992b, 56)

This time only women lawyers brought the proposal to the convention. It was sponsored by the National Association of Women Lawyers, the National Conference of Women's Bar Associations, and forty-one women delegates to the House, who made explicit their feminist concerns. Saying that "not since the ABA's shameful 'neutrality' on civil rights in the late 50's and 60's has the Association shrunk from its historic and honored role as a leading participant in the nation's dialogue on pressing legal issues," they reminded their male colleagues that "the women who are members of the ABA and most of the daughters and granddaughters of ABA members will continue to control their reproductive lives because the funds will be found to ensure that our teenagers do not enter adulthood with the crushing burden of an unwanted child—or, worse, with infection or sterility from an unsafe abortion. *Our* daughters and granddaughters, for the most part, will not risk their lives because safe and legal abortions will continue to be available to persons of means. But the lawyers of America have a duty to ensure that the daughters and granddaughters of *all* Americans—not just those with professional-level incomes—enjoy the same basic rights, unfettered by laws designed to impose the morality and religious beliefs of others on the women of America" (American Bar Association 1992a, 1).

The CMA and CBA

As in the United States, abortion reform in Canada was due less to a groundswell of public opinion than to a lobbying campaign from above, but the similarity ends there, especially insofar as organized medicine and the legal establishment are concerned. The Canadian political landscape was characterized by Morton (1992, 19) this way: "Two professional groups, the Canadian Medical Association [CMA] and the Canadian Bar Association [CBA], spearheaded the effort. They received moral support from the United Church, the largest Protestant denomination in Canada, which began to support wider access to abortion in 1960. Surprisingly, women's groups played only a marginal role at this stage of the reform movement." Feminist scholars Brodie, Gavigan, and Jenson (1992, 25) concur that women did not mobilize behind abortion reform because "in the mid-sixties [they] did not have the political resources to press their positions or even a language in which they could express them."

Apparently the CMA first acted on abortion at the behest of the Canadian Bar Association. In 1965 the General Council of the CMA, its governing body, was informed that its Committee on Maternal Welfare had "prolonged discussion of the problem associated with therapeutic and criminal abortion" and "agreed that it would be desirable to discuss this question with the Canadian Bar Association before the Canadian Bar Association recommended any new legislation to government." The committee offered resolutions, which were accepted, to solicit information on the "incidence of therapeutic abortions" and "procedures for therapeutic abortions in the various provinces" throughout Canada and also to send representatives to join a study committee formed by CBA to assess the Criminal Code (Canadian Medical Association 1965, 78–79).

The following year the CBA had prepared a resolution for its annual meeting (which was adopted) to recommend that Section 237 of the Criminal Code be amended to allow a "Termination Board" to authorize an abortion where pregnancy endangered the physical or mental health of the woman, where the pregnancy resulted from a criminal act (rape), or where there existed "substantial risk" that the child would be born with grave mental or physical disabilities. But the CMA in 1966 would go no further than to approve a resolution to allow abortions "after consultation with and approval of a hospital-appointed therapeutic abortion committee" in cases "where the continuance of the pregnancy may endanger the life or the physical health or mental health of the mother." Interestingly, the recommendation also stipulated that "the written consent of the patient" must be obtained as well as "the consent of the spouse or guardian" where deemed necessary by the Therapeutic Abortion Committee (Canadian Medical Association 1966, 62–63).

Discussions within the CBA began as early as 1963, when a resolution from the British Columbia subsection asked that abortions performed pursuant to authority from a provincial board be legalized, but the Catholic Lawyers' Guild of British Columbia entered a brief opposing that resolution, and the matter was delayed to allow more study by other provincial subsections (Canadian Bar Association 1963, 177). Two years later the Criminal Justice Section proposed to amend the Criminal Code to allow abortions authorized by a termination board in cases where the "physical or mental health" of the woman was endangered, where pregnancy resulted from criminal assault, and where a "substantial risk" existed that the child "may be born with a grave mental or physical disability." It provoked minimal debate, but one member, who held the floor for his allotted ten minutes, talked about how a pregnant girl, under age sixteen might "become panicky" and flee to a big city, where she would "eventually find someone who will, for a fee, attempt to abort her" even though abortion was "extremely risky at any time," even under hospital conditions. He urged his colleagues "that the time has now come that this is a pressing problem in Canada that can no longer be ignored" and invited them to speak to doctors who "have seen what has happened when a girl is brought into the emergency room of a hospital because she has attempted to commit an abortion." In nine of ten cases, he alleged, the girl faces "permanent sterility, permanent injury, and, as if that was not bad enough ... when the child is born there is a tremendous psychological shock that attacks the child who is not mature enough, sometimes not even physically mature enough to give birth, but in any event, the emotional shock and scar remains with this child all through its life." But at least three speakers were cautious, suggesting that organized medicine be consulted, and others argued that the entire membership should be apprised of such a policy change. An amendment to distribute the report to the rank and file carried, and a final decision was postponed until the next year (Canadian Bar Association 1965, 90–99).

No doubt because of the publicity surrounding the abortion resolutions, debate at the 1966 annual meeting of the CBA was prolonged, filling forty-seven pages of minutes (Canadian Bar Association 1966, 74–120), and ultimately the three justifications for abortion—risk to the mother's health and life, grave mental or physical disability of the fetus, and criminal assault—were approved as well as the creation of termination boards in each province. Except for some amendments that adjusted specific language, the recommendation was approved intact, though the floor debate was pretty much dominated by opponents who raised moral and religious arguments against killing the fetus.

One referenced the position of the Roman Catholic Church "that the unborn child is a human being" (Canadian Bar Association 1966, 83); another said a "large body of people in Canada ... views man as having a spiritual component—a soul. They regard every man as possessing his right to life from God—not from man or society. They believe that no human authority can justify the deliberate and 'direct' destruction of 'innocent' human life" (Canadian Bar Association 1966, 99–100). Those defending liberalization talked about the collaboration between the CBA and the CMA. One speaker told his colleagues that "there can be nothing more immoral, nothing more irreligious than turning medical practitioners and decent people into criminals in the way which our present legislation does," and he reminded them that the CMA "has seen fit to endorse this sort of proposition" on therapeutic abortion (Canadian Bar Association 1966, 102). Another statement by a proponent, who was a member of the CBA-CMA study committee, recollected that

> our essential feeling could be expressed best in an article which we had examined prior to our gathering in Ottawa. This was an article by Mandeville Williams which was printed in the British Journal of Criminology in October of 1964, and the major concerns which we thought should influence us—and I'll mention a few as he did in his article prior to the discussions in England—were these: The prime social evil, he says, is the large number of abortions performed by unskilled operators. This will remain so long as we have only limited legislation for the medical profession. (Canadian Bar Association 1966, 112–13)

Only the final speaker, a woman who identified herself as an attorney in the welfare department of a large city, urged the general meeting not to "take the narrow view that legislation has only legal implications"; rather, it "has far-reaching social implications, and this matter of abortion has probably the farthest implications of any of it." Then she pointed out the social pathologies from ill-conceived pregnancies: "If the infant does not experience maternal love in this early stage of its life, the child at its adulthood is never able to feel real love as human beings know it as distinct from the animal species. And I would put to you that in many instances where a mother who is mentally unfit to rear a child or unfit to rear a child because she is too young will produce this type of psychopathic child unless a substitute mother is found for it" (Canadian Bar Association 1966, 111).

In 1967 the CMA endorsed essentially the same grounds for abortion that had been adopted by the CBA one year earlier, but the provincial termination boards were scrapped and replaced with hospital-based therapeutic abortion committees. Its Committee on Maternal Health recommended that the Criminal Code be amended so that the termination of a pregnancy would be lawful

(a) If continuation of the pregnancy will endanger the life or health of the pregnant female or there is substantial risk that the child may

be born with a grave mental or physical disability, and the operation is performed by a duly qualified and licensed medical practitioner, in a hospital accredited by the Canadian Council on Hospital Accreditation after approval by a Therapeutic Abortion Committee of such hospital, or
(b) Where there are reasonable grounds to believe that a sexual offence has been committed from which pregnancy has resulted. (Canadian Medical Association 1967, 69)

A motion to limit abortions to endangerment of the "life and health" of the woman was rejected, and it was recorded that "several" members of the General Council spoke against the amendment, including one who praised the report and said that "reform in therapeutic abortion was long overdue and ... it was the responsibility of the medical profession to lead this reform" (Canadian Medical Association 1967, 69–70).

In hearings on abortion before a committee of the House of Commons in 1967, the CMA sent a delegation that one Progressive Conservative MP called "distinguished lawbreakers" and a Liberal MP referred to as "the biggest gathering of abortionists ever held in Canada"—apparently a reaction to the admission by one physician that "I and my colleagues have been breaking the law now for a long time" by doing abortions and giving advice on contraception (quoted in de Valk 1974, 17). Thereupon ensued this exchange between Dr. Douglas Cannell, of the CMA, and the Liberal MP Robert Stanbury:

> MR. STANBURY: Is it then fair to say that ... Canadian doctors have indeed, on compassionate grounds, been performing abortions for some years?
> DR. CANNELL: I think that is a fair statement.
> MR. STANBURY: I am glad that they have but it is unfortunate that you have been exposed to criminal prosecution by so doing. I gather the main purpose of your resolution is to try to clarify the fact that it is permissible for doctors to do what they have indeed been doing and to encourage the availability of such treatment on a more equal basis in all hospitals across Canada rather than just in some, as has been the case.
> DR. CANNELL: I would say that is correct. (Brodie, Gavigan, and Jenson 1992, 27)

The CMA representatives affirmed that three conditions were appropriate reasons for a therapeutic abortion, but organized medicine was opposed to the notion of abortion on request as Dr. Henry Morgentaler advocated in his testimony on behalf of the Humanist Fellowship of Canada (Brodie, Gavigan, and Jenson 1992, 27). It would be four more years before organized medicine endorsed nontherapeutic abortions, though not without provoking considerable debate within the General Council. In 1971 the newly formed Council on Community Health Care created a study committee to focus on family planning issues, including sterilization and abortion. Its lengthy report included so many recommendations on abortion that the Board of Directors of the CMA invited the General Council to debate the fundamental proposition.

Its recommendation, which was barely accepted (on a 78–74 vote) by the General Council after much debate, declared: "The C.M.A. recognizes that there is justification on non-medical social grounds for the deliberate termination of pregnancy." Immediately a substitute was offered by a member: "The C.M.A. agrees that there is occasional justification on non-medical social grounds for the deliberate termination of pregnancy and recognizes that this involves the voluntary taking of a human life." Most discussion went against the substitute, including comments from one member that this "amendment does exactly what the resolution of the Board had tried to overcome and that is the inclusion of any emotional, religious or moral bias in the discussion of this problem" and that it was to be hoped that the "Council, as a group of responsible, intelligent citizens with a specific expertise and a specific area of knowledge . . . would consider the recommendation of the Board in that light: logically, sensibly, rationally and unemotionally." Other speakers went even further. One said, "The profession offers medical advice on social decisions which society must make," while another member echoed that sentiment, saying, "If society wants abortion on demand, society must provide facilities and due process within the law for proper controls." The objectionable substitute was defeated, so it was clear that the majority agreed with the Board of Directors, and apparently also with the logic of the final speaker, who argued that "there is no law in Canada at the present time that will allow an abortion on social grounds so, in effect, the C.M.A. will be saying that we recognize there are social indications but having said that the next step is for us to define those indications. It is up to society, through government, to bring in the legislation. Doctors across Canada have had to 'prostitute' themselves under the guise of performing therapeutic abortions when in reality there were no medical indications" (Canadian Medical Association 1971, 59–61).

Among the other eleven abortion-related resolutions adopted by the CMA in that 1971 meeting were recommendations to delete the therapeutic abortion committee requirement from the Criminal Code *but* to apply all applicable sections of the Criminal Code to those (even licensed MDs) performing abortions "in facilities other than approved hospitals" and, additionally, to provide for a right of refusal when "a physician whose moral or religious beliefs prevent him from recommending and/or performing this procedure" so long as the patient is told she may consult another physician.

Some pressure for reform came from organized religion. As early as 1960 the United Church favored abortions for health reasons but not socio-economic ones, and the Anglican Church in Canada also favored some liberalization (de Valk 1974, 10, 20). The 1967 resolution adopted by the Presbyterian Church in Canada opposed legalizing abortion "to reduce the number of illegal abortions, or as a method of population control" but nonetheless recommended that the Criminal Code be revised to legalize therapeutic abortions "when the continuance of a pregnancy endangers the mother's life or is likely seriously to impair her physical or mental health, when authorized by a panel of qualified medical authorities" (Muldoon 1991, 117–18). The position of the churches was to defer to the professional judgment of physicians on matters of abortion.

As would be expected, the primary opposition to abortion reform came from the Roman Catholic Church, but during those years its pro-life advocacy was less effective. It failed to mobilize a quick response against the legislation (de Valk 1974, ch. 8) because of "social and doctrinal upheaval associated with the Vatican Council and the papacy of John XXIII. While Catholics themselves were debating doctrinal and social questions, their interventions in the public and Parliamentary discussions tended to reflect a certain hesitancy to promote traditional positions with complete enthusiasm" (Brodie, Gavigan, and Jenson 1992, 32). On the floor of the House of Commons, the Créditiste MPs from Quebec expressed the Catholic viewpoint, but with no effect. Even Catholic MPs in the Liberal Party did not accept the logic of their position.

The largest organization of women—the National Council of Women—in 1964 became the first national organization to endorse legal abortion and twice, in 1965 and 1966, urged the government to establish a royal commission to provide "an objective and non-partisan basis for amending the law," which it called "confused, conflicting, outdated, and in certain instances, cruel and unjust" (quoted in de Valk 1972, 22). However, with the exception of feminists aligned with the emerging "women's liberation" movement (de Valk 1974, 41) and of course Dr. Morgentaler's Humanist Fellowship of Canada, few organizations agitating for reform had argued for abortion on demand as a requisite for reproductive freedom. Women were not major players in the development of abortion reform in Canada, as Brodie, Gavigan, and Jenson observe:

> Doctors and lawyers concerned for their medical clients, then, organized the movement toward reform. The proposals with the greatest impact on the deliberations of the Parliamentary Committee came from the CBA and CMA.

> Because of the perception that doctors and lawyers were the experts on the topic and because of the privileged access they had to the legislative process, their testimony was received with deference and their preferred discourses of medicalization and liberalization shaped the reform. As a result, the reform was interpreted at the time to be one addressing *doctors'* difficulties with an ambiguous law. Women's needs and women's voices counted for little and the themes their groups expressed about fairness, equity, and social justice were taken up by very few. (Brodie, Gavigan, and Jenson 1992, 32)

Morton (1992, 19) agrees that the CMA was the leading advocate, with the CBA's help, though for both the "principal motivation appears to have been neither sexual equality nor social engineering but professional self-interest: to protect doctors against the legal uncertainties of the current law."

Summary

This review of the events that led to abortion reform in Canada and the United States shows more parallels between the two countries than departures. In both countries the reform agitation dates from the 1960s and the leading advocates were physicians, though in the United States it was mainly activists outside the AMA who were involved, while in Canada the leading proponents of reform were within the ranks of organized medicine. The Canadian bar was prominently involved, but not the ABA. This pattern indicates that women's groups, especially in Canada, were marginal forces during the 1960s and explains why the debate over abortion reforms in Canada, as in the United States, was devoid of "rights" rhetoric. In both countries humanitarian concerns were important, but the driving force was the need to reconcile medical practice with the law. Canada was able to enact a reformed code on abortion in 1969, and by the end of that year eleven American states had liberalized their antiabortion laws, more or less following the "therapeutic" guidelines of the American Law Institute. Canadian and American reformers were thinking in tandem.

What was fortuitous was the restrained opposition of the Roman Catholic Church at this juncture. With some exceptions (such as in New York), most American states that reformed or repealed their abortion laws had small concentrations of Catholics, whereas the Catholic Church in Canada had been neutralized due to internal theological debate. Cross-cultural research by Field (1979, 776) on twenty-two non-Communist regimes in 1972 found that the "size of the Roman Catholic population accounts for nearly two-thirds of the (total) variation across nations in liberalness of abortion policies." In the House of Commons, Liberals from Quebec voted their party, not religion, in backing Prime Minister Trudeau (who was a French Quebec

Catholic). Had the church fully mobilized its constituency, the Liberal ranks in Parliament might have weakened considerably.

Legal developments in Canada and United States point to abortion reforms as being elite-driven rather than the consequence of popular demands, though a caveat hinges on the agenda-setting role of the mass media. During the late 1950s and early 1960s there was very little coverage given to the abortion "problem" in Canada, while in the United States there was a shared concern and concerted effort by the media to assist the reformers. In the process they undoubtedly persuaded the American people that therapeutic abortions were morally and legally tenable, because a virtual consensus emerged in public opinion behind that goal. The majority of Canadians and, most assuredly, the majority of Americans endorsed the reform objectives (see chapter 4).

Three other conclusions are more tentative. First, because reformers in Canada had to pressure only Parliament to achieve their goals, whereas their American counterparts had to focus energies on each state legislature, in the United States it would be more essential as a political strategy to engage the mass media to "nationalize" the debate over abortion reform in order to reach citizens across the fifty states. Second, getting national organizations such as the AMA to endorse abortion reform is another way to mobilize state-level constituent groups (state medical associations) to lobby state legislatures. By implication, coalition building among organized interests would be more extensive in the United States given the greater political and social fragmentation of the U.S. polity (see chapter 4). Third, political parties—certainly the Liberals under Prime Minister Trudeau—were vital to the fashioning of abortion policy in Canada. In the United States the Republicans and Democrats were not forced to deal with this issue until 1973, when *Roe* was handed down, and there was no political incentive for either party to take the policy initiative since jurisdiction over abortion rested solely with the states.

The next chapter discusses a profound difference in these two regimes. In the United States the abortion issue has come to symbolize the excesses of judicial activism, but in Canada the development of abortion policy has been accompanied by a measure of judicial restraint. Close scrutiny of abortion jurisprudence and the nature of judicial decision making will illustrate how much more the Supreme Court of the United States has politicized this conflict.

2

Judicial Activism and Judicial Activity

Is Canada Becoming Like the United States?

The argument of this chapter is that there is a fundamental difference between what the U.S. Supreme Court did in its 1973 *Roe v. Wade* decision and what the Supreme Court of Canada subsequently did in its 1988 ruling in *Morgentaler v. The Queen*. In the United States the high court created a constitutional right to an abortion, thus barring any governmental regulation unless it could withstand the highest judicial standard of strict scrutiny (and few could), whereas in Canada the high court declared the existing statute unworkable and, furthermore, invited Parliament to rework that legislation. To say that today both countries have legalized abortion as an elective procedure is to miss the point. In the United States elective abortions during the first trimester have been constitutionalized as a right; in Canada elective abortions are legal only because Parliament thus far has refused to act. If Congress wanted to overturn *Roe v. Wade,* it would have to garner two-thirds votes in the House and Senate and then obtain the approval of three-fourths of the states for a constitutional amendment. Parliament, to reverse the effect of *Morgentaler v. The Queen* (1988), would need only to enact new legislation (which presumably also would be challenged in court). In other words, the legal status quo in Canada is the result of legislative default—the failure of Parliament to act in the affirmative.

American Judicial Activism

What led the Supreme Court in 1973 to legalize abortion during the first trimester of a pregnancy was the privacy doctrine articulated in *Griswold v.*

Connecticut (1965) and its extension via the equal-protection clause in *Eisenstadt v. Baird* (1972). *Griswold v. Connecticut* (1965) was a birth control case in which contraceptive use was declared to be a privacy right inferred from various provisions of the Bill of Rights and the language of the Ninth Amendment, which reads: "The enumeration in the Constitution, of certain rights, shall not be construed to deny or disparage others retained by the people." Neither privacy nor abortion is mentioned anywhere in the Constitution or the Bill of Rights, so Justice Douglas in *Griswold v. Connecticut* (1965) resorted to finding "penumbras" and "emanations" from the First, Third, Fourth, Fifth, and Ninth Amendments. As he declared:

> [Prior] cases suggest that specific guarantees in the Bill of Rights have penumbras, formed by emanations from those guarantees that help give them life and substance. . . . Various guarantees create zones of privacy. The right of association contained in the penumbra of the First Amendment is one, as we have seen. The Third Amendment in its prohibition against the quartering of soldiers "in any house" in time of peace without the consent of the owner is another facet of that privacy. The Fourth Amendment explicitly affirms the "right of the people to be secure in their persons, houses, papers, and effects, against unreasonable searches and seizures." The Fifth Amendment in its Self-Incrimination Clause enables the citizen to create a zone of privacy which government may not force him to surrender to his detriment. The Ninth Amendment provides: "The enumeration in the Constitution, of certain rights, shall not be construed to deny or disparage others retained by the people."

Though the vote was 7–2, only one other justice joined Douglas's opinion. Instead, Chief Justice Warren and Justice Brennan joined the concurrence by Justice Goldberg, which entirely relied upon the Ninth Amendment. Justice Harlan also concurred but believed that "the proper constitutional inquiry in this case is whether this Connecticut statute infringes the Due Process Clause of the Fourteenth Amendment," so "while the relevant inquiry may be aided by resort to one or more of the provisions of the Bill of Rights, it is not dependent on them or any of their radiations." Justices Stewart and Black joined in each other's dissent. Black's position, which anticipated much of the scholarly criticism that would follow (mainly by conservatives but not entirely), bluntly stated: "I get nowhere in this case by talk about a constitutional 'right of privacy' as an emanation from one or more constitutional provisions. I like my privacy as well as the next one, but I am nevertheless compelled to admit that government has a right to invade it unless prohibited by some specific constitutional provision." As for Justice Stewart's dissent in *Griswold,* while he agreed that the Connecticut law was "silly" and "obviously unenforceable, except in the oblique context of the present case," he dared the majority to show him how it violated the Constitution: "In the course of its opinion the Court refers to no less than six Amendments to the Constitution: the First, the Third, the Fourth, the Fifth, the Ninth, and the Fourteenth. But the Court does not say which of these Amendments, if any, it thinks is infringed by this Connecticut law."

An important article by Roy Lucas (1968, 753–54) argued that "the constitutional issues implicit in the enactment and application of abortion laws have received scant judicial attention" in the 150 years preceding *Griswold.* Once that precedent was created, state and federal courts began extending the privacy doctrine, which in *Griswold* involved birth control, to abortion cases. Two cases of note, one state and one federal, were decided in the years prior to *Roe v. Wade.* In *People v. Belous* (1969), the California supreme court invalided its pre-1967 ("original") antiabortion law on the grounds that its stipulation that the procedure be "necessary to preserve life" was so vague as to violate the due process requirements for criminal law and, more important, that the law violated a woman's fundamental rights to life and to choose whether to bear children.

United States v. Vuitch

The first ruling by a federal court came shortly thereafter in *United States v. Vuitch* (1969), where the District Court for the District of Columbia ruled that the federal law governing abortion in the District of Columbia was unconstitutional. The ruling, by Judge Gerhard A. Gesell, argued that the word *health* in the statute was unconstitutionally vague, that the burden of proof rested with the physician to persuade a jury that his actions were necessary to preserve the mother's life or health, thus limiting his professional responsibility, and that the language prevented a woman from avoiding childbirth for any reason. The U.S. government appealed his ruling directly to the Supreme Court. In 1971 the justices, voting 5–4, let the District of Columbia abortion law stand, as Chief Justice Burger and Justices Harlan, White, and Blackmun joined the majority opinion, written by Justice Black. The law, as amended in 1953, read:

> Whoever, by means of any instrument, medicine, drug or other means whatever, procures or produces, or attempts to procure or produce an abortion or miscarriage on any woman, unless the same were done as necessary for the preservation of the mother's life or health and under the direction of a competent licensed practitioner of medicine, shall be imprisoned in the penitentiary not less than one year or not more than ten years. (D.C. Code Ann. @ 22–201)

However, the original statute of 1901 had allowed abortions only "for the purpose of preserving the life of any woman pregnant," and Justice Black relied heavily on that distinction in his argument in *United States v. Vuitch* (1971).

Noting that the "statute does not outlaw all abortions, but only those which are not performed under the direction of a competent, licensed physician, and those not necessary to preserve the mother's life or health," Justice Black reminded us that "as a general guide to the interpretation of criminal statutes that when an exception is incorporated in the enacting clause of a statute, the burden is on the prosecution to plead and prove that the defendant is not within the exception." Observing that Congress had amended the 1901 law in 1953, he concluded: "Because abortions were authorized only in more restrictive circumstances under previous D.C. law, the change must represent a judgment by Congress that it is desirable that women be able to obtain abortions needed for the preservation of their lives or health. It would be highly anomalous for a legislature to authorize abortions necessary for life or health and then to demand that a doctor, upon pain of one to ten years' imprisonment, bear the burden of proving that an abortion he performed fell within that category. Placing such a burden of proof on a doctor would be peculiarly inconsistent with society's notions of the responsibilities of the medical profession. Generally, doctors are encouraged by society's expectations, by the strictures of malpractice law, and by their own professional standards to give their patients such treatment as is necessary to preserve their health. We are unable to believe that Congress intended that a physician be required to prove his innocence." Thus the Court ruled that under the District of Columbia criminal code, "the burden is on the prosecution to plead and prove that an abortion was not 'necessary for the preservation of the mother's life or health.' "

Justice Black then made quick work of the view that the word *health* is unconstitutionally vague. Admittedly, he said, "the legislative history of the statute gives no guidance as to whether 'health' refers to both a patient's mental and physical state," but then Black cited a recent judicial ruling in the District of Columbia that "accords with the general usage and modern understanding of the word 'health,' which includes psychological as well as physical well-being. Indeed Webster's Dictionary, in accord with that common usage, properly defines health as the 'state of being . . . sound in body [or] mind.' Viewed in this light, the term 'health' presents no problem of vagueness. Indeed, whether a particular operation is necessary for a patient's physical or mental health is a judgment that physicians are obviously called upon to make routinely whenever surgery is considered."

Justice Black noted that the "appellee has suggested that there are other reasons why the dismissal of the indictments should be affirmed," namely "this Court's decision in *Griswold v. Connecticut,*" and "although there was some reference to these arguments in the opinion of the [district] court," the majority opinion did not feel obliged to address that aspect; "since that question of vagueness was the only issue passed upon by the District Court it is the only issue we reach here."

On this point Justice William O. Douglas, a liberal who authored the "right to privacy" doctrine in *Griswold,* offered his long dissent. Douglas's argument in *Vuitch* was that the law was too vague because psychological considerations were not more explicitly stated and because women had a right to choose whether or not to terminate their pregnancies. Justice Douglas asked several hypothetical questions, including: "Is any unwanted pregnancy a 'health' factor because it is a source of anxiety? Is an abortion 'necessary' in the statutory sense if the doctor thought that an additional child in a family would unduly tax the mother's physical well-being by reason of the additional work which would be forced upon her? Would a doctor be violating the law if he performed an abortion because the added expense of another child in the family would drain its resources, leaving an anxious mother with an insufficient budget to buy nutritious food? Is the fate of an unwanted child or the plight of the family into which it is born relevant to the factor of the mother's 'health'?" All this led inevitably to Douglas's making the kind of analogy with *Griswold* that two years later was codified in *Roe:*

> Abortion touches intimate affairs of the family, of marriage, of sex, which in *Griswold v. Connecticut* . . . we held to involve rights associated with several express constitutional rights and which are summed up in "the right of privacy." They include the right to procreate . . . the right to marry across the color line . . . the intimate familial relations between children and parents. . . . There is a compelling personal interest in marital privacy and in the limitation of family size. And on the other side is the belief of many that the fetus, once formed, is a member of the human family and that mere personal inconvenience cannot justify the fetus' destruction. This is not to say that government is powerless to legislate on abortions. Yet the laws enacted must not trench on constitutional guarantees which they can easily do unless closely confined.

Roe v. Wade

At least eight times prior to 1973 the Supreme Court had declined to review rulings against state antiabortion laws, including the landmark *Belous* decision in California. By the time *Roe v. Wade* was decided, conflicting precedents could be cited from eighteen state and federal abortion cases. During those years the antiabortion statutes of Connecticut, Georgia, Texas, North

Dakota, Illinois, Kansas, New Jersey, Wisconsin, California, and Florida had been nullified, while existing laws in Kentucky, Louisiana, North Carolina, Ohio, Utah, Indiana, Mississippi, and South Dakota had been upheld. Usually the Supreme Court, when faced with conflicting rulings from appellate courts around the country, will respond, and it did so here by ruling on the arguments posed by the original 1854 Texas antiabortion law in *Roe v. Wade* (1973) and the 1968 Georgia therapeutic reform law in *Doe v. Bolton* (1973).

The task for the plaintiff attorneys in *Roe v. Wade* was to convince at least five justices that the privacy doctrine could logically be extended to reproductive freedom—in this case, the freedom to abort an unwanted pregnancy. That was accomplished even though Justice Blackmun, who spoke for the majority in *Roe,* acknowledged that "the Constitution does not explicitly mention any right of privacy. In a line of decisions, however, going back perhaps as far as [1891], the Court has recognized that a right of privacy, or a guarantee of certain areas or zones of privacy, does exist under the Constitution." Thereupon he cited eleven cases; they are listed below along with the issue involved in each.

Boyd v. United States (1886)	unreasonable search and seizure (private papers)
Meyer v. Nebraska (1923)	English language for public/private instruction
Pierce v. Society of Sisters (1925)	public-school attendance law
Skinner v. Oklahoma (1942)	sterilization of habitual criminals
Prince v. Massachusetts (1944)	child labor laws and sale of religious materials
Griswold v. Connecticut (1965)	birth control advice to married couples
Loving v. Virginia (1967)	miscegenation law
Katz v. United States (1967)	unreasonable search and seizure (wiretapping)
Terry v. Ohio (1968)	unreasonable search and seizure ("stop and frisk")
Stanley v. Georgia (1969)	possession of obscene materials in home
Eisenstadt v. Baird (1972)	birth control advice to unmarried persons

Clearly *Griswold,* and its extension to unmarried persons in *Eisenstadt,* was *the* essential precedent that *Roe v. Wade* required. None of the previous cases pertained to marital sex, let alone abortions, and, absent the "zone of privacy" doctrine of *Griswold,* it would have taken quite a leap of liberal faith (and jurisprudence) to argue that this variety of previous cases—to allow parents to arrange private instruction for their children *(Meyer* and *Pierce),* or to prevent the sterilization of persons with multiple felonies *(Skinner),* or to marry somebody of another race *(Loving),* or to protect criminal defendants from unreasonable searches and seizures *(Katz* and *Terry)*—would logically lead to a woman's right to choose to abort her pregnancy. Appellate court judge Henry J. Friendly (1978), though sympathetic to the pro-choice side, was troubled by the ruling in *Roe v. Wade.* He stated that courts sometimes have to deal with social policy but nonetheless believed that the court should "rest its decision on an ascertainable jural principle rather than support its decision on the basis of its conception of what is desirable social policy" (p. 21) and, specifically with regard to *Roe,* that "one must face the question of how a case of such overwhelming social import could be translated into a principle of constitutional law, particularly in the face of what we now know to be deeply felt contrary views" (p. 33). Thus Friendly claimed that *Roe* did not really have "precedential support" and said it was "a bit disingenuous" (p. 34) for the Supreme Court to rest its decision on a right to privacy. But however tenuous the legal thread might seem to pro-lifers, conservatives, proponents of judicial restraint, and probably many ordinary citizens, by a 7–2 vote the justices reasoned that "privacy" in marital sex could be extended on similar legal grounds to abortion.

In his majority opinion in *Roe,* Justice Blackmun distinguished among the three trimesters of pregnancy. During the first trimester, he argued, "the attending physician, in consultation with his patient, is free to determine, without regulation by the State, that, in his medical judgment, the patient's pregnancy should be terminated. If that decision is reached, the judgment may be effectuated by an abortion free of interference by the State." It is during the second trimester that the "State's important and legitimate interest in the health of the mother" allows government to "regulate the abortion procedure to the extent that the regulation reasonably relates to the preservation and protection of maternal health." Finally, during the third trimester, "the State's important and legitimate interest in potential life . . . is at viability. This is so because the fetus then presumably has the capability of meaningful life outside the mother's womb. State regulation protective of fetal life after viability thus has both logical and biological justifications. If the State is interested in protecting fetal life after viability, it may go so far as to proscribe abortion during that period, except when it is necessary to preserve the life or health of the mother."

Justice William Rehnquist authored a dissenting opinion in *Roe* that was joined by Justice Byron White. In it Rehnquist "marshaled a strict constructionist argument against the Court's extension of the right of privacy and supported his interpretation of the Fourteenth Amendment by drawing on history. Contrary to Blackmun's reading of the text and historical context of the Fourteenth Amendment, Rehnquist concluded that the fact that several states had restrictive abortion laws in 1868, when the Fourteenth Amendment was adopted, is evidence that the amendment was not intended to bar states from regulating abortion" (Craig and O'Brien 1993, 30–31). Rather than accept an unabridged version of the incorporation doctrine based on a loose reading of the Fourteenth Amendment, Rehnquist countered that "the Due Process Clause of the Fourteenth Amendment undoubtedly does place a limit, albeit a broad one, on legislative power to enact laws such as this. If the Texas statute were to prohibit an abortion even where the mother's life is in jeopardy, I have little doubt that such a statute would lack a rational relation to a valid state objective. . . . But the Court's sweeping invalidation of any restrictions on abortion during the first trimester is impossible to justify under that standard, and the conscious weighing of competing factors that the Court's opinion apparently substitutes for the established test is far more appropriate to a legislative judgement than to a judicial one."

Critiques of Roe

More than one observer might concur with the early commentary by Tatalovich and Daynes (1981b, 644) that the "Supreme Court's landmark 1973 rulings . . . did not resolve this dispute but rather aggravated it to the point where the very fabric of democratic politics is threatened." The counts against judicial activism in this instance are five. The U.S. Supreme Court (1) used a nontextual, interpretive, and open-ended jurisprudence on which to base the right to abortion, (2) ruptured the social and political consensus that was developing during the 1960s around "therapeutic" abortion, (3) denied the legislative authorities their policy-making role to fashion new legislation on abortion, (4) polarized the abortion debate by disregarding any legal protections for the fetus in favor of a woman's right of privacy, and (5) unleashed a political backlash as the pro-life counteroffensive was mobilized.

The first critique was made almost immediately after *Roe v. Wade* was announced, by Ely (1973). The second lies at the heart of the policy analysis by Tatalovich and Daynes (1981a). Especially the third but also the fourth critique was systematically developed by Glendon (1987) in her comparative study of abortion laws. The fifth is typified by the work of Tushnet (1989, 413), who argues that "the Court's decision in *Roe* had a number of effects that combine to suggest why appeals to [abortion] rights may sometimes be politically debilitating." Tushnet (1989, 413–14) gives four reasons to support that conclusion: (1) *Roe* "stimulated the growth of the antichoice movement," (2) "prochoice advocates tended to rely more and more substantially on the courts to protect their interests," (3) pro-life advocates "were able to add new arguments to their appeals," namely their "appeal to democracy" against judicial activism, and (4) *Roe* "handed an issue that a politically important segment of the society cared deeply about to the Republican party, and it did so for free. Republicans could adopt antichoice positions at almost no political cost." For now, I will focus extensively on the Ely and Glendon critiques and defer my own additional comments on consensus building (the second critique) until the conclusion of this section.

It is John Hart Ely (1973) who, though sympathetic to the outcome in *Roe,* goes beyond the standard criticism—that the Court nullified the state law on broad grounds rather than because of statutory vagueness—to level his chief complaint that "the Court claims no mandate to second-guess legislative balances [the woman and the fetus], at least not when the Constitution has designated neither of the values in conflict as entitled to special protection. But even assuming it would be a good idea for the Court to assume this function, *Roe* seems a curious place to have begun." Then Ely explains:

> Laws prohibiting the use of "soft" drugs or, even more obviously, homosexual acts between consenting adults can stunt "the preferred life styles" of those against whom enforcement is threatened in very serious ways. It is clear such acts harm no one besides the participants, and indeed the case that the participants are harmed is a rather shaky one. Yet such laws survive, on the theory that there exists a societal consensus that the behavior involved is revolting or at any rate immoral. Of course the consensus is not universal but it is sufficient, and this is what is counted crucial, to get the laws passed and keep them on the books. Whether anti-abortion legislation cramps the life style of an unwilling mother more significantly than anti-homosexuality legislation cramps the life style of a homosexual is a close question. But even granting that it does, the *other* side of the balance looks very different. For there is more than simple societal revulsion to support legislation restricting abortion: Abortion ends (or if it makes a difference, prevents) the life of a human being other than the one making the choice. (Ely 1973, 923)

Without knowing it, Ely's reference to antisodomy laws was prophetic. *Griswold* was the linchpin for the future of this kind of jurisprudence, but in fact the Supreme Court has not been bound by that precedent when confronting other issues that directly involve personal privacy in sexual relations. Indeed, the Supreme Court *refused* to extend the logic of privacy rights to consenting homosexuals in *Bowers v. Hardwick* (1986), and the National Right to Life Committee, as amicus in the 1989 *Webster* case, took notice of that judicial retreat and asked the high court to "be guided by the analysis of *Bowers v. Hardwick* . . . and find that there is no constitutional right to abortion." A reasonable person would be hard-pressed not to comprehend, rightly or wrongly, that a consistently straightforward jurisprudence extends from the "right" of couples to have privacy in birth control matters to the "right" of women to get abortions during the first trimester to the "right" of homosexuals to enjoy consenting relationships. Certainly advocates of gay rights see the *Bowers* decision as "inconsistent with treating privacy as autonomy" (Samar 1991, 36). What seemed bizarre was the logic of Justice Byron White, who voted with the majority in *Bowers.*

He began his *Bowers* opinion by stating that "we first register our disagreement with the Court of Appeals and with respondent that the Court's prior cases have construed the Constitution to confer a right of privacy that extends to homosexual sodomy and for all intents and purposes have decided this case." This listing of precedents cited by the court of appeals included these same precedents cited by the Supreme Court in its *Roe* decision (indicated with an asterisk) plus two newer cases, *Roe* and *Carey.*

Meyer v. Nebraska (1923)*	*Loving v. Virginia* (1967)*
Pierce v. Society of Sisters (1925)*	*Stanley v. Georgia* (1969)*
Skinner v. Oklahoma (1942)*	*Eisenstadt v. Baird* (1972)*
Prince v. Massachusetts (1944)*	*Roe v. Wade* (1973)
Griswold v. Connecticut (1965)*	*Carey v. Population Services International* (1977)

(In *Carey* the Supreme Court nullified a New York State law prohibiting the advertising and sale of contraceptives to minors.) However, White focused squarely on *Griswold, Eisenstadt,* and *Roe* because they "were interpreted as construing the Due Process Clause of the Fourteenth Amendment to confer a fundamental individual right to decide whether or not to beget or bear a child." But he denied there was a linkage between those rulings and the case at hand.

Accepting the decisions in these cases and the above description of them, Justice White's *Bowers* opinion concluded that:

> we think it evident that none of the rights announced in these cases bears any resemblance to the claimed constitutional right of homosexuals to engage in acts of sodomy that is asserted in this case. No connection between family, marriage, or procreation on the one hand and homosexual activity on the other has been demonstrated, either by the Court of Appeals or by the respon-

dent. Moreover, any claim that these cases stand for the proposition that any kind of private sexual conduct between consenting adults is constitutionally insulated from state proscription is unsupportable.

White's position is a tenuous and disingenuous argument on which to abandon privacy as a fundamental right via the incorporation doctrine that links the Bill of Rights to the Fourteenth Amendment. Four justices who were reliable pro-choice votes on abortion—Blackmun, Brennan, Marshall, and Stevens—would have overturned the Georgia law, whereas White and Rehnquist (both dissenters in *Roe*) along with O'Connor, Burger, and Powell formed the majority. Simply put, the votes were there to uphold the Georgia law, and this tortured logic was devised to do so, just as the precedent that yielded *Roe v. Wade* in 1973 was itself grounded on a series of cases that had no direct bearing on birth control, let alone abortion.

Glendon (1987) argues that *Roe v. Wade* created the most one-sided abortion policy found in twenty Western democracies (table 2.1) by denying any positive legislative role to the states. In this, she contrasts the *Roe* ruling against the only other constitutional case on abortion in the developed West, a 1975 ruling by the West German constitutional court invalidating that country's abortion law. Whereas "the court in the United States held that restrictive state legislation impinged on a fundamental right of the pregnant woman," the "West German court found that a liberal federal statute did not sufficiently protect unborn life." Moreover, "the West German court left the legislature with considerable room to devise . . . abortion policy, providing only that abortion is not to be completely decriminalized unless adequate alternative preventive measures are in place, and that the total effect of the laws in the area is to support and protect the value of human life. Within this framework, the Bundestag was able to work out a compromise typical of that reached at this stage in history by most other Western nations" (Glendon 1987, 33–34). A very different scenario affected the United States:

> *Roe v. Wade* and succeeding cases . . . have virtually closed down the state legislative process with respect to abortions prior to viability. Legislative attempts to provide for more information, deliberation, and counseling, more participation by others in the woman's decision-making process, and even protection for the fetus after viability have regularly been struck down. (Glendon 1987, 34)

Ruth Bader Ginsburg, now a Supreme Court justice, had expressed reservations about *Roe v. Wade* in print (1985) and in a lecture at New York University School of Law (1992), though she was the first nominee since

Table 2.1

Abortion Policy in Twenty Developed Nations by 1986

Abortion Illegal	Medical Grounds Only	Socioeconomic Conditions	Elective in Early Pregnancy	Elective Until Viability	No Abortion Law
Belgium	Canada (after 1969)	England	Austria	United States	Canada (after 1988)
Ireland	Portugal	Finland	Denmark		
	Spain	France	Greece		
	Switzerland	West Germany	Norway		
		Iceland	Sweden		
		Italy			
		Luxembourg			
		Netherlands			

Source: Adapted from Mary Ann Glendon, *Abortion and Divorce in Western Law* (Cambridge: Harvard University Press, 1987), p. 14.

O'Connor to publicly defend abortion rights and has been reliably liberal on the bench. Her earlier writings revealed that, on the one hand, Ginsburg believed that abortion should have been viewed as an equality right rather than a privacy right, yet, on the other hand, she was concerned that the broad-based judicial attack on state abortion laws was based on weak precedent and, moreover, short-circuited the trend by states to liberalize their abortion laws (Greenhouse 1993b). As Ginsburg stated:

> Roe, I believe, would have been more acceptable as a judicial decision if it had not gone beyond a ruling on the extreme statute before the Court. The political process was moving in the early 1970s, not swiftly enough for advocates of quick, complete change, but majoritarian institutions were listening and acting. Heavy-handed judicial intervention was difficult to justify and appears to have provoked, not resolved, conflict. (Ginsburg 1985, 385–86)

Seven years later Ginsburg (1992, 1198) expressed the similar view that courts "do not alone shape legal doctrine but . . . they participate in a dialogue with other organs of government, and with the people as well"— which is why, she continued, "doctrinal limbs too swiftly shaped, experience teaches, may prove unstable. The most prominent example in recent decades is *Roe v. Wade*." Then Ginsburg explains more fully what the Court should have done in 1973:

> The seven to two judgment in *Roe v. Wade* declared "violative of the Due Process Clause of the Fourteenth Amendment" a Texas criminal abortion statute that intolerably shackled a woman's autonomy; the Texas law "except[ed] from criminality only a *life-saving* procedure on behalf of the [pregnant] woman." Suppose the Court had stopped there, rightly declaring unconstitutional the most extreme brand of law in the nation, and had not gone on, as the Court did in *Roe,* to fashion a regime blanketing the subject, a set of rules that displaced virtually every state law in force. Would there have been the twenty-year controversy we have witnessed. . . . A less encompassing *Roe,* one that merely struck down the extreme Texas law and went no further on that day, I believe . . . might have served to reduce rather than to fuel controversy. (Ginsburg 1992, 1199)

What If?

I agree with Ginsburg's analysis but would put the turning point back two years earlier. The ruling by the Supreme Court majority in *United States v. Vuitch* (1971) was designed to salvage the District of Columbia abortion law, but clearly the grounds it established to successfully prosecute a doctor for doing an abortion would be difficult to surmount. In Canada, the refusal of Quebec juries in 1973, 1975, and 1976 to convict Dr. Henry Morgentaler for performing clinic abortions ultimately (and despite adverse judgments from higher courts) had the effect of allowing him to operate freely and openly in that province. The *Vuitch* case may arguably be viewed, in retrospect, as a lost opportunity for the judiciary to join the emerging consensus favoring therapeutic abortions and thus settle the abortion dispute before it broke out as political war. Certainly the narrow grounding of *Vuitch* in "vagueness" could have been extended to other pending cases so that state legislatures would have been encouraged to revise their abortion statutes in light of the "minimum standard" of including mental as well as physical health of the woman, which the Court established in *Vuitch*. It would have given rise to lawsuits challenging most original state abortion laws as unduly restrictive (since most allowed abortions only to save the mother's life) and forced reluctant state legislatures to confront abortion policy at a time when the American Law Institute reform proposals were gaining acceptance among medical professionals, state political elites, and the public. The judicial requirement that mental as well as physical health be included in order to pass constitutional muster would have opened a gaping hole in abortion codes under which pregnancies could be terminated in a host of circumstances under the guise of medical standards and the physician-patient relationship. Moreover, this approach would have brought the Supreme Court in line with the reform agenda that stressed therapeutic abortions, thus promoting the consensus-building process that, eventually, would have led some states to enact elective abortion laws on their own. To argue retrospectively that most states would not have done so, given the retrenchment that followed the *Webster* (1989) decision allowing more abortion restrictions, is to do history an injustice (Fung 1993; also see Dworkin 1993, 9). To argue that if *Roe* is overturned, states would choose between very permissive abortion laws (like those of New York) or very restrictive ones (like those of Louisiana) simply shows how much this society has been polarized by political events following the 1973 landmark decision. Anticipating future developments on the eve of *Roe,* however, shows an emerging policy consensus in which the majority of states would probably have adopted laws allowing "therapeutic" abortions to safeguard the woman's life as well as her physical and *mental* health, in cases of rape, and where serious fetal disabilities are indicated. To make the counterfactual argument that "even if such compromise laws had been established, there would have been large regional variations in abortion access and the result would have been less access overall than under *Roe*" (Fung 1993, 496–97) is beside the point, and purely speculative. Not knowing how history would have unfolded had the high court adopted a *Vuitch* approach rather than its *Roe* methodology, no alternative historical scenario—however plausible—can discount the fact that, more than two decades after *Roe,* we face a situation where legalized abortion is the norm but access to abortion services is the exception (see chapter 7) across large stretches of the United States. Every indication is that the problem of access will worsen year by year, to the point where *Roe* will become a legal dead issue, not because it was overturned but because it has been ignored.

Roe *and Its Progeny*

In the more than two decades since the high court constitutionalized a right of abortion, pro-choice activists have looked to the judiciary to protect their newfound liberty. Except for those rulings that upheld state or local bans on public funding and the use of public facilities for abortions—*Beal v. Doe* (1977), *Maher v. Roe* (1977), *Poelker v. Doe* (1977)—as well as the 1980 decision in *Harris v. McRae* (which supported the Hyde Amendment, by which Congress refused to fund most abortions under Medicaid), the Supreme Court has yielded little ground to the pro-lifers. The judiciary has not reneged on abortion as a woman's constitutional right, has refused to acknowledge that the unborn is a "person" in any legal sense, and has fairly regularly struck down obstacles designed to prevent women from obtaining abortions. Since 1973 there have been twenty-three major Supreme Court abortion rulings (table 2.2); all but *Harris v. McRae* (1980) and three cases during 1993–1994 involved state or local regulations on abortion (the most recent decisions pertained to protests around abortion clinics). Taking my rough itemization of the state and local restrictions being challenged in those cases, during the period between 1974 and 1992, 26 of 44 (59 percent) restrictions on the abortion procedure were struck down, but there was a dramatic change beginning in 1989. For the period from 1974 to 1988, 25 of 33 regulations (76 percent) were invalidated, but from 1989 to 1992 the Court nullified only 1 of 11 (9 percent), thus highlighting the consequences of the ruling in *Webster v. Reproductive Health Services* (1989). Since then, moreover, the most important cases have involved efforts by pro-choice activists and abortion clinic operators to function without facing serious harassment from such direct-action groups as Operation Rescue. In two of the three decisions the Supreme Court sided with the clinics despite objections from conservatives, notably Justice Scalia, that those legal remedies infringe upon the protesters' free-speech guarantees under the First Amendment.

Webster *and Its Aftermath*

Webster resulted because there was turnover on the high court and Republicans had owned the White House for all but four years between 1973 and 1989. With a new partisan lineup, pro-choice advocates feared that *Roe*

Table 2.2

U.S. Supreme Court Abortion Cases, 1973–1994

Date	Case	State	Ruling	Vote	Legal Issues
1973	*Roe v. Wade*	TX	O	7–2	Abortion to save life of mother only
1973	*Doe v. Bolton*	GA	O	7–2	Abortion in cases of rape/incest and to save mother's life; required Georgia-licensed doctor; hospital accreditation and review committee; residency requirement
1975	*Bigelow v. Virginia*	VA	O	7–2	State law prohibiting newspaper ads for abortions and abortion services
1976	*Planned Parenthood of Central Missouri v. Danforth*	MO	O	5–4	Saline abortion method; spousal and parental consent; records and reports; doctor must preserve life of fetus; viability definition
1976	*Bellotti v. Baird*	MA	O	9–0	Parental consent with judicial bypass
1977	*Beal v. Doe*	PA	U	6–3	Medicaid funding limits challenged as illegal under Social Security Act
1977	*Maher v. Roe*	CT	U	6–3	Medicaid funding limits challenged under equal-protection clause of 14th Amendment
1977	*Poelker v. Doe*	MO	U	6–3	Public hospital refused to do abortions
1979	*Bellotti v. Baird*	MA	O	8–1	Parental consent with judicial bypass for "good cause"
1979	*Colautti v. Franklin*	PA	O	6–3	Use abortion methods that would enhance the survival of fetus

(continued)

Table 2.2 *(continued)*

Date	Case	State	Ruling	Vote	Legal Issues
1980	*Harris v. McRae*	—	U	5–4	Constitutionality of Hyde Amendment limits on Medicaid funds for abortions
1981	*M.L. v. Matheson*	UT	U	6–3	Parental notification
1983	*City of Akron v. Akron Center for Reproductive Health*	OH	O	6–3	Second-trimester abortions only in hospitals; parental consent; 24-hour waiting period; informed consent; pathology report; second physician; humane disposal of fetal remains
1983	*Planned Parenthood of Kansas City v. Ashcroft*	MO	O	6–3	Second-trimester abortions in hospital
			U	5–4	pathology report; second doctor after viability; parental consent with judicial bypass
1983	*Simopoulos v. Virginia*	VA	U	8–1	Second-trimester abortions only in state-licensed facilities
1986	*Thornburgh v. American College of Obstetricians and Gynecologists*	PA	O	5–4	Lecture on risk and fetal development; informed consent; 24-hour waiting period; records/reports; use abortion methods that would enhance the survival of fetus; second physician after viability
1987	*Zbaraz v. Hartigan*	IL	O	4–4	Parental notification; waiting period
1989	*Webster v. Reproductive Health Services*	MO	U	5–4	Preamble defined life; prohibited use of public funds for abortion counseling; no use of public facilities or employees for abortions; viability tests required
1990	*Hodgson v. Minnesota*	MN	U	5–4	Two-parent notification with judicial bypass

(continued)

Table 2.2 *(continued)*

Date	Case	State	Ruling	Vote	Legal Issues
1990	*Ohio v. Akron Center for Reproductive Health*	OH	U	6–3	Parental notification
1990	*Rust v. Sullivan*	—	U	5–4	1st Amendment (free speech) challenge to executive branch regulation against abortion counseling by agency getting federal family planning grants
1992	*Planned Parenthood of Southeastern Pennsylvania v. Casey*	PA	U	5–4	24–hr. waiting period; records; parental consent; counseling/informed consent
			O	5–4	spousal consent
1993	*Bray v. Alexandria Women's Health Clinic*	—	O	6–3	Use of 1871 Civil Rights Act to enjoin protesters from blocking abortion clinics as "conspiracy" to violate civil rights
1994	*National Organization for Women v. Scheidler*	—	U	9–0	Abortion clinics can use the federal Racketeer-Influenced and Corrupt Organizations Act (RICO) to sue antiabortion protest groups for damages
1994	*Madsen v. Women's Health Center*	—	U	6–3	1st Amendment (free speech) challenge to Florida state court injunction creating a buffer zone between abortion clinic and protesters

Note: O, overturned existing legal provision; U, upheld legal provision.

would be overturned, and pro-lifers relished the thought. The 5–4 vote in *Webster* did neither. While the constitutional right to abortion was not directly repudiated, its practical effect was narrowed because Chief Justice Rehnquist, along with Justices Kennedy and White, abandoned the trimester framework of *Roe,* O'Connor applied her "undue burden" standard to uphold the regulations, and Scalia favored outright reversal of *Roe.* Indeed, those chilling prospects led pro-choice litigants to informally resolve, and not appeal to the high court, their suit against Illinois's use of its medical practice laws to impose regulations on abortion clinics (Mezey, Tatalovich, and Walsh 1994).

Because the 1973 *Roe* decision had established a "fundamental" right to abortion and thus required "strict scrutiny" of any state or local regulations that prevented or deterred women from obtaining abortions, few laws could withstand that legal hurdle. So *Webster* is a turning point in abortion jurisprudence and paved the way for the Court—three years later—to approve state antiabortion restrictions that previously had been struck down. Various questions were at issue in *Planned Parenthood of Southeastern Pennsylvania v. Casey* (1992). The Pennsylvania Abortion Control Act required an unmarried woman under eighteen to obtain written consent from at least one parent, or from a judge, and also required a parent to accompany the woman for abortion counseling. After giving her informed consent, the woman had to wait twenty-four hours before getting the abortion. Prior to getting her written consent, doctors had to counsel the woman on the risks of abortion, detail the stages of fetal development, and supply her with a list of facilities that offered alternatives to abortion. Doctors also had to report each abortion performed to the state, including copies of the informed consent and, where appropriate, the parental consent forms, and those documents were to be open to the public. All these provisions were *upheld* by the Supreme Court except the spousal notification requirement. It stipulated that a married woman had to certify that she had notified her husband, but with exceptions allowed: where the husband did not father the child, or if the father could not be located, or when pregnancy resulted from a "spousal sexual assault" that was reported to the police, or where the woman feared "bodily injury" if she told her husband.

Several features of this new Pennsylvania law—counseling on risks and fetal development, informed consent, a twenty-four-hour waiting period, recordkeeping, and reports—were virtually identical to provisions of an earlier Pennsylvania statute that the Supreme Court had struck down in 1986 in its *Thornburgh* decision (see table 2.2). This turnabout shows that the ideological center of gravity on the Court had shifted to the right. Both *Thornburgh* and *Casey* were decided by 5–4 votes, but the Court's composition had changed with new appointments. President Reagan elevated Justice William Rehnquist to be the new chief justice and appointed Antonin Scalia and Anthony Kennedy as associate justices; then President Bush secured confirmation for his nominees, David Souter (who has become extremely liberal in his voting behavior) and Clarence Thomas (as conservative as Justice Scalia).

Although *Casey* technically overturned an injunction against the state law issued by federal district judge Daniel H. Huyett III, Huyett would not lift the injunction until he received "implementing regulations in each of Pennsylvania's 67 counties by their courts of Common Pleas and departments of Welfare" so that "judicial bypass procedures are available for minors, both to protect their privacy and to provide their Supreme-Court-mandated redress from potentially abusive family situations" (quoted in Hansen 1993a, 11). Then Huyett agreed with Planned Parenthood that, in light of the *Casey* ruling, a new trial should be held to allow them to show how the statute places "undue burdens" on women seeking abortions. This action by Huyett was blocked when the attorney general appealed to the U.S. Court of Appeals for the Third Circuit, which ruled unanimously that Huyett had overstepped his authority. "The [Supreme] Court did not intend the lower courts to consider additional issues or to undertake proceedings other than routine, ministerial ones necessary to carrying out its mandate," declared the three-judge panel (quoted in Hinds 1994, 10). Not until March 21, 1994, did the first woman in Pennsylvania seeking an abortion have to comply with the *Casey* decision that was handed down on June 29, 1992.

The final three Supreme Court cases involved attempts by abortion clinic operators to stop antiabortion protesters from harassing their clients and to make them liable for lost income and damages. The first attempt in *Bray v. Alexandria Women's Health Clinic* (1993) was unsuccessful (Greenhouse 1993a). The 1871 Civil Rights Act, known as the Ku Klux Klan Act, was a Reconstruction-era bill meant to protect freed slaves from any "conspiracy" to deny them their civil rights. Here abortion clinic operators had sued to enjoin Operation Rescue protestors from demonstrating at their facilities on the grounds that they were conspiring to deprive women seeking abortions of their civil rights. In the majority opinion, by Justice Scalia, the Court made the argument that "opposition to voluntary abortion cannot possibly be considered such an irrational surrogate for opposition to (or paternalism toward) women." On this, Justice O'Connor dissented because she believed that women are a "protected class" within reach of that law (Greenhouse 1993a).

But the crescendo of demonstrations, pickets, sit-ins, and confrontations nationwide by antiabortion forces may have had an effect on the justices, even some of the conservative ones. In *Bray* O'Connor—the important swing vote in abortion cases—joined the pro-choice bloc (Blackmun and Stevens) in filing dissents. But in January 1994 a unanimous Supreme Court gave abortion clinics a powerful new legal weapon to combat violence in ruling on *National Organization for Women v. Scheidler*. Later, in June, a 6–3 majority (with Scalia, Thomas, and Kennedy dissenting) supported the pro-choice side in *Madsen v. Women's Health Center*. It was politically significant that Chief Justice Rehnquist authored both those opinions.

The National Organization for Women (NOW) accused Operation Rescue and others of organizing a nationwide conspiracy to force abortion clinics to cease operations by means of a "pattern of racketeering activity," including intimidation, bombings, harassment of staff, vandalism, and other violent acts. The decision in *National Organization for Women v. Scheidler* (1994) was a shocker since two lower federal courts had dismissed the suit on the grounds that the Racketeer-Influenced and Corrupt Organizations Act (known as RICO) applied only to such activities when the motivation was economic gain, not protest. Indeed, Congress had enacted the legislation to combat the infiltration of legitimate businesses by organized crime, not to deter protest. The outcome hinged on Rehnquist's assertion that no economic motive was required by the statute, so that showing that the "affairs" of an "enterprise" are conducted through a "pattern of racketeering activity" is sufficient enough. As the protesters argued that the application of RICO would infringe on their First Amendment rights, Justices Souter and Kennedy joined in a separate concurrence to address that issue (Greenhouse 1994a).

The *Madsen* ruling involved an injunction by a state judge designed to prevent disruptive antiabortion protesters from blocking access to an abortion clinic in Melbourne, Florida. Again protesters raised free-speech objections, but Chief Justice Rehnquist said the thirty-six-foot buffer zone around the clinic "burdens no more speech than necessary to accomplish the governmental interest at stake." He also upheld a ban on excessive noise during clinic operating hours but struck down as too broad and excessive a three-hundred-foot buffer zone within which protesters could not make uninvited approaches to patients or employees. The Supreme Court acted because the Florida Supreme Court had upheld the injunction but the U.S. Court of Appeals for the Eleventh Circuit struck it down. Justice Kennedy, though he had voted with the majority in *Scheidler,* had filed a concurrence with Justice Souter to reassure the protesters that they could sue again if RICO powers were abused in such a way as to curb their First Amendment rights. But in *Madsen* Justices Kennedy and Thomas joined with Justice Scalia's dissent in charging that "the judicial creation of a 36-foot zone in which only a particular group, which has broken no law, cannot exercise its rights of speech, assembly, and association, and the judicial enactment of a noise prohibition, applicable to that group and that group alone, are profoundly at odds with our First Amendment precedents and traditions." So angry was Justice Scalia that, after the chief justice finished reading his majority opinion, Scalia took his turn and gave a rendition of his dissent, which at one point referred to "abortion mills" even though that phrase did not appear in Scalia's written opinion (Greenhouse 1994b).

If the twin legal developments of the post-*Webster* era continue, they may indicate that the Supreme Court is trying to forge a new policy consensus on abortion: allow restrictions on abortions so long as they do not impose an "undue burden" on women and foster the growth of abortion clinics as the only viable delivery mechanism for abortion services. To sustain an "absolute" right to abortion and disallow all restrictions (as was virtually the situation following *Roe*) will not serve the cause of reconciliation and consensus building. To attempt to require that all hospitals, physicians, and health care personnel provide abortion services would cause a serious escalation of political turmoil. Ordinary citizens would not understand why women should be guaranteed their right to choose an abortion when, at the same time, health care facilities and professionals are denied their right to refuse to terminate a pregnancy.

Canadian Judicial Activity

The Canadian Supreme Court, compared to the U.S. Supreme Court, has not displayed full-blown judicial activism, notwithstanding its *Morgentaler* ruling that nullified the 1969 Criminal Code on abortion. The 1988 decision by the high court was a dramatic about-face from its refusal thirteen years earlier to intervene affirmatively in the abortion controversy. That 1975 abortion ruling illustrated that "the Canadian court's reluctance to intervene can be traced to the ambiguous nature of the 1960 Canadian Bill of Rights and its status as a 'simply statutory instrument' and not part of an established constitution" (Mezey 1983, 700). The 1960 Bill of Rights was passed by Parliament as ordinary law but provided that no federal statute could violate its enumeration of human rights. So "the Bill of Rights established a code of conduct to which all federal statutes were obliged to conform" (Mezey 1983, 700), but what about the judiciary? At that time, the Canadian Constitution was embodied largely in the British North America Act of 1867, which outlined the reach of legislative and judicial authority. The Constitution Act of 1982, approved by the British Parliament at the request of the Canadian Parliament, now contains the Charter of Rights and Freedoms, which has replaced the 1960 Bill of Rights.

Thus the story of the March 26, 1975, *Morgentaler* ruling involved his appeals on the basis of the 1960 statutory Bill of Rights. On August 15, 1973, Morgentaler's abortion clinic in Montreal was raided by police during the performance of an abortion on a graduate student from abroad who could not afford the fee charged by local hospitals. He alleged that Section 251 of the 1969 Criminal Code was limited by the British North America Act and, in addition, that it violated the due process clause of the Canadian Bill of Rights. He also invoked Section 45 of the Criminal Code and the

"Bourne Defence" (or "defence of necessity"), which had evolved in common law from the famous *R. v. Bourne* (1939) case in Britain, when Justice Macnaghten instructed the jury that an abortion could be performed in good faith to safeguard the life and health of the mother despite the fact that British law then made no such exceptions. Similarly, the elements of a Section 45 defense meant that a surgical procedure was performed for the benefit of the patient with reasonable care and skill and with regard to the health of the patient. "In other words, as a matter of law, the section 45 and the 'necessity' defences supplemented the provisions of section 251(4) of the Criminal Code which allowed legal abortion only after approval by the therapeutic abortion committee of a hospital" (Mezey 1983, 703).

A British jury acquitted Dr. Bourne in 1939, and Dr. Morgentaler was acquitted by a Quebec jury in 1973. But the Crown prosecutor appealed that decision to the Quebec Court of Appeal, which reversed the acquittal and ordered the trial judge to sentence Morgentaler, ruling that Section 45 was not applicable to abortion because to do so would categorize abortion like any other surgical procedure. Also, the Court of Appeal ruled that evidence supporting the "defence of necessity" was not offered during the trial. At this point Morgentaler appealed to the Supreme Court of Canada based on both the "defence of necessity" and constitutional claims, but his appeal was rejected and he was ordered to face sentencing.

His constitutional appeal was a gamble, and Morgentaler lost: "Morgentaler alleged that the Canadian Bill of Rights 1960, derived from the US Constitution, imported American common law decisions into Canadian law, and thus *Roe v. Wade* case law should be followed in Canada. He urged that women had a right to privacy under the Canadian Bill of Rights which encompassed the decision to terminate a pregnancy, especially during the first trimester" (Mezey 1983, 704). The high court unanimously dismissed his constitutional claims and then, by a 6–3 vote, affirmed the Court of Appeal ruling that Section 45 did not displace Section 251(4) and, furthermore, that the trial judge had erred in allowing the jury to consider the "defence of necessity" because there was no evidence at trial to show that an emergency existed. In his opinion, the chief justice took note that "what is patent on the face of the prohibitory portion of s. 251 is that Parliament has in its judgment decreed that interference by another, or even by the pregnant woman herself, with the ordinary course of conception is socially undesirable conduct subject to punishment. That was a judgment open to Parliament in the exercise of its plenary criminal law power, and the fact that there may be safe ways of terminating a pregnancy, or that any woman or women claim a personal privilege to that end, becomes immaterial." At base, says Mezey (1983, 705), "by rejecting the constitutional argu-

ments and declining to question the constitutionality of the legislative enactment, the Canadian Supreme Court showed a degree of judicial restraint"
and "defined its role with respect to constitutional adjudication in a very
narrow sense."

The 1975 ruling involved Morgentaler in the modern era of Canadian
abortion politics. In 1988 the Supreme Court voted 5–2 to remove abortion
from the Criminal Code. Section 251 of the 1969 statute had restricted
abortions to accredited or approved hospitals and only where pregnancy
·terminations were certified by the majority of a hospital therapeutic abortion committee. While the immediate effect of its ruling was to make abortion a medical issue between the woman and her doctor, all five justices in
the majority indicated that they would accept some federal restrictions on
abortion. The provinces, while they could not make abortion a criminal
offense, could try—and various provinces did try—to regulate abortion as
they do any health service.

The difference between 1975 and 1988 was the 1982 Canadian Charter
of Rights and Freedoms, and Morgentaler mounted his second legal
challenge pursuant to Section 7, which states: "Everyone has the right to
life, liberty and security of the person and the right not to be deprived
thereof except in accordance with the principles of fundamental justice." In
1983 Morgentaler and two other physicians were charged with unlawfully
doing abortions in his Toronto clinic. When appealed to the high court, the
fundamental legal issue was whether the Criminal Code infringed on a
woman's right to "life, liberty and security of the person" as guaranteed by
Section 7 of the Charter. The *Morgentaler v. The Queen* (1988) judgment
was comprised of three opinions, which may be outlined as follows:

- Section 287 (then 251) of the *Criminal Code* infringed a woman's
  right to security of the person;
- The process by which a woman was deprived of that right was not
  in accord with fundamental justice;
- The state interest in protecting the fetus was sufficiently important
  to justify limiting individual Charter rights at some point; and
- The right to security of the person of a pregnant woman was infringed
  more than was required to achieve the objective of protecting the fetus,
  and the means were not reasonable. (Dunsmuir 1991, 11)

To summarize the point of law, Dunsmuir (1991, 11) read the decision to
mean "that the legislation interfered with the security of the person of a
woman in limiting, by criminal law, her effective and timely access to
medical services when her life or health was endangered. This criminaliza-

tion was not in accordance with fundamental justice." Three majority opinions in *Morgentaler* were authored: by Chief Justice Dickson with Justice Lamer, by Justice Beetz with Justice Estey, and by Justice Wilson alone. A dissent was filed by Justice McIntyre, joined by Justice LaForest.

Dickson argued that the *Criminal Code* (Section 251) "clearly interferes with a woman's physical and bodily integrity. Forcing a woman, by threat of criminal sanction, to carry a foetus to term unless she meets certain criteria unrelated to her own priorities and aspirations, is a profound interference with a woman's body and thus an infringement of security of the person. A second breach of the right to security of the person occurs independently as a result of the delay in obtaining therapeutic abortions caused by the mandatory procedures of s. 251 which results in a higher probability of complications and greater risk. The harm to the psychological integrity of women seeking abortions was also clearly established."

Beetz argued that "before the advent of the Charter, Parliament recognized, in adopting s. 251(4) of the *Criminal Code,* that the interest in the life or health of the pregnant woman takes precedence over the interest in prohibiting abortions, including the interest of the state in the protection of the foetus, when 'the continuation of the pregnancy of such female person would or would be likely to endanger her life or health.' This standard in s. 251(4) became entrenched at least as a minimum when the 'right to life, liberty and security of the person' was enshrined in the *Canadian Charter of Rights and Freedoms* at s. 7." Moreover, he continued, "security" of the person within the context of Section 7 "must include a right of access to medical treatment for a condition representing a danger to life or health without fear of criminal sanction" and, furthermore, "according to the evidence, the procedural requirements of s. 251 of the *Criminal Code* significantly delay pregnant women's access to medical treatment resulting in an additional danger to their health, thereby depriving them of their right to security of the person." Such deprivation violates the principles of fundamental justice.

Beetz then observed that "the primary objective of s. 251 . . . is the protection of the foetus," which "does relate to concerns which are pressing and substantial in a free and democratic society and which, pursuant to s. 1 of the *Charter,* justify reasonable limits to be put on a woman's right." The means utilized in Section 251 "are not reasonable and demonstrably justified" but "it is possible that a future enactment by Parliament that would require a higher degree of danger to health in the latter months of pregnancy, as opposed to the early months, for an abortion to be lawful, could achieve a proportionality which would be acceptable under s. 1 of the *Charter.*" In other words, says Morton (1992, 245), the Beetz-Estey opinion, unlike that by Dickson and Lamar, "rejected the claim that 'threat of health' was unconstitutionally vague" and so "explicitly accepted the principle of limiting abortions to 'therapeutic' reasons (reasons of health), and also the use of some sort of third-party determination to ensure 'a reliable, independent and medically sound opinion in order to protect the state interest in the fetus.' This implied that a revised section 251 with a 'streamlined' determination process would be acceptable. In sum, for Beetz and Estey, section 251 violated section 7 because it imposed 'unnecessary rules [that] impose delays which result in additional risk to women's health.' The problem with section 251 was not what it tried to achieve, but how it went about it."

Justice Wilson (the first woman appointed to the high court, by Liberal prime minister Trudeau) agreed that the Criminal Code posed a threat to the physical or psychological security of pregnant women, but she went beyond therapeutics: "The right to 'liberty' contained in s. 7 [of the Charter] guarantees to every individual a degree of personal autonomy over important decisions intimately affecting his or her private life. Liberty in a free and democratic society does not require the state to approve such decisions but it does require the state to respect them." Thus Wilson believed that "a woman's decision to terminate her pregnancy falls within this class of protected decisions" because it "will have profound psychological, economic and social consequences for her," "deeply reflects the way the woman thinks about herself and her relationship to others," and "is not just a medical decision; it is a profound social and ethical one as well." Section 251 thus deprives the pregnant woman of her "security of the person" under Section 7 of the Charter and, in addition, "offends freedom of conscience guaranteed in s. 2(a) of the *Charter*. The decision whether or not to terminate a pregnancy is essentially a moral decision and in a free and democratic society the conscience of the individual must be paramount to that of the state. "The decision to abort was, according to Justice Wilson, a matter of conscience," and criminalizing such a decision violated the freedom of conscience guaranteed by Section 2(a) of the Charter.

As to the unborn, Wilson said, "the value to be placed on the foetus as potential life is directly related to the stage of its development during gestation," which therefore "supports a permissive approach to abortion in the early stages where the woman's autonomy would be absolute and a restrictive approach in the later stages where the state's interest in protecting the foetus would justify its prescribing conditions. The precise point in the development of the foetus at which the state's interest in its protection becomes 'compelling' should be left to the informed judgment of the legislature which is in a position to receive submissions on the subject from all the relevant disciplines."

In sum, this ruling, unlike *Roe,* was not grounded in privacy rights and did not preclude parliamentary restrictions on abortions. Rather, the reasoning of the Canadian Supreme Court hinged on the unworkable nature of the existing abortion law, which posed a threat to the "security" of women, unlike the U.S. Supreme Court opinion, which made virtually no mention of abortion services. "Much of [plaintiff's lawyer Morris] Manning's case centered on his argument that the law created unequal access to abortion—coupled with distressing, often dangerous delays" (Janigan 1988, 10). Of the five-person majority, only Justice Wilson was receptive to the appellant's argument that, following the U.S. example, a constitutional right to abortion should be established.

Lest we forget, there were two dissenting justices in *Morgentaler,* which indicated that there may well be enough votes on the nine-member Canadian Supreme Court to uphold "reasonable" restrictions on abortions based on gestational development (as suggested by Wilson) should Parliament make the attempt (which it did with Bill C-43; see chapter 3).* In *Morgentaler,* Justices McIntyre and LaForest defended judicial restraint and gave a traditional interpretation by declaring that "the power of judicial review of legislation, although given greater scope under the *Charter,* is not unlimited. The courts must confine themselves to such democratic values as are clearly expressed in the Charter and refrain from imposing or creating rights with no identifiable base in the *Charter."* Therefore, "the proposition that women enjoy a constitutional right to have an abortion is devoid of support in either the language, structure or history of the constitutional text, in constitutional tradition, or in the history, traditions or underlying philosophies of our society." And any failure to gain access to abortion services cannot be attributed to the *Criminal Code* per se, because "this machinery was considered adequate to deal with the type of abortion Parliament had envisaged. Any inefficiency in the administrative scheme is caused principally by forces external to the statute—the general demand for abortion irrespective of the provisions of s. 251. A court cannot strike down a statutory provision on this basis."

Her reading of this case led Glendon to agree that "the justices in the Canadian majority, by contrast (except for Justice Wilson), were quite content to leave for another day such questions as to what extent and under what circumstances might the legislature give priority to the interests of the pregnant woman, or to those of the fetus, or to social concerns for maternal

---

*Since one member was incapacitated when *Morgentaler* was decided and the Canadian Supreme Court avoids hearing cases with an even number of justices, one justice was excused from the deliberations and the other seven were empaneled.

health and developing life. Declining to second-guess Parliament on the substance of abortion regulation, the Court confined itself to ruling that certain procedural features of the existing system violated a pregnant woman's right to 'security of the person' under section 7 of the Canadian Charter of Rights and Freedoms" (Glendon 1989, 575).

Trilogy of Abortion Cases

The 1988 *Morgentaler* case was the first of a trilogy of important abortion decisions issued by the Canadian Supreme Court. The *Tremblay v. Daigle* (1989) case began when Jean-Guy Tremblay won a temporary injunction preventing Chantal Daigle, his former girlfriend, from aborting her pregnancy, a request upheld by the Quebec Superior Court and the Quebec Court of Appeal, whereupon Daigle appealed to the high court. By the time the Supreme Court ruled, Daigle's attorney informed the justices that she, at the twenty-fourth week of her pregnancy, had decided to have the abortion. Even though the case was moot, the Supreme Court invalidated Tremblay's injunction on various grounds, primarily legislative intent. That is, "the Court is not required to enter the philosophical and theological debates about whether or not a foetus is a person, but, rather, to answer the legal question of whether the Quebec legislature has accorded the foetus personhood" because "ascribing personhood to a foetus in law is a fundamentally normative task" and "decisions based upon broad social, political, moral and economic choices are more appropriately left to the legislature." Ultimately the justices in *Tremblay* ruled that the National Assembly of Quebec did not choose to do so because "the *Quebec Charter*, considered as a whole, does not display any clear intention on the part of its framers to consider the status of a foetus." In other words, the high court would not ascribe personhood to the fetus and, once again, deferred to the legislative branch in resolving that issue.

The third case involved a direct attempt to force the Canadian Supreme Court to grant legal protection to the unborn. *Borowski v. Canada* (1989) was litigated by Morgentaler's nemesis, Joe Borowski, an ex–union activist and former Manitoba NDP cabinet member who became Canada's foremost pro-life crusader. Though his original legal efforts preceded the Charter of Rights and Freedoms of 1982, his final appeal argued that Section 7, granting "everyone" the "right to life, liberty and security," should be extended to the unborn.

The Saskatchewan Court of Queen's Bench in 1983 ruled that the fetus was not a legal person, and its judgment was upheld by the Saskatchewan Court of Appeal in 1987, setting the stage for a high-court review. On

March 9, 1989, the Canadian Supreme Court sidestepped the constitutional issue of whether the fetus has a right to life under the Charter, arguing instead that Borowski's appeal was moot since Section 251 of the Criminal Code already had been nullified by its *Morgentaler* decision. That the controversy was moot hinged on three constitutional doctrines articulated in *Borowski,* the third of which is based on "the need to demonstrate some sensitivity to the effectiveness or efficacy of judicial intervention." That is, "what the appellant seeks is to turn this appeal into a private reference. . . . To accede to this request would intrude on the right of the executive or order a reference and pre-empt a possible decision of Parliament by dictating the form of legislation it should enact. To do so would be a marked departure from the traditional role of the Court." Of course Borowski was devastated, complaining that "it would be a waste of my time to ever go back before those gutless . . . judges who wasted ten years of our time" (quoted in Brodie, Gavigan, and Jenson 1992, 95). But an option remained insofar as all three rulings in the trilogy of abortion cases of 1988–1989 encouraged the legislative branch to write a new law on abortion and specify the legal status of the fetus.

Summary

Three conclusions seem paramount from this chronicle of Canadian constitutional case law as compared to the U.S. experience. First, *Morgentaler* (1988) did not constitutionalize an abortion right in the manner of *Roe v. Wade.* Second, judicial concern about the fetus and even fetal rights colored the justices' opinions. Third, Parliament was virtually invited by the Supreme Court to rewrite the law to balance the competing values of a woman's rights and the potential of life. The first point is aptly summarized by feminist scholar Janine Brodie:

> Contrary to popular perceptions that the *Morgentaler* decision had granted women reproductive rights, only one judge cast abortion as a question of women's reproductive rights. Moreover, all judges recognized that the state may have a legitimate interest in protecting the fetus. Women did have rights but these were rights to health-care free from potentially harmful regulations and third-party interference. Only within a universal health-care system could these rights be read as a code for reproductive freedom, and the pro-choice movement certainly interpreted the decision in this way. Like the *Roe* decision, the *Morgentaler* decision guaranteed nothing. From a strictly legal perspective, the Court simply struck down the 1969 regulatory regime without providing guidelines for a new national policy. In fact, the Court explicitly argued that a new regulatory regime, one which balanced the interests of the woman and the fetus, would have to be negotiated in the political sphere. (Brodie 1994, 131)

On the second point, Donna Greschner brings an explicitly feminist perspective to assess how the high court handled the *Tremblay v. Daigle* case, not so much the outcome as its failure to address, "other than implicitly through its comments on the 'ordeal' [experienced by Daigle], . . . the consequences for women of bestowing constitutional or statutory rights to foetuses or potential fathers. Foetal rights are discussed without any attention to the context in which they would operate if recognized: the specific, material and immediate context of an individual woman's body and the general pervasive context of the subordination of women. The court does see the inseparability of the woman and her foetus: 'A foetus would appear to be a paradigmatic example of a being whose alleged rights would be inseparable from the rights of others, and in particular, from the rights of the woman carrying the foetus.' Yet the court does not set out the negative ramifications for women of enforcing a concept of foetal rights. A more empathic approach would likely have led the court to openly consider the impact on women of the concept of foetal and potential father's rights" (Greschner 1990, 660).

The third point is made by Mary Ann Glendon, who brings a decidedly antifeminist viewpoint to this issue. "Since six of the seven judges in *Morgentaler* (1988) indicated they were prepared to accord considerable latitude to the legislature in working out a new legal approach to abortion" (Glendon 1989, 581), Glendon fully expected Parliament to fill the abortion policy void. Because not only "is the court-legislature relationship in Canada situated within a parliamentary system of government, but the limitations on legislative power that were imposed by the Charter in 1982 are significantly less drastic than those that have come to be accepted in the American constitutional tradition. Whatever a 'free and democratic society' as those words are used in the Charter may be, therefore, it will take shape within a tradition which has reposed more confidence in elected representatives and less in judges than has been the case in the United States" (Glendon 1989, 587).

The constitutional developments that accompanied the abortion controversy in Canada and the United States are strong testimony to the fact that the U.S. Supreme Court is the outlier among high courts in the common-law world (Holland 1991). For that reason, the evidence is conclusive that much of the blame for the resulting furor over abortion policy must be attributed to the excessive level of judicial activism by the U.S. federal courts, and principally the high court. But before a too sanguine view of judicial activity in Canada is accepted, it must be noted that ominous trends can be sensed on the legal horizon. Since 1988 federal or provincial high courts have intervened to stop virtually every effort by provinces to impose "time, place or manner" restrictions on abortions (see chapter 7), so perhaps the rhetoric of the Canadian Supreme Court's restraint in the trilogy of abortion cases may conceal an ideological commitment to the pro-choice position. One scholar who suggests this possibility is F.L. Morton, who notes that "the Court's sharply contrasting approaches to Charter interpretation in the *Daigle* and *Morgentaler* cases also raised questions about judicial bias. Why did the Court adopt a narrow and legalistic approach to determine fetal rights, but a broad, purposive approach to decide abortion rights?" (Morton 1992, 287). A closer look at those cases indicates that "at the most explicit and obvious level, this [prevailing] view of judicial self-restraint was accurate. But at a more subtle level, there was contradictory evidence. The *Daigle* majority used the methods of the *Morgentaler* minority. Why had the Court exercised the techniques of judicial self-restraint when ruling on the rights of the unborn, but the tools of judicial activism when dealing with the rights of the mother?" (Morton 1992, 288–89).

3

The Legislative Response

Abortion in Congress and Parliament

Abortion has been a convulsive political issue for many parliamentary governments. In Germany, it caused a breach between East and West following unification, and then the German constitutional court in 1993 declared the new abortion law to be unconstitutional. In the wake of its successful democratization movement, the Polish Parliament in 1993 moved to tighten abortion restrictions, thus undoing a 1956 law that allowed virtually unlimited abortions. Abortion has been a periodic issue in the Parliament of the United Kingdom; it led to popular referenda in Italy and Ireland; and it persists as a divisive issue in the U.S. Congress, the latest episode being legislation (which was vetoed) in 1996 to ban a gruesome procedure known as "partial-birth" abortion, which is performed after the twentieth week of a pregnancy. Is the Canadian Parliament an exception to this pattern?

There is little research on how moral policies affect Canada's lawmaking process. Distinctions among Canadian policies are made on other grounds (Pal 1987; Brooks 1989; Coleman and Skogstad 1991), and abortion is not usually included in those analyses. To extend theoretical insights and empirical findings from European parliamentary contexts to Canada is a fairly straightforward matter. More innovative, however, is the task of evaluating whether the U.S. Congress has operated in a fashion similar to the Canadian Parliament.

First, what is needed are qualitative indexes that evaluate formal procedures and legislative rules in order to signal whether abortion provoked more "abnormal" (as opposed to "normal") deliberations. Second, legislative voting on abortion in Congress and Parliament can be compared to assess whether similar forces affected the outcome. Third, because moral conflict calls forth such emotional commitment, it would be revealing to identify the activists who are promoting the pro-life legislative agendas in both countries.

Cohan (1986, 27, 30) argues that "for most Western democracies abortion . . . is a marginal [issue] and . . . treated differently by decision-makers than core [economic] issues," due to its civil liberties and rights dimensions and, furthermore, "mechanisms [Private Members' Bills, or PMBs] have evolved to take the steam out of such issues by permitting resolutions to problems that impose minimal obligations on the core decision-making bodies." However, he cautions that "the use of peripheral mechanisms makes that [policy] resolution less authoritative than had it been stamped with the mark of core [legislative] decision-making bodies in their respective countries" (Cohan 1986, 46), and here he draws parallels between the use of PMBs in Great Britain and judicial activism in the United States. To the degree that moral conflicts such as abortion are transformed into economic disputes, presumably the core decision makers—Parliament and Congress—would become involved more directly in conflict resolution.

Much of Cohan's insight comports with my formulation of the process hypotheses (see the introduction to this volume) but not his speculation that issue evolution may affect abortion. Tatalovich and Daynes (1988) allege that moral conflicts are fundamentally unlike other policies in this regard. Abortion has staying power because the zero-sum quality of that debate does not basically change over time. From this perspective, a resolution of the abortion controversy would have to depend more on institutional (or social) forces rather than alterations in policy content. This chapter begins with Canada, where the legislative history of abortion policy is relatively brief, and continues with coverage of the more-than-two-decade-long debate in the U.S. Congress.

Parliament Confronts Abortion

No concerted attempt was made to amend the reformed Criminal Code of 1969 until the issue was forced onto the legislative agenda by the Canadian Supreme Court. Updating this policy history requires that attention be given to the parliamentary deliberations that led to a series of roll call votes on May 23 and May 29, 1990, with respect to Bill C-43, a government proposal to recriminalize abortion after *Morgentaler v. The Queen* (1988).

On May 20, 1988, a three-pronged motion was placed before the Parliament so that the government could get the sense of the House on a free vote about a new abortion policy. The main resolution (called the "gestational approach") stated that abortions could be legally obtained by any women from a qualified physician in the earlier stages of pregnancy so long as the doctor believed that the continued pregnancy posed a threat to her physical or mental well-being, but abortions at any subsequent stage of pregnancy required approval by two physicians. Amendment A (the pro-life option) would have tightened up the original motion by allowing abortions only when two physicians agreed that the continued pregnancy endangered the life of the woman, or seriously and substantially endangered her health, and there was no alternative for alleviating the risk. Considerations of health related to stress, anxiety, or any other socioeconomic reasons were disallowed by Amendment A. On the other hand, Amendment B (the pro-choice option) would have eased all restrictions in the original motion by legalizing abortions at any stage of pregnancy if performed by a qualified physician (Day, Heaton, Byfield, and Stevenson 1988).

But the maneuver failed. The government "didn't expect the ferocious reaction it received from both sides of the abortion spectrum. Feminist lobbies denounced any attempt to restore Criminal Code sanctions against abortion. On the other hand, pro-life spokesmen from across the nation heaped scathing condemnation of all three options including the so-called 'pro-life' choice" (Day, Heaton, Byfield, and Stevenson 1988, 11). Since the government faced dissension within the Tory caucus and because debate would be limited and amendments prohibited, both Liberals and New Democrats denounced the procedures as antidemocratic and illegal, and as a result, the government "sheepishly withdrew its proposal" (Morton 1992, 251). On July 26 a second attempt was made when the identical wording of the main resolution of May was reintroduced but without the optional amendments. This time, however, the government would permit amendments from the floor as well as a free vote by the MPs. The formal motion was proposed by MP Doug Lewis. Declaring its goal of defending "the fundamental value and inherent dignity of each human being and the inherent worth of human life" and achieving "a balance between the right of a woman to liberty and security of her person and the responsibility of society to protect the unborn," the motion stated:

> Such legislation should prohibit the performance of an abortion, subject to the following exceptions:
> When, during the earlier stages of pregnancy: a qualified medical practitioner is of the opinion that the continuation of the pregnancy of a woman would, or would be likely to, threaten her physical or mental well-being; when the woman in consultation with a qualified medical practitioner decides to terminate her pregnancy; and when the termination is performed by a qualified medical practitioner; and

> When, during subsequent stages of pregnancy: the termination of the pregnancy satisfies further conditions, including a condition that after a certain point in time, the termination would only be permitted where, in the opinion of two qualified medical practitioners, the continuation of the pregnancy would, or would be likely to, endanger the woman's life or seriously endanger her health. (*Statutes of Canada* 1988, 17964)

In all, twenty-one amendments were offered, but the Speaker of the House of Commons, for procedural reasons, accepted only five for a formal vote. The first, from MP Mary Collins, a Progressive Conservative (PC), made an early abortion a decision between the woman and her physician; regarding later abortions, it would have required the determination by only one doctor that the continued pregnancy endangered the woman's "mental and physical" health. It was defeated, 29–191. The second, from MP Ken James (PC), would have changed "earlier stages" to "first trimester," and for later abortions would have required agreement by two physicians that the pregnancy would or would likely endanger the life of the woman or "seriously and substantially endanger her health" because "there is no other commonly accepted medical procedure for effectively treating the health risk." It too was defeated, 17–202.

The third, by MP Gus Mitges (PC), was absolutely pro-life and allowed abortions only when two or more physicians believed that continuation of the pregnancy would or would be likely to endanger the woman's life. An initial voice vote implied that it had passed, but then a recorded vote showed that it had narrowly lost, 105–118. Ninety-two percent of the votes for the Mitges Amendment were supplied by Progressive Conservatives, and all by men. The fourth, from MP Barbara Sparrow (PC), would have defined "earlier stages of pregnancy" to mean "up to and including the 18th week of pregnancy" (beyond the first trimester). It was defeated on a voice vote. The fifth and final motion, from MP John W. Bosley (PC), was pro-choice insofar as his one-line proposal stipulated only that "legislation should prohibit the performance of an abortion except when performed by a qualified medical practitioner." It lost, 20–198. In the end, the House of Commons even rejected the government's proposal on a 76–147 vote. While "the voting crossed all party lines, female MPs from all parties voted consistently for the pro-choice positions" (Morton 1992, 251). Soon thereafter Prime Minister Brian Mulroney dissolved the 33rd Parliament and called for elections on November 21, 1988.

Mulroney also decided that no more efforts to forge an abortion policy would be made pending the outcome of other abortion cases before the Supreme Court of Canada, namely the *Borowski* suit. However, those continuing lawsuits "had embarrassed the Tory government. Prime Minister

Mulroney, viewing them as a consequence of the post-*Morgentaler* policy vacuum, saw them as posing an issue of leadership" (Morton 1992, 290). So in late 1989 the Mulroney government tried one last time to resolve the legal tangle over abortion policy.

The prime minister formed a caucus committee of pro-life and pro-choice MPs to find a compromise position, and what they agreed upon eventually became Bill C-43. It was introduced to the House of Commons on November 28, 1989, when Mulroney made a speech imploring both sides to compromise on the issue. Moreover, he indicated that only PC backbenchers would be allowed a free vote, whereas "Cabinet Ministers and those aspiring to Cabinet were sent a clear message to hold their noses and pass the bill" (Brodie, Gavigan, and Jenson 1992, 99). Bill C-43 passed its second reading on a 164–114 vote; then a parliamentary committee received testimony and briefs from organizations and individuals from January through March 1990.

Those testifying gave three points of view. Pro-life opponents believed that the law permitted too many abortions; pro-choice advocates argued against criminalization; and CMA representatives objected to specific aspects of the legislation. The various spokespersons had proposed twenty-four amendments, but only one, from NDP member of Parliament Dawn Black, was openly pro-choice (Brodie, Gavigan, and Jenson 1992, 108). All proposed amendments were rejected by the committee; the next stage was formal debate and still more amendments from the floor of the House of Commons.

According to Brodie, Gavigan, and Jenson (1992, 109), "the passage of the bill seemed to be a foregone conclusion. The government had exerted strong pressure on its caucus to toe the party line and the debate itself was not well attended." But outside Parliament, pro-choice activists organized rallies against Bill C-43 in Toronto and fifteen other Canadian cities. Pro-life forces were "inactive in the face of this eleventh-hour campaign," suggesting that "their confidence had been visibly shaken both because their committed proponents proved unable to change the legislation in committee and because many self-proclaimed pro-life MPs now appeared willing to support the bill" (Brodie, Gavigan, and Jenson 1992, 109). Though all efforts to amend Bill C-43 were turned aside, in the end it was approved "with a surprisingly small majority" (Brodie, Gavigan, and Jenson 1992, 110).

According to Morton (1992, 291), "the legislative process did not operate in the manner observed by Glendon [1987] in most European regimes. Instead, the pro-life and pro-abortion extremes, which had dominated the earlier stage of courtroom politics, continued to play a leading role in the legislative arena." Thus Bill C-43 barely survived, argues Morton (1992,

292), because "both pro-life and pro-abortion MPs voted against it. This alliance of extremes against the middle failed largely because the 'free vote' did not apply to the cabinet, which maintained its solidarity and voted *en masse* in favour of the bill."

The sixteen votes on Bill C-43 included all roll calls from the beginning to the end of the lawmaking process. A vote is required to authorize a bill to be introduced to the Canadian House of Commons, and then a vote accompanies the second reading, after which the bill is referred to committee. When the bill is reported to the floor of the House of Commons, amendments may be offered; on C-43 there were eleven motions from the floor and all were rejected, whereupon the unamended bill was accepted during the report stage and passed on to the third reading, which is the equivalent of final passage. Ten motions were from pro-life MPs to strengthen the prohibitions against abortion, and one pro-choice motion proposed to decriminalize abortion entirely.

Bill C-43 would have repealed Sections 287 and 288 of the Criminal Code and substituted new language, as follows:

> 287. (1) Every person who induces an abortion on a female person is guilty of an indictable offence and liable to imprisonment for a term not exceeding two years, unless the abortion is induced by or under the direction of a medical practitioner who is of the opinion that, if the abortion were not induced, the health or life of the female person would be likely to be threatened.
>
> (2) For the purposes of this section, "health" includes, for greater certainty, physical, mental and psychological health; "medical practitioner," in respect of an abortion induced in a province, means a person who is entitled to practise medicine under the laws of that province; "opinion" means an opinion formed using generally accepted standards of the medical profession.
>
> (3) For the purposes of this section and section 288, inducing an abortion does not include using a drug, device or other means on a female person that is likely to prevent implantation of a fertilized ovum.
>
> 288. Every one who unlawfully supplies or procures a drug or other noxious thing or an instrument or thing, knowing that it is intended to be used or employed to induce an abortion on a female person, is guilty of an indictable offence and liable to imprisonment for a term not exceeding two years. (*Statutes of Canada* 1989–90)

From the floor of the House of Commons, the first three motions were proposed by Liberal MP Don Boudria of Ontario. His first motion (#4) would have provided for "imprisonment for a term not exceeding twenty years" in place of the "two years" mentioned in the first paragraph. His second motion (#5) would have eliminated the words "or under the direction of" in the first paragraph. His third motion (#10) would have removed the first paragraph's reference to the "health" of the woman. Here the purpose was to impose more severe punishments against violators, restrict the performance of abortions to only physicians, and remove "health" as grounds for abortion.

Fearing that the inclusion of "health" as a "psychological" condition would allow greater access to abortions, other motions were designed to remove this legal loophole. Motion 12, by Ross Belsher, a Progressive Conservative MP from British Columbia, would substitute the words "seriously threatened" for "threatened" in the first paragraph. Motion 13, by John Reimer, a Progressive Conservative MP from Ontario, would add the wording "threatened and the medical practitioner has concluded that there is no other medically acceptable treatment to alleviate the health risk" to the end of the first paragraph. And the fourth motion by Boudria (#14) would have struck out the part of subsection 2 that defines health.

A motion (#16) by Liberal MP Rey Pagtakhan from Manitoba—a physician—to replace the wording "physical, mental and psychological" in subsection 2 with "considerations of physical and mental factors as they cause a serious threat to life and [health]" was designed to eliminate "psychological" reasons for justifying abortions. Like motivations led to motion 17A, by Liberal MP Francis G. LeBlanc, from Nova Scotia, to remove "psychological" from the second paragraph and the motion by Bill Attewell, a Progressive Conservative MP from Ontario, specifying that "health" includes "physical and mental health, and does not include psychological" (#17B). The last pro-life amendment (#19), also by Pagtakhan, would have elaborated upon the language of subsection 2 by adding to the end of the paragraph the phrase "medical profession, developed from a solid body of scientific knowledge."

Motion 24, by NDP MP Dawn Black, of British Columbia, would have scrapped the entire bill with this rewrite—"Sections 287 and 288 of the *Criminal Code* are repealed." This would have prevented any law from being enacted and would thus decriminalize abortion within Canada.

Voting on Abortion

Most of the literature on how Private Members' Bills (Bromhead 1956; Marsh and Read 1988) and "unwhipped" free votes (Hibbing and Marsh 1987; Marsh and Chambers 1981; Moyser 1979) are used to push controversial laws through Parliament deals with the British House of Commons. Several reforms on moral policy issues of the 1960s (pornography, divorce, homosexuality, and abortion) were enacted with implicit but not explicit British Labour government support (Richards 1970; Pym 1974; Marsh and Read 1988).

Analysis of the lawmaking process in Canada tends to focus more on the government, and free voting is mentioned only in passing (Franks 1987; Jackson and Atkinson 1980). But moral controversies, including divorce and capital punishment, have been handled through Private Members' Bills, whereupon the government either adopts that bill or introduces its own measure (Van Loon and Whittington 1971; Campbell and Pal 1989). Contrary to normal Canadian practice, where legislation is officially sponsored by the government, a free vote usually is allowed (Thorne 1990).

Abstentions on issues such as abortion are not uncommon, given the obvious political reasons for trying to avoid the question. When the Liberal government of Prime Minister Trudeau recommended the abortion reforms of 1969, he allowed only one free vote on a motion to eliminate that provision entirely. Says Morton (1992, 26–27): "In a classic display of political cowardice, sixty-eight of the 155 Liberal members of Parliament somehow managed to be absent. . . . The Conservatives were no better. Of the seventy-two members, forty were absent. Indeed, in the vote that was to determine Canada's new abortion law, the 'absents' outnumbered both the 'ayes' and the 'nays.' "

There has been research on what factors influence voting on abortion or other matters of conscience in the United Kingdom (Moyser 1979; Marsh and Chambers 1981; Hibbing and Marsh 1987; Marsh and Read 1988). In general, party is one of the two most important predictors of legislative behavior, the other being religion: Conservative MPs and Roman Catholics are more to the right on abortion. The most recent analysis of abortion voting in Britain (Marsh and Read 1988) found that a two-variable model (party and religion) performed well in explaining voting behavior on eight abortion votes in the House of Commons over the period from 1966 to 1988, though the explainable variance was not high. As Marsh and Read (1988, 98–99) concluded: "Party is a good predictor of vote but it is a far from perfect predictor." Other predictors that surfaced as important in one or more studies included region (Scotland and Wales are more conservative) and the religious makeup the of constituency (MPs from areas with more Catholics vote more conservatively). Also, MPs with smaller victory margins, who are older, who are less educated, or who had less prestigious occupations tend to vote pro-life, though in general women MPs favored more liberal abortion policies. Ideology has some influence within the Labour Party, with the left wing of the party being more supportive of abortion. But abortion is a conscience issue that tends to split parties more than other kinds of issues.

It would seem that each party in Canada viewed Bill C-43 from differing perspectives (table 3.1). On the pro-life motions the prevailing pattern was

Table 3.1

Votes by Party on Amendments to Bill C-43 on Abortion, 1990 (in percent)[*]

Vote	Outcome	Conservatives	Liberals	New Democrats
Introduction	25–7–68	28–0–72	32–1–67	0–44–56
First reading	26–7–67	28–0–72	34–1–65	0–44–56
Second reading	56–39–5	87–7–7	21–76–3	0–95–5
Motion 4	3–71–26	1–85–14	7–46–46	0–71–29
Motion 5	15–62–23	7–81–11	36–23–42	0–69–31
Motion 10	20–54–25	20–66–14	24–31–45	0–69–31
Motion 12	20–54–26	22–65–13	26–27–46	0–67–33
Motion 13	21–54–25	20–66–14	32–24–44	2–71–26
Motion 14	20–54–25	20–67–13	31–24–45	0–69–31
Motion 16	10–58–32	6–75–19	21–25–54	0–69–31
Motion 17A	12–59–28	4–77–19	29–20–51	0–69–31
Motion 17B	19–54–27	20–64–16	24–25–51	2–64–33
Motion 19	10–58–32	8–72–20	23–23–55	0–69–31
Motion 24	13–62–25	1–87–12	7–45–48	69–0–31
Report stage	45–29–26	79–5–16	1–56–43	0–69–31
Third reading	47–44–8	83–10–7	2–88–10	0–98–2

[*]For the outcome and vote by party the three statistics are, in order, the percentage favoring, the percentage opposing, and the percentage not voting. Percentages may not equal 100 due to rounding.

for a majority of Progressive Conservatives (from 54 percent to 71 percent) and upward of two-thirds (64 percent to 71 percent) of New Democrats to oppose those amendments. But the Liberal Party was divided over the issue; most Liberals chose to abstain, and among those who voted, a small plurality were pro-choice on motions 4, 10, 12, 16, and 17B but pro-life on motions 5, 13, and 17A. Yet on the pro-choice motion 24 almost equal numbers of Liberal MPs voted pro-life or abstained, while 87 percent of the Progressive Conservatives were opposed and 69 percent of New Democrats were supportive.

On final enactment there was a marked increase in the number of MPs who voted (273, compared to an average of 215 on the ten pro-life motions), and the result was a strong partisan showing. Though Bill C-43 was approved by a 47 percent–44 percent margin (with 9 percent abstaining), 83 percent of the Progressive Conservatives favored the bill, whereas 88 percent of Liberals and 98 percent of New Democrats were opposed. In parliamentary regimes a "party vote" would occur when 90 percent of each major party votes either in opposition or in favor, so in Canada the free vote on

Bill C-43 yielded a degree of party cohesion that is close to the norm for parliamentary systems but would be exceptional in the U.S. Congress.

In summary, Progressive Conservatives voted consistently *against* the pro-life motions but *for* Bill C-43, thus defending the government, whereas the New Democrats, who formally endorsed the pro-choice position, acted as the loyal opposition. What caused Liberal MPs to rally against C-43 after showing great uncertainty in dealing with the pro-life motions is a question that deserves further attention. A multivariate analysis of voting on these sixteen roll calls (Overby, Tatalovich, and Studlar 1995) offers a clue.

All votes factor-analyzed into three clusters except motion 4 (omitted from the analysis). Voting to permit introduction of C-43 and the first reading, after which the bill is printed, are pro forma votes for the government, though at this stage of the legislative process the majority party can prevent consideration of Private Members' Bills. The critical stages are the votes on second reading to authorize that a bill be referred to a legislative committee, during floor debate when motions to amend are considered, at the report stage when the House of Commons accepts or rejects amendments to the committee report, and third reading, which is equivalent to final enactment.

Votes on the introduction and first reading of Bill C-43 had only 32 percent and 33 percent, respectively, of the MPs voting, with very few opposed. Voting on all nine pro-life motions clustered together, though their support levels and turnouts varied somewhat. No more than 19 percent of the House of Commons supported motions 5, 16, 17A, and 19, and turnout averaged 71 percent, hinting both that pro-life MPs may not have been enthusiastic about such relatively mild restrictions and, moreover, that these motions were not viewed as a serious threat to the government's program. The remaining pro-life motions got nearly identical divisions, and the pro-life minority rose to 26 or 27 percent of the vote along with a 74 percent turnout. The most important cluster of roll calls included second reading, report stage, and third reading, as well as pro-choice motion 24. Almost all MPs recorded a vote during second reading (94 percent) and the report stage (92 percent), while 74 percent did so at the anticlimactic third reading. Motion 24 was the most direct threat to the government program, and though only 13 percent of the House of Commons backed this proposal, voting turnout represented 75 percent of its membership.

Overby, Tatalovich, and Studlar (1995) first developed a seventeen-variable model that included personal characteristics, riding (district) characteristics, and each MP's party identification, electoral margin of victory, and whether or not he or she was a member of the cabinet (Progressive Conservative MPs in the cabinet were whipped on these votes). It was hypothesized that MPs from Quebec might face crosspressures—party loyalty versus religious faith—on the abortion issue, insofar as during the 1969 parliamentary debate pro-life critics of the Liberal government "intimated that the silence of the Quebec Liberals was a betrayal of French Quebec and its Catholic heritage" (Morton 1992, 25).

But few of the seventeen variables were statistically significant, so a reduced regression model was derived based on the most important predictors (see the appendix, table A1), and the overall results hardly changed. However, changing relationships among the five variables confirm that a different political dynamic affected each stage of the lawmaking process. First, members of the cabinet voted to support the government on all three clusters of roll calls; they favored introduction and first reading, opposed the pro-life motions, and then backed enactment of C-43 as originally drafted by the government. Second, the Progressive Conservatives, more than the Liberals or New Democrats, voted on introduction and first reading (cluster one) to support the government position and especially so on the key votes of the third cluster. A substantial increase in party voting on motion 24, second reading, the report stage, and third reading took place, but party affiliation was not a significant predictor of voting on the nine pro-life motions. Third, Catholic and Greek Orthodox MPs were more inclined to favor the government on introduction and first reading, but then MPs identified with those pro-life churches disproportionately backed the various pro-life motions in the House of Commons. On the key roll calls, moreover, Catholic and Greek Orthodox MPs were *less* likely than Protestants and Jews to endorse Bill C-43. Having failed to strengthen its anti-abortion restrictions, apparently these MPs abandoned the government rather than accept its liberalized policy on abortion.

Thus the regression analysis (see the appendix, table A1) shows two cleavages of paramount importance. The first involves party affiliation and membership in the cabinet. Progressive Conservatives, particularly frontbenchers, supported C-43. It was the cabinet that remained unified against the pro-life motions; this was less true for the backbenchers, although on the key procedural votes the rank-and-file membership rallied behind the government. Overall partisanship was the strongest predictor of free voting and apparently was a stronger influence in Canada than in Great Britain (Overby, Tatalovich, and Studlar 1995; also Tatalovich, Overby, and Studlar 1993).

The Canadian Senate

Bill C-43 survived the House of Commons but ultimately was defeated on a 43–43 tie vote in the 104-member Canadian Senate. Senators are not elected;

Table 3.2

Votes on Bill C-43 by Party and Religion in the Canadian Senate[*]

	Yes	No
Liberals	2 (5%)	36 (95%)
Catholic[†]	2 (13%)	13 (87%)
Non-Catholic[†]	0 —	22 (100%)
Progressive Conservatives	41 (85%)	7 (15%)
Catholic[†]	24 (89%)	3 (11%)
Non-Catholic[†]	14 (78%)	4 (22%)

[*]The 104 Senators are appointed by the governor general, who, by constitutional convention, acts on the advice of the prime minister, so the party of the prime minister when each senator was appointed is used to indicate each senator's party. Eighteen senators did not vote.

[†]The four religious groups equal 82 because the religious affiliations of Senators Berntson (voted yes), Oliver (voted yes), Waters (voted yes) and Stollery (voted no) were not available in biographical sources.

they are appointed by the governor general on the advice of the prime minister and, under current law, serve until age seventy-five. So they are immune from the exigencies of electoral politics, though not from political pressures by the government. On Bill C-43 the Mulroney government permitted a "free vote" in the Senate, and "there had been very little pressure exerted on Conservative Senators to toe the party line" (Brodie, Gavigan, and Jenson 1992, 115). Morton (1992, 292) contends the absence of cabinet members meant that unlike in Parliament, where the vote by frontbenchers was whipped, a "similar critical mass supporting the legislation did not exist in the Senate" to salvage the outcome.

The tie vote brought confusion, being without precedent in the history of the Senate, and it was the first defeat in thirty years of a government bill by the upper chamber (Brodie, Gavigan, and Jenson 1992, 115). Attorney General Kim Campbell announced that the government would not make another attempt to formulate a new law on abortion. Perhaps she sensed that defeat in a Senate dominated by Progressive Conservatives was due to lukewarm support among her partisans. Examining how senators voted according to their party and religious affiliations (table 3.2) shows that the Liberals were more unified against C-43 than were Progressive Conservatives in favor. Also, the percentage of Catholic Progressive Conservatives voting for C-43 was barely higher than for Progressive Conservatives irrespective of their religion, and the percentage of Catholic Liberals who opposed the measure was only slightly lower than for Liberals irrespective of religion. So party was more determinative than religion, and the government would have salvaged the day had one fewer PC senator voted for the bill.

Pro-Life Agenda

Without Private Members' Bills, the best measure of pro-life activism would be those MPs who tried to tighten the restrictions on the government's abortion proposals. In 1988, motion 36, offered by the government, prompted twenty-one amendments (none accepted) from the floor of the House of Commons, and Bill C-43, as noted, provoked eleven motions by backbenchers. The MPs who offered motions on these two occasions can be taken as an indication of what type of legislator represents the pro-life position, the pro-choice stand, or a compromise supporting therapeutic abortions.

According to Tremblay (1991, 459), in 1988 ninety MPs debated motion 36; her analysis by party and gender showed that "the 'pro-choice' and 'compromise' options have united all women, regardless of party affiliation, and men of the New Democratic Party, whereas the 'anti-choice' viewpoint has been promoted by a majority of Liberal and Conservative men." To offer amendments involves a more visible advocacy than speaking to the issue on the floor, however, and my data indicate a caveat to Tremblay's conclusion based on how the Liberals behaved (table 3.3). Two amendments from NDP MPs firmly endorsed the pro-choice position, whereas pro-lifers would seem to be overrepresented among the Progressive Conservatives, given the fact that the vast majority of its rank and file embraced Bill C-43 on third reading. But only three Liberals, all Catholics, offered amendments to restrict abortions. Indeed, Catholic MPs—both Liberal and Progressive Conservative—tried to advance the pro-life agenda even though *none* had ridings in Quebec. This finding suggests that party, more than religion, may be the dominant consideration for this group of potentially crosspressured MPs from Quebec.

Congress and Abortion

In the decade prior to *Roe,* the first abortion bill introduced in Congress was in 1970, with six more in 1971 and three more in 1972 (Tatalovich 1988, 200). There had been a surge in legislative activity as the number of bills sponsored rose to 571 through 1988,* and 94 percent advanced the pro-life

---

*The number of bills introduced between 1973 and 1985 in Tatalovich (1988, 201) has been updated through 1988 by the author from information in the *Congressional Record,* 1986–1988.

Table 3.3

Sponsors of Amendments to Motion 36 (1988) and Bill C-43 (1990) in the House of Commons by Party and Religious Affiliation

	New Democratic Party			Liberal			Progressive Conservative		
	PL	MP	PC	PL	MP	PC	PL	MP	PC
Catholic		1		3			5		
Non-Catholic		1					11	3	2
Total		2		3			17*	3	2

Source: House of Commons Debates.
Note: PL (pro-life) was usually the view that life is sacred from conception and that abortions be allowed only to safeguard the woman's life; MP (middle position) represented acceptance of abortions for health and other therapeutic reasons or articulated the need to balance fetal considerations with the well-being of the woman; PC (pro-choice) articulated the position that women ought to have a right to choose in consultation with one physician.
*Religious affiliation was not available in biographical sources for MP Gordon E. Taylor (PC), who offered a pro-life amendment.

agenda, mainly through proposals to amend the Constitution (293, or 54 percent, of pro-life measures between 1973 and 1988 were proposed constitutional amendments).

Few of those bills were passed, but some enactments imposed substantial restrictions on abortion policy. The pro-life agenda targeted a broad range of federal programs. The Family Planning Services and Population Research Act of 1970 (PL 91-572), for example, prohibited the use of federal funds for programs where abortion is a method of family planning. Under the Health Programs Extension Act of 1973 (PL 93-45), judges and public officials were barred from ordering recipients of federal funds to perform abortions or from making facilities available for this purpose where the moral convictions or religious beliefs of these persons are violated. Amendments to the Public Health Service Act of 1977 (PL 95-215) mandated that the secretary of health, education, and welfare (HEW, now designated Health and Human Services, or HHS) examine whether medical, nursing, or osteopathic schools discriminated against applicants who, because of their religious beliefs or moral convictions, were either willing or unwilling to counsel, assist with, or perform abortions or sterilizations. This antibias statement was later codified in the Public Health Service Act, 1979 Amendments (PL 96-76). The Pregnancy Disability Amendment of 1977 to Title VII of the 1964 Civil Rights Act (PL 95-555) stipulated that employers are not required to fund any health insurance benefits for abortion except where necessary to save the mother's life (though they may do so voluntarily).

The instances of other antiabortion riders are too numerous to mention (see Rubin 1987, 151–83). Prohibitions on the use of foreign aid to perform abortions have existed since 1979; beginning in 1982 the Defense Department has been barred from providing abortions to military personnel at military hospitals; and laws stipulate whether the District of Columbia can allocate any of its federal subsidies, sometimes even its own revenues, for abortions. In 1981 Congress prohibited the District of Columbia from using federal funds for abortions except to save the mother's life and in cases of rape or incest; in 1985 the exemption for rape and incest was eliminated; and in 1988 Washington, DC, was barred from spending local revenues for abortions (Craig and O'Brien 1993, 112–13). Of course, the most famous illustration is the ongoing controversy over which abortions Congress will fund under the federal-state Medicaid program. Title XIX of the Social Security Act established the Medicaid program under which the federal government provides grants to states (except Arizona and the District of Columbia, which at the time did not participate in the program) for certain types of medical expenses for needy persons. When the federal government began funding abortions pursuant to the 1973 *Roe* decision, Congressman Henry J. Hyde (R-Illinois) determined that the Department of Health, Education, and Welfare was paying for 250,000 to 300,000 abortions a year at a cost of $45 million (*Congressional Quarterly Weekly Report* 1980, 1038).

The original Hyde Amendment of 1976 was a rider to H.R. 14232, the Departments of Labor and of Health, Education, and Welfare appropriations bill, and stipulated that *no* funds under that act could be used to fund abortions or to promote or encourage their commission. When that bill arrived in the Senate, this prohibition was deleted by a majority and the bill was forced into conference committee. The conferees compromised by banning abortion funding "except where the life of the mother would be endangered if the fetus were carried to term" (*Congressional Quarterly Almanac* 1976, 802–3). After enactment, Public Law 94-439 was delayed through legal challenges and did not take effect until August 4, 1977.

Since the Hyde Amendment is a rider attached to appropriations bills funding the Department of Health and Human Services, Congress must annually reenact this legislation. The years since 1976 have been a replay of that first abortion struggle. The House routinely passed a restrictive Hyde Amendment, while pro-choice forces in the Senate softened the prohibition. In the past, what resulted was hard bargaining by conferees who often failed in their efforts to compromise, so that Congress frequently was unable to enact a regular appropriations bill for HHS. In 1980 the Supreme

Court ruled the Hyde Amendment to be constitutional, and it remains the law to this day.

The abortion controversy continues to impact the lawmaking process. It sidelined for nearly three years congressional efforts to pass the Civil Rights Restoration Act of 1988 and threatened to derail efforts (which ultimately failed anyway) by the Clinton administration to reorganize America's medical care system and establish universal health insurance. Both episodes involved heavy lobbying from the National Conference of Catholic Bishops (NCCB), which originally had been sympathetic to both goals (Segers 1995a, 98–99). The civil rights bill was designed to "restore" expansive guidelines protecting women from sex discrimination by educational institutions that receive federal aid. A Supreme Court ruling in *Grove City College v. Bell* (1984) narrowed the interpretation of Title IX of the Education Amendments of 1972 whereby only "programs" that discriminated against women were legally liable, rather than the whole educational institution, as congressional liberals had intended. Since a broad reading of the prohibition would encompass pregnancy and abortion services, the NCCB demanded (and got) the "abortion-neutral" Danforth Amendment, named for Senator John Danforth (R-Missouri), which excluded abortion services from coverage under the antidiscrimination law.

For the most part, pro-choice forces in Congress have fought a rearguard battle, trying to prevent or modify the most restrictive antiabortion bills, though recently the pro-choice cause won legislative victories when Democratic majorities of the 103rd Congress joined forces with President Clinton, the first Democrat to hold the White House in twelve years. One success with far-reaching implications was the enactment of the Freedom of Access to Clinic Entrances Act (FACE), which was designed to impose penalties on groups such as Operation Rescue that use direct-action tactics against women seeking abortions at clinic facilities. The other legislative advance, albeit minor in the scheme of things, was changing the Hyde Amendment. Since 1981 the law had said that no federal Medicaid moneys could be used to perform abortions "except where the life of the mother would be endangered if the fetus were carried to term." The 1994 enactment, which added rape and incest, read: "None of the funds appropriated under this Act shall be expended for any abortion except when it is made known to the Federal entity or official to which funds are appropriated under this Act that such procedure is necessary to save the life of the mother or that the pregnancy is the result of an act of rape or incest." This convoluted wording and a Clinton administration edict mandating coverage for rape and incest provoked a rebellion by some state Medicaid officials who believed that Congress permitted them flexibility in the matter (Pear 1994). At least thirteen states went to federal court asserting their administrative prerogatives, but in all cases their claims were rejected.

Yet pro-lifers gained the political advantage when the 104th Congress, with Republican majorities in both chambers, enacted (and Clinton signed) legislation to foster major structural changes in the communications industry, but which included another proviso by Representative Hyde that banned abortion information from electronic information networks. Civil libertarians and information technology companies immediately promised to challenge that provision on free-speech grounds. In early 1996 Congress enacted legislation prohibiting a gruesome procedure known as "partial-birth" abortions, performed after twenty weeks of pregnancy. The fetus is partly extracted feet first and its brain is then suctioned out to allow the head to pass through the birth canal. The first statute to target a specific abortion method, and providing a maximum imprisonment of two years and fines up to $250,000 for any doctor convicted under the law, the bill had strong backing from pro-lifers and the Roman Catholic hierarchy.

Fewer than 1.5 percent (about 19,500) of the 1.3 million abortions done in 1993 involved this procedure. The only exception to the ban was endangerment of the life of the woman, but President Clinton wanted more latitude to "avert serious health consequences" as well. The issue promised to become a political football during 1996, a presidential election year. Clinton vetoed the bill in a public session with a group of women who had had to terminate their pregnancies by this means, and the GOP nominee, Robert Dole (R-Kansas), blasted Clinton for having "rejected a very modest and bipartisan measure reflecting the values of the great majority of Americans," adding: "A partial-birth abortion blurs the line between abortion and infanticide and crosses an ethical and legal line we must never cross. President Clinton now stands on the wrong side of this line" (quoted in Purdum 1996). To a point Dole was right, because apparently many Democrats and Republicans in the House of Representatives shared his moral qualms. The bill was enacted by a veto-proof majority of 286–129 in the House of Representatives, with 72 Democrats (including the minority leader, Richard A. Gephardt) joining 214 Republicans in favor while 113 Democrats, 15 Republicans, and 1 independent voted no, but it narrowly passed the Senate on a 51–47 roll call.

Congressional Votes on Abortion

Does abortion voting in Congress have a partisan or religious dimension? One assumes that Catholics, irrespective of party, would have a special concern about abortion, yet Catholic Democrats may feel crosspressured:

Table 3.4

Type of Party Division and Pro-Life Victories on Abortion Votes in the House of Representatives and the Senate, 1973–1988

	House of Representatives				Senate			
	1973–80	1981–88	Total	Pro-life Wins	1973–80	1981–88	Total	Pro-life Wins
Party Vote*	14	12	26	18	12	18	30	4
Bipartisan Vote	6	0	6	5	9	2	11	2
Conservative Coalition	16	4	20	20	11	9	20	10
Unclassified	0	2	2	2	7	2	9	2
Totals	36	18	54	45 (83%)	39	31	70	18 (26%)

Source: Derived from *Congressional Quarterly Almanac* (Washington, D.C.: Congressional Quarterly, 1973–1988).

*Party Vote: majority of northern Democrats and southern Democrats oppose majority of Republicans; Bipartisan Vote: majority of northern Democrats, southern Democrats, and Republicans vote together; Conservative Coalition: majority of Republicans and majority of southern Democrats oppose majority of northern Democrats.

led by their consciences, official church teachings, and constituency pressures to oppose abortion, while the Democratic Party platforms and Democratic leadership of Congress strongly endorse the pro-choice position (see table 3.5). So Catholic Democrats may not wish to openly contradict official doctrine or disrupt party unity by promoting pro-life legislation, whereas pro-life Republican Catholics are able to act consistently with both their party ideology and their religious convictions.

The polarization of the abortion controversy since *Roe* has transformed the political environment inside Congress. The change is revealed by classifying abortion roll calls according to whether they reflected a partisan, bipartisan, or "conservative coalition" voting cleavage (table 3.4). The patterns also show, first, that the type of voting bloc in Congress affects the odds of passing antiabortion legislation and, second, that the Senate has been more liberal on abortion while the House is much more conservative. The accounting of pro-life victories is a relative measure of winning, since many roll calls involved efforts to forge some kind of compromise position. Since these efforts typically occurred in the Senate (where more recorded votes were cast), it may understate the political clout of pro-life forces. For example, pro-choice advocates would be opposed to any ban on Medicaid funding of abortions, but the best they can hope for is to prevent enactment of absolute prohibitions in favor of therapeutic exceptions. Yet Congress has never excluded the mother's life as grounds for funding abortions under Medicaid.

In both House and Senate the best chance for pro-lifers to win a roll call depended on the emergence of the "conservative coalition" between Republicans and southern Democrats. There was little bipartisan voting on abortion in either chamber, but any vote that brought together all three party groups meant that pro-lifers were more likely to win in the House of Representatives but less likely to do so in the Senate. A party vote signaled slightly fewer pro-life wins in the House and many fewer in the Senate. At base, about seven of ten party votes in the House resulted in pro-life victories even though the Democratic Party had been solidly in control during these two decades. Voting that unites southern and northern Democrats ought to imply that the number of pro-choice victories would be higher, but the party votes usually resulted in slim majorities among the Democrats, which were inadequate to assure victory. A sizable number of Democrats were defecting to the pro-life side on these votes. Who were they?

Research on congressional voting on abortion point to some critical predictors. An analysis by Vinovskis (1980a) of three House votes taken on the original Hyde Amendment in 1976 concluded that party was not a primary determinant; most important was an index of domestic "liberalism," and second was religion. Peltzman (1984) also found that ideology was the strongest predictor of abortion voting, and similar results were found in a systematic examination of abortion votes in the House across two decades (Tatalovich and Schier 1993). In the eight Houses studied, ideology was consistently the most important predictor of voting on abortion; religion was the second most important factor (non-Catholics were more pro-choice than Catholics), and constituency variables had little if any effect on congressional votes.

Tatalovich and Schier (1993) further validated the notion that deviations from party voting are due to religion—but that most defectors are Catholic Democrats, not Catholic Republicans. A statistical analysis done separately on Republicans and Democrats indicated, as expected, that liberals and non-Catholics voted pro-choice more often than Catholics or conservatives, but comparing the strength of ideology versus religion shows that ideology had roughly the same impact on both parties although religion was a stronger influence on Democrats.

Eccles (1978) was the first to observe that in the Senate, party affiliation did *not* seem to be an overriding factor in voting on abortion. Though a couple of hundred pro-life constitutional amendments have been introduced since 1973, only once has a committee of either chamber cleared such a proposal for a floor vote. On June 28, 1983, the Senate defeated the Hatch-Eagleton Amendment (HEA), which read: "A right to abortion is not secured by this Constitution." The objective was to return abortion policy to Congress and to the states, but the 49–50 vote was far short of the two-thirds needed for approval. Granberg (1985, 127) found that the odds of a pro-HEA vote increased "if the Senator was a *Catholic,* if the Senator was a *Republican,* if the Senator's state had a relatively *low income,* and if the Senator represented a state *not* in the *New England, Pacific,* or *Middle Atlantic* region" (emphasis in original).

The HEA also was analyzed by Strickland and Whicker (1986), who compared it to the vote on a pro-life bill sponsored by Senator Jesse Helms (R-North Carolina). Voting was affected more by social rather than political variables, and constituency makeup exerted more influence than did the senators' personal attributes, but no measure of ideology was included. However, both ideology and party were used in the latest examination of the HEA by Chressanthis, Gilbert, and Grimes (1991), who found that party was insignificant and that "ideological measures may be more important than constituent interests in voting outcomes on abortion legislation" (p. 596). Religion also exerted an important influence on how senators voted on the HEA.

The most systematic analysis of seventy Senate roll calls on abortion during the period 1973–1988 (Wattier and Tatalovich 1995) shows that by substituting a "partisanship" variable (which combines party affiliation with ideological orientation) for party affiliation alone, the resulting variable is a stronger predictor of voting behavior. That is, more-partisan (meaning liberal) Democratic senators voted pro-choice more frequently, and more-partisan (conservative) Republican senators voted pro-life more frequently. Religion seemed to be *less* salient for Senate voting—though, as it was with the House, every relationship signified that non-Catholic senators were more liberal on abortion policy than Catholic senators. And where research on the House of Representatives found virtually no relationship between the makeup of congressional districts and voting on abortion legislation, senators from more-affluent states tended to vote pro-choice.

It may be that the demographic characteristics of ridings, congressional districts, and states do not adequately capture popular sentiment regarding abortion policy. General elections are supposed to signal the intentions of constituents, and one analysis of the 1990 senatorial elections, for example, indicates that abortion was a significant predictor of vote choice in nine states but had marginal or no influence on six other Senate elections. In most instances, moreover, the views of the candidates mirrored the official positions of their national parties (Cook, Jelen, and Wilcox 1994b), although this study did not attempt to match the winners' position on abortion with their subsequent voting on Senate abortion roll calls. An additional reason why Republican senators are generally less liberal than Democratic senators on abortion is that in order to gain the nomination, they need to pay particular attention to the views of voters in primary elections. Many observers note that conservatives tend to dominate Republican primaries while liberals predominate among Democratic primary voters, and this applies as well to abortion. Indeed, an extensive analysis of primary and general election voters in senatorial elections from 1972 to 1988 found that over that period, "Democratic primary voters also [like the general electorate] became less pro-life with the exception of Southern Democrats who were about the same over the time period. Republican primary voters clearly became more pro-life thus placing themselves at a distance from both Democrats and more importantly the November electorate" (Brady and Schwartz 1995, 37). In other words, given the gradual shift in public attitudes on abortion, strong pro-life Republican senatorial candidates who win the GOP primaries face obstacles in trying to appeal to more centrist voters in November, whereas the pro-choice leanings of Democratic senatorial candidates are more compatible with the general electorate.

Leaders and Followers

For parliamentary parties, cohesion rates exceeding 90 percent are commonplace, because too many deviations from party loyalty could result in a vote of no confidence and thus force the government to call new elections. That congressional scholars consider it to be a party vote anytime 51 percent of Republicans oppose 51 percent of Democrats underscores both the ideological diversity of congressional parties and the lack of formal sanctions by legislative leaders to enforce discipline. Whereas free votes are rare in Canada, it is not beyond credibility to conceptualize, for Congress, that virtually *all* roll calls are unwhipped votes. Loyalty to party may depend more on the constellation of political forces than leadership, but one important cue guiding legislative behavior is the position taken by the majority and minority party leaders and the whips.

In paliamentary governments, frontbenchers and backbenchers vote in lockstep because the rank and file were elected to uphold the programmatic objectives of their party, but observers of Congress are never sure whether members are influenced by leaders or vice versa. If leaders are to have any leverage over the party membership, presumably they cannot be unduly unrepresentative of rank-and-file attitudes. As a rough assessment of this

Table 3.5

Mean Scale Scores on Abortion Votes by Republican Party and Democratic Party Leaders and Members in the House of Representatives, 1973–1988[*]

	Democratic Party			Republican Party		
Congress	Leader	Whip	Members	Leader	Whip	Members
93rd	0.33[†]	1.00	0.40	0.25	0.33	0.20
94th	0.00	0.50	0.43	0.00	0.00	0.17
95th	0.71	1.00	0.55	0.00	0.29	0.23
96th	0.50	1.00	0.53	0.00	0.00	0.17
97th	0.33	0.75	0.61	0.00	0.00	0.24
98th	0.50	0.80	0.48	0.00	0.25	0.24
99th	1.00	0.80	0.64	0.00	0.00	0.20
100th	1.00	1.00	0.67	0.00	0.00	0.19

Source: Derived by author.

[*]Leader: majority leader or minority leader

[†]Each score is the mean value on an additive scale based on the number of votes cast by each person (nonvotes excluded). Since the number of votes differed among members within each house of Congress and across time between Congresses, the "raw" score on each scale was divided by the number of votes included in that scale in order to derive a comparative measure ranging from 0.0 (pro-life) to 1.0 (pro-choice). Since the mean value reflects the number of votes in each scale, one cannot draw longitudinal conclusions that any particular party group is becoming more pro-choice or more pro-life. However, comparisons between party groups can be made within each Congress.

relationship, the mean values on all abortion roll calls were derived for party leadership and party membership in the House of Representatives for 1973–1988 (table 3.5).

Data imperfections prevent us from making comparisons between Congresses, but the consistency within each Congress points to one conclusion: Republican leaders are more conservative than the GOP rank and file, and Democratic leaders are more liberal than rank-and-file Democrats. Certainly these findings are plausible. On an issue such as abortion, leaders are most ideologically committed to the party position, but the rank and file must balance the needs of party against those of the constituency, especially where crosspressures exist. However important party leaders may be as a general voting cue for members (Bond and Fleisher 1990), these comparisons suggest that Republican and Democratic members of the House are *not* following in lockstep behind their leadership. That is not say that the rank and file, notably Democrats, are openly rebellious toward their party leadership. To answer that question involves looking at the sponsors of pro-life bills.

Pro-Life Sponsors

That Representative Henry J. Hyde is a Republican and a Catholic might underscore how the abortion debate links party and religion in the House of Representatives. It was already noted that religious affiliation is a weaker influence on senatorial abortion voting and that the Senate institutionally is more pro-choice than the House. It would appear that, even in the Senate, Republicans were more conspicuous than Democrats on both sides of the question. Jesse Helms (R-North Carolina), Mark O. Hatfield (R-Oregon), Orrin Hatch (R-Utah), and John Danforth (R-Missouri) were determined pro-lifers (and none are Catholics), just as Lowell P. Weicker (R-Connecticut) and Robert Packwood (R-Oregon) were steadfast defenders of the pro-choice position.

Since abortion is a prominent issue for Catholics, Catholic legislators may feel a special responsibility to promote the pro-life agenda. How party and religion interact with regard to sponsorship of pro-life legislation may be especially telling given the finding that, among representatives, religion causes more deviations by Democrats than Republicans. To untangle this dynamic, the sponsors and cosponsors of the nineteen pro-life bills that were introduced into the House during the 100th Congress (1987–1988) were categorized according to party and religion (table 3.6).

The 122 Republican sponsors of those pro-life bills represented 69 percent of the GOP membership in the 100th Congress, while the 49 Democratic sponsors were but 19 percent of its membership. Pro-life legislative activists much more closely "represent" the congressional Republicans than they do congressional Democrats, but when a Democrat does sponsor pro-life legislation, the odds are that he or she will be a Catholic. Within the partisan groupings of pro-life activists, Catholics are overrepresented among Democrats but *not* among Republicans. Catholics equaled 33 percent of all House Democrats but 59 percent of the Democratic pro-life sponsors. Among congressional Republicans, Catholics were equally represented (at 23 percent) both among the rank and file and among the pro-life legislative activists.

What seemingly matters more is the political party to which a Catholic member of the House belongs. Catholic Republicans were much more actively involved in agenda setting than Catholic Democrats. Seven of ten Catholic Republicans were pro-life sponsors, but only 35 percent of the Catholic Democrats assumed that legislative role. Another notable difference between the parties is that where 68 percent of non-Catholic Republicans sponsored antiabortion bills, only 11 percent of non-Catholic Democrats did so. Thus, non-Catholics Republicans were as committed as

Table 3.6

Sponsors of Pro-Life Bills in the House of Representatives, 100th Congress (1987–1988), Categorized by Party and Religion

	Republicans		Democrats	
	N	%	N	%
Pro-Life Sponsors	122		49	
Catholics	28	(23)	29	(59)
Non-Catholics	94	(77)	20	(41)
Frequency of Sponsorship	429		101	
Catholics	114	(27)	63	(62)
Non-Catholics	315	(73)	38	(38)
Average Frequency of Sponsorship	3.5		2.1	
Party Composition of the House of Representatives (N = 435)	178	(41)	257	(59)
Sponsors as Percentage of Party Membership		69		19
Religious Composition of the House of Representatives (N = 435)				
Catholics	40	(23)	83	(33)
Non-Catholics	138	(77)	174	(67)
Catholic Sponsors as Percentage of Catholic Membership		70		35
Non-Catholic Sponsors as Percentage of Non-Catholic Membership		68		11

Source: Based on nineteen pro-life bills introduced in the House of Representatives, as reported in the index to the *Congressional Record,* 100th Congress, 1987–1988. Tabulations include original sponsor and cosponsors identified by Legi-slate, a computer software package.

Catholic Republicans to promoting the pro-life agenda in Congress, whereas non-Catholic Democrats were not involved in this legislative effort; for that matter, Catholic Democrats did not show very much enthusiasm, either. At base, two-thirds of the Catholic Democrats did *not* throw their formal support behind antiabortion legislation in the 100th Congress.

In sum, the congressional Republican Party is decidedly more unified in its advocacy of the pro-life agenda. Democrats are a less cohesive group but arguably may be characterized as opposed to promoting the antiabortion agenda. These findings, when coupled with the voting research, imply that Catholic Democrats are reluctant pro-lifers who do not promote that agenda but vote alongside Catholic Republicans when a floor vote is demanded. The reluctance of Catholic Democrats to sponsor antiabortion bills but their apparent readiness to vote pro-life on the House floor means that these representatives, though they are generally liberal on various social welfare policies, in all likelihood experience cross-pressures when dealing with the abortion issue.

Summary

As was expected, free votes were allowed in the House of Commons and even in the Canadian Senate when Bill C-43 was debated. Surely the failed attempts in 1988 by the Mulroney government to gauge the sense of the House with respect to pro-choice, pro-life, and moderate resolutions, and later through motion 36, is not the usual approach by which governments author legislation in parliamentary regimes. Even the tie vote on C-43 in the Senate was unprecedented, the first defeat of a government bill in thirty years.

As to Congress, what happened with the Hyde Amendment in 1976 seems to have become the preferred legislative strategy by pro-lifers. Invariably the conflict over abortion spills onto the floors of the House and Senate because the issue cannot be resolved in committee. With Democratic majorities able to block consideration of any pro-life bill in standing committee, Republicans have added antiabortion riders on the floor of the House of Representatives. Not only does this strategy bypass the standing committees but, by forcing a recorded vote, the GOP put tremendous pressure on Catholic Democrats to back their pro-life agenda.

Bill C-43, which the Mulroney government had crafted, was a very permissive policy on abortion as compared to the policy outcomes in Congress. That all pro-life amendments were defeated by the House of Commons does imply that its political center of gravity on abortion was to the left of the U.S. House of Representatives, even perhaps the U.S. Senate. No doubt U.S. pro-choice advocates would have been thrilled if legislation along the lines of Bill C-43 had cleared Congress.

On voting patterns, analysis of roll calls on Bill C-43 are consistent with the British findings that political party *is* the strongest predictor in the parliamentary system, whereas evidence is equally convincing that party is *not* the salient consideration in congressional voting. Most analyses of House and Senate voting point to political ideology. Party affiliation fails to predict abortion votes because the essential ideological dimension is missing, and the implication (see Wattier and Tatalovich 1995) is that cohesion among Republicans and particularly Democrats depends upon taking into account how the abortion issue affects liberals and conservatives within both parties.

A methodological problem that bars direct comparisons between Congress and Parliament is that there is no independent measure of ideology for the Canadian House of Commons. Unlike the situation with the British House of Commons, there are no readily identifiable ideological factions within the parties or across parties. Ideology may be implicit in the ordering of the three Canadian parties, with the NDP on the left, the Liberals more or less in the middle, and the Progressive Conservatives on the right. Even though since 1980 the Republican platform has included a pro-life plank and the Democratic platform has embraced pro-choice orthodoxy (see chapter 5), commitments that bind the two presidential candidates have not extended to their congressional partisans.

If the speculation with regard to Catholic Liberals is tenable, then those MPs were acting similarly to Catholic Democrats in Congress. The Liberal Party was opposed to the government position, but Catholic Liberals did not challenge party unity by offering pro-life amendments in the House of Commons. Among U.S. representatives, Catholic Democrats are not the primary source of pro-life legislation, though when confronted with an abortion roll call they generally voted with the conservatives more often than the liberals. Both these groups of cross-pressured legislators try to resolve the conflict in ways protective of their party.

4

Public Opinion and Organized Interests

Consensus Building or Mobilization of Bias?

A democratic government is supposed to be responsive to public opinion without disparaging the rights of minorities, but oftentimes public policy is shaped by organized interests without regard to the majority view. This political dilemma lies at the heart of the debate over abortion. What exists is a situation where two "intense" minorities have polarized views of abortion policy that do not represent the feelings of the majority of Americans or Canadians. In both countries the majority stands to the right of the strongest pro-choice position but left of the absolutist pro-life position. That conclusion is apparent from survey data indicating that the contours of public opinion on abortion have been generally unchanged over the past two decades.

Public Moderation on Abortion

In the United States, even before *Roe,* there was a virtual consensus favoring therapeutic abortions under specified medical conditions but resistance to abortion on demand. One analysis of Gallup polls during the 1960s found that "abortion to preserve the mother's health or prevent child deformity may be said to be publicly well accepted, while abortion for discretionary ('selfish') reasons receives minimal but, nonetheless, rapidly growing support. Legal freedom of elective abortion, however, is rejected by the non-Catholic majority" (Blake 1971, 544; see also Blake 1973; Pomeroy and Landman 1973). In Canada, a 1965 poll found that nearly three-fourths of those surveyed supported therapeutic abortions when the mother's health was endangered (Boyd and Gillieson 1975, 55–56).

A key to understanding public-opinion data is consistency over time. On three specific questions there is longitudinal data that show general stability and coherency in public attitudes toward abortion. Gallup polls ask whether "abortions should be legal under any circumstances, legal only under certain circumstances, or legal in all circumstances." In 1993, 13 percent of Americans favored an absolute prohibition against all abortions, 32 percent endorsed legalized abortion for any reason, and a majority of 51 percent approved abortions under certain conditions (see table 4.1). In 1992 slightly fewer Canadians endorsed the pro-life or pro-choice options, whereas more favored allowing abortion for therapeutic reasons. Quite similar results were reported by Gallup back as far as 1975 for both the United States and Canada (table 4.1). Their review of these data led Nevitte, Brandon, and Davis to conclude that

> a substantial majority of both publics consistently fall into a very large middle ground; most Americans and Canadians are prepared to support the legalization of abortion "under certain circumstances." The precise nature of this middle ground . . . turns out to be a crucial source of variation in public opinions about abortion. When respondents are asked if abortion should be legalized when health concerns come into play . . . over three-quarters reply "yes." Support for legalizing abortion drops off dramatically when such "discretionary considerations" as low family income are at issue. (Nevitte, Brandon, and Davis 1993, 20)

Also, research in the 1988 American National Election Study and the 1988 Canadian National Election Study indicated that "Canadians are very slightly more supportive of legal abortion than are residents of the United States: On the three-point abortion item, the Canadian mean is 2.35, while the mean abortion attitude for the United States is 2.25" (Chandler, Cook, Jelen, and Wilcox 1994, 136).

The overwhelming support for "hard" or "therapeutic" reasons for abortion (mother's life at risk, rape, deformed child) is corroborated by surveys of Americans by the National Opinion Research Center (NORC) and of Canadians by Gallup. This question was first used by NORC in 1972, allowing us to gauge how much public opinion has changed in the United States over the past two decades (table 4.2).

The 1972 NORC survey found 83 percent approving abortion where the mother's health was seriously endangered, while 74 percent supported abortion in cases of rape or if there was a strong chance of a "serious defect in the baby." Since then, support for abortion never fell below 87 percent when the mother's life was endangered, 77 percent in cases of rape, and 76 percent when fetal deformity was indicated. A minority favored abortion for

Table 4.1

Abortion Attitudes in the United States and Canada (in percent)

Year	Country	Distribution of Public Attitudes		
		Legal Under Any Circumstances	Legal Under Certain Circumstances	Illegal Under All Circumstances
1993	United States	32	51	13
1992*	United States	33	51	14
1992	Canada	31	57	10
1991*	United States	33	50	16
1991	Canada	24	60	14
1990*	United States	31	53	12
1990*	Canada	27	60	12
1989*	United States	28	51	18
1989*	Canada	27	61	12
1988	United States	24	57	17
1988*	Canada	24	60	14
1983	United States	23	58	16
1983	Canada	23	59	17
1981	United States	23	52	21
1980	United States	25	53	18
1979	United States	22	54	19
1978	Canada	16	69	14
1977	United States	22	55	19
1975	United States	21	54	22
1975	Canada	23	60	16

Source: Gallup United States and Gallup Canada, as reported in Neil Nevitte, William P. Brandon, and Lori Davis, "The American Abortion Controversy: Lessons from Cross-National Evidence," *Politics and the Life Sciences* 12 (February 1993), p. 21. The 1993 data are from *Gallup Poll Monthly* (April 1993), p. 38. The question was: "Do you think abortions should be legal under any circumstance, legal only under certain circumstances, or illegal in all circumstances?"

*Indicates that for each year the results of two surveys were averaged to derive mean percentages in each category except for Canada in 1988, when three surveys were averaged to derive mean percentages in each category.

Table 4.2

Public Support for Therapeutic and Socioeconomic Reasons for Abortions in the United States and Canada (in percent)

Year	Mother's Health	Fetal Defect	Rape	Unmarried†	No More Children†	Too Poor	Any Reason‡	Before 3 Months§	Before 5 Months§
				United States*					
1972	83	74	74	41	38	46			
1973	91	82	81	47	46	52			
1975	88	80	80	46	44	51			
1977	88	83	80	47	44	52	36		
1980	88	80	80	46	45	50	39		
1982	89	81	83	47	46	50	39		
1984	87	77	77	43	41	44	37		
1985	87	76	78	40	39	42	36		
1988	89	78	81	40	40	42	37		
1990	89	78	81	43	43	45	42		

Canada[||]

1988	78	64	69	29	41	36	24
1989 (February)	80	67	73	36	47	41	30
1989 (August)	84	75	78	39	55	49	31
1990	82	69	73	38	50	45	30

Sources: National Opinion Research Center (NORC) data for 1972–1985, reported in Raymond Tatalovich and Byron W. Daynes, eds., *Social Regulatory Policy: Moral Controversies in American Politics* (Boulder, CO: Westview, 1988), p. 188, and updated by author. Gallup (Canada) data for 1988–1990 reported in Maureen Muldoon, *The Abortion Debate in the United States and Canada: A Source Book* (New York: Garland Publishing, 1991), p. 40.

*The NORC question was "whether or not *you* think it should be possible for a pregnant woman to obtain a *legal* abortion if (a) there is a strong chance of a serious defect in the baby? (b) if she is married and does not want any more children? (c) the woman's own health is seriously endangered by the pregnancy? (d) the family has a very low income and cannot afford any more children? (e) she became pregnant as a result of rape? (f) she is not married and does not want to marry the man? (g) the woman wants it for any reason?"

[||]The Gallup question was "In which of these specific cases would you think an abortion should be legal? If there is a strong chance of a serious defect in the baby; If the woman's health is endangered by the pregnancy; If agreed upon by a woman and her physician; If the family has a very low income and cannot afford any more children; If it is within 5 months of conception; If it is within 3 months of conception; If conception is due to rape or incest."

[†]The "unmarried" and "no more children" questions were not asked in the Canadian survey in 1988–1990.

[‡]The "any reason" question was not asked in the U.S. survey in 1972–1975.

[§]The "before 3 months" and "before 5 months" questions were not asked in the U.S. survey in 1972–1990.

"soft" or socioeconomic reasons, with one possible exception: The 46 percent in 1972 who approved of abortions for families who could not afford any more children rose to a slim majority from 1973 through 1982 but then fell again to the 42 percent level in 1985. So these trend data show a slight retrenchment in support by Americans for nontherapeutic abortions after 1982.

Abortion for "any reason" was supported by no more than 39 percent of the NORC samples. In the mid-1970s nearly two-thirds of Canadians would allow the woman and her physician to decide whether or not to abort a pregnancy (Boyd and Gillieson 1975, 55–56), and that sentiment was expressed by 75 percent of Canadians in a 1982 Gallup poll (Oliver 1983, 42). One item in the 1984 Canadian National Election Study showed most Canadians reacting favorably to a general statement that abortion should be a woman's personal decision. On that occasion 69 percent agreed in varying degrees with the view that "the decision to have an abortion should be the responsibility of the pregnant woman" (Simpson 1994, 153).

A 1977 regional study of the Edmonton area (Hartnagel, Creechan, and Silverman 1985, 417), generally a more conservative locale than other parts of Canada, found that large numbers of respondents favored abortion when the woman's health was endangered (93 percent), when serious defects in the baby were indicated (89 percent), and when pregnancy resulted from rape (85 percent), but again support levels dropped to barely a majority (51 percent) in cases where the family had a low income and could not afford more children and eroded further in cases where a married woman did not want additional children (48 percent) or where an unmarried woman did not want to marry the father (47 percent). The authors thus concluded "that the current statement of the Canadian abortion statute . . . is generally congruent with public opinion" (Hartnagel, Creechan, and Silverman 1985, 424), though their multivariate analysis also indicated that "membership in either a subordinate status Protestant denomination [meaning Baptist, Lutheran, or Pentecostal] or in the Catholic church is strongly related to opposition to unconditional support for legal abortion (abortion on demand)" (ibid., 422).

Another information source is the World Values Survey of 1981 and 1990, which had a question on therapeutic or socioeconomic indications for abortion (Nevitte, Brandon, and Davis 1993, 22). On each occasion (1981 and 1990, respectively) there was consensus among Canadians (92 percent and 91 percent) and Americans (86 percent and 89 percent) for abortion when the mother's health was at risk, and roughly three in five Canadians (63 percent and 64 percent) and Americans (54 percent and 61 percent) agreed abortion was permissible when the child would be born physically handicapped. But the question of whether abortion was acceptable simply because the woman was unmarried showed in Canada (32 percent and 23 percent) and the United States (29 percent and 27 percent) that supporters of such a position are a distinct minority, and the same applied to cases where a married couple did not want any more children. In 1981 such abortions were acceptable to 24 percent of Canadians (30 percent in 1990) and to 27 percent of Americans (up one point from 1990). These longitudinal and cross-national comparisons hint that "Canadians were slightly less likely than Americans to support discretionary abortions, but by 1990 they were more supportive" (Nevitte, Brandon, and Davis 1993, 22)

The longitudinal NORC data for the United States have been given close scrutiny to assess changes in public attitudes toward abortion. Because the largest increases in public support for abortion came before *Roe,* between 1965 and 1970, Gillespie, Ten Vergert, and Kingma (1988, 324) argue that the "Supreme Court decisions of 1973 . . . have had little or no effect on public opinion. Instead, the enactment of the Supreme Court decisions may have been a response to shifts in North American and European public opinion on sexual and related issues in the 1960s." And earlier, in 1980, Uslander and Weber (1980, 214) agreed that "the abortion policies of *Roe* and *Doe* have not been legitimized. We have not seen substantial increases in public support for abortion after the Court decisions; instead, we have witnessed a hardening of positions by many who were opposed to abortions."

Since pollsters do not find high support for abortion as an elective procedure, does that necessarily mean that the American people are opposed to the *Roe* decision by the Supreme Court and wish to see that ruling overturned? The Harris survey and Gallup poll used nearly identical questions to track public support for the *Roe* decision (Tatalovich 1988, 189). In six of the eight polls taken during the decade following *Roe,* between 50 percent and 54 percent favored "the U.S. Supreme Court decision making abortions up to three months of pregnancy legal," but the 1985 and 1986 polls divided the public 45 percent to 45 percent on this issue. Those opposing the decision ranged between 37 percent and 45 percent, so while all people opposed to *Roe* may not be committed pro-lifers, nonetheless there is a substantial number of Americans who may be receptive to the arguments of the antiabortionists.

Blake and Del Pinal (1981) estimated that people between the pro-life and pro-choice extremes or who have inconsistent positions represent one-half to two-thirds of the American public. The "fact that high proportions of respondents can be found to approve at least one reason for legalizing abortion does not, apparently, constitute very meaningful public support. People who equivocate, who wish to fine-tune the justifications for abortion, apparently are more negative than positive in their views about legalizing abortion. In fact, it may be fair to say that these respondents are 'closet negatives' " (Blake and Del Pinal 1981, 314–15).

A 1989 Gallup poll assessed public support for *Roe* and found that 58 percent supported the ruling though a sizable minority (37 percent) favored its repeal (*Gallup Report* 1989, 18). But short of repealing *Roe,* the 1989 *Webster* decision suggests the likelihood that *Roe* may be eroded by future state regulations rather than directly repudiated by the high court. In a Gallup poll commissioned by *Newsweek* (1989a, 15), 53 percent disapproved of "this week's Supreme Court decision allowing states to pass laws that restrict abortion," but 37 percent approved; a Yankelovich Clancy Shulman survey commissioned by Cable News Network and *Time* (*Time* 1989, 63) found 61 percent disagreeing with the recent ruling "that states can pass laws restricting women's ability to have abortions." When questioned about specific restrictions, however, a different picture emerges (*Newsweek* 1989b, 15; *Time* 1989, 63). Both these polls found seven of ten respondents supporting parental consent before a teenager could get an abortion; 81 percent in the Gallup poll and 88 percent in the Yankelovich Clancy Shulman survey believed that doctors should inform the woman about alternatives to abortion; and people who favored testing for fetal viability outside the womb totaled 54 percent in the Gallup poll and 48 percent in the survey by Yankelovich Clancy Shulman. A *New York Times–* CBS News poll (Apple 1989, 8) confirmed that a large majority (70 percent) was in favor of requiring parental consent for a girl under eighteen to have an abortion, and 65 percent supported a "test in a pregnancy of 20 weeks or more to make sure the fetus is not developed enough to live outside the womb before a woman could have an abortion."

Acceptance of abortion also rises when its legality is cited or when abortion is defined as a medical decision between a woman and her doctor, yet most people also view the unborn as human, meaning that a moral dilemma is involved here. As early as 1977 Gallup found that after the first trimester, the majority was not willing to sanction abortions except to save the mother's life (*Gallup Opinion Index* 1978). Canadians have similar reservations about late-term abortions (see table 4.2), since abortions within three weeks of conception are supported by 11 percent to 18 percent more people than are abortions within five weeks of conception. This pattern of response implies that people are weighing the mother's right to an abortion against the "right" of the unborn to live.

The preamble to Missouri's statute declared life to begin at conception, and eight years prior to *Webster* a 1981 Gallup poll found that 54 percent of Americans felt that "human life begins at the moment of conception" while only 17 percent believed that "human life does not begin until the baby is actually born." But, curiously, 42 percent supported (and 51 percent opposed) a federal law to declare that "human life begins at conception, and therefore abortion at any time could be considered a crime of murder" (*Gallup Report* 1981a, 19, 22). *Time* in 1989 reported that 50 percent "personally believe[d] having an abortion is wrong" (Lacayo 1989, 21), and the moral concerns that surround the debate over abortion were extensively probed by a *Los Angeles Times* survey also taken that year (Skelton 1989). Most people surveyed (57 percent) agreed that "abortion is murder," though their responses to other questions indicated that this sentiment may not be the critical factor influencing how people assess the need for abortion. That is, although 61 percent expressed the view that abortion was "morally wrong," 74 percent also said that while "I personally feel that abortion is morally wrong . . . I also feel that whether or not to have an abortion is a decision that has to be made by every woman for herself" (Skelton 1989, 12). Yet these same respondents further qualified their opinions, as 81 percent believed that "minors should have to get their parents' permission before they get an abortion" and 53 percent favored "requiring a woman to get the consent of the natural father before she has an abortion" (Skelton 1989, 14).

The question of the father's consent has special relevance for Canada since there were cases in Alberta, Manitoba, Ontario, and Quebec—the last reaching the Canadian Supreme Court as *Tremblay v. Daigle* (1989)—involving fathers who sought court injunctions to prevent their partners from aborting their pregnancies (Morton 1992, 275–89). When asked by Gallup, "Should an abortion be allowed if the woman requests one but the man disagrees?" 57 percent said yes, including majorities of Protestants and Catholics, men and women, and residents of Quebec, Ontario, British Columbia, and even the prairies (51 percent). Only those living in the Atlantic provinces divided at 45 percent against and 38 percent for the woman in this situation (Muldoon 1991, 41).

Who Favors or Opposes Abortion?

Opinion analysts generally agree that upper socioeconomic groups and specifically people with more education are more supportive of abortion. "The closest we come to a deep division by social characteristics," Blake (1973, 455) observed, based on 1960s data, "is the educational differential, where the college-educated are decidedly more in favor of nonmedical reasons for abortion than are those of lesser education." A comprehensive study of abortion attitudes in the United States drew the same conclusion:

> Of all the social characteristics that help us understand abortion attitudes, education is the strongest predictor. Opposition to legal abortion is highest

among those who have dropped out of high school and lowest among college graduates. The effects of education are generally strong and exist across the entire range of educational attainment, with each increasing year of education leading to more liberal beliefs about abortion. (Cook, Jelen, and Wilcox 1992, 48)

Obviously there is a religious cleavage, but its dynamics might suggest less opposition to abortion in Canada than here. The first studies showed that Catholics were somewhat more opposed to abortion than Protestants (Blake 1971, 540–49; see also Tedrow and Mahoney 1979; Pomeroy and Landman 1973; Jones and Westoff 1973), though the sectarian gap has narrowed since the 1960s (McIntosh and Alston 1977). For Canada, in the final month of 1989 Gallup reported that more Protestants (29 percent) than Catholics (19 percent) would legalize abortions in any circumstance and that slightly more Catholics (14 percent) than Protestants (10 percent) would make abortion illegal in all circumstances. On the other hand, more Catholics (63 percent) than Protestants (58 percent) accepted abortions under certain circumstances (Muldoon 1991, 39).

More important than dogma, according to recent studies, is religious commitment, because Catholics and Protestants who are frequent church attenders are decidedly more opposed to abortion. One of the first American researchers to identify this religiosity variable was Alice Rossi (1967), but others have confirmed the relationship in the United States (Legge 1983; Baker, Epstein, and Forth 1981; McIntosh, Alston, and Alston 1979; Petersen and Mauss 1976; McCormick 1975, 57–69) and Canada (Hartnagel, Creechan, and Silverman 1985). The use of multiple-classification analysis to examine abortion attitudes among the 1984 and 1988 Canadian national electorates determined that "the greatest correlation to position on abortion in both elections was church attendance. The only other variables that were significant in both 1984 and 1988 were religiosity and region, the latter distinguished by a pro-life tendency in Atlantic Canada and greater pro-choice support in Quebec" (Kay, Lambert, Brown, and Curtis 1991, 151). Going a step further, Cook, Jelen, and Wilcox (1992, 124) determined that "direct religious socialization about abortion is more evident among Catholics and evangelicals. Among evangelicals and Catholics, abortion attitudes seem at least partially based on the interpretation of biblical passages." The fact that Canada has many more Catholics, though fewer fundamentalists, than the United States begs the question of why the U.S. debate over church–state separation is not being replicated to the north.

Recent cross-cultural research assessed how an array of variables affected abortion attitudes in Canada and the United States. Using the World Values Survey for 1990, Nevitte, Brandon, and Davis (1993) found three strong relationships. The importance of God and church attendance were the most powerful predictors in both countries. Canadian Catholics more than non-Catholics disapproved of abortions for health and discretionary reasons, whereas American Catholics were more opposed only with respect to aborting a handicapped child. In both countries postmaterialist values, feminism, and education predicted attitudes regarding discretionary abortions, particularly in Canada, and the study's authors estimated that in 1990 26 percent of Canadians and 10 percent of Americans qualified as postmaterialists. Third, socioeconomic cleavages had mixed impact insofar as American blacks opposed but francophone Canadians supported abortions for health reasons, and gender had no decisive effect in either culture.

The comparative study by Chandler, Cook, Jelen, and Wilcox (1994) again showed that religious variables dominate. Roman Catholicism was related to opposition to abortion in the United States and Canada; in both contexts religiosity, subjective interpretations of the Bible, and the saliency of religion were negative influences; but belonging to an evangelical church was related to antiabortion attitudes only in Canada. In sum, "the effects of religious variables appear slightly stronger in Canada, although Canadians are more supportive of legal abortion than are respondents from the United States" (Chandler, Cook, Jelen, and Wilcox 1994, 137).

Although organized religion is more pervasive in the United States, the study's authors suggest a trade-off between the forces of religion and political culture. The United States "is a highly religious country, but the effects of religion on abortion attitudes seem to be reduced by the pervasive individualism of the U.S. political culture," and in Canada "while antiabortion attitudes are not suppressed by individualistic values, such attitudes are inhibited by the relative lack of religiosity among Canadians" (Chandler, Cook, Jelen, and Wilcox 1994, 139). This study also gave attention to regional variations in Canada and the United States. Quebec and the American South are unique, for different reasons: "Southerners are less supportive of access to legal abortion than are nonsoutherners in the United States" but "residents of Quebec are more supportive of abortion rights than are respondents residing in the English-speaking provinces" (Chandler, Cook, Jelen, and Wilcox 1994, 140).

Questions on abortion funding are regularly asked in the United States but rarely in Canada. One recent exception was a provincial-government-backed nonbinding plebiscite in Saskatchewan where the majority of voters rejected public funding for abortions—although public authorities there have not acted accordingly (Brodie 1994, 135). Discerning the popular will from the myriad of U.S. surveys is not so easy. ABC News polls indicated that 57 percent in 1981 and 55 percent in 1985 were against the government's paying for abortions (*Family Planning Perspectives* 1985a, 77), but during the same time frame Gallup reported 56 percent to be opposed to "a ban on federal financing of abortions" (*Gallup Report* 1982, 19). Legge (1987, 76–77) analyzed a 1981 *Washington Post*–ABC News poll that found 56 percent disagreeing with the statement "Abortion is something that government should not pay for even if a woman seeking an abortion is very poor." Most predictive of attitudes were scales on conservatism-liberalism and on women's rights; in addition, socioeconomic "class is significant but it is in an opposite direction from what one might expect—those identifying themselves as middle class are more supportive of public funding than the working class."

Nobody has suggested that the Canadian Constitution be amended to prohibit abortions, but those proposals are often heard in the United States. If American public opinion can be neatly summarized, overall most people are opposed to abortion in general, although they might be sympathetic so long as abortions for therapeutic reasons are allowed.

New York Times–CBS News surveys found that 56 percent in 1976 (Blake 1977, 59) and 68 percent in 1982 (Clymer 1982) were opposed to any constitutional amendment making *all* abortions illegal, while seven years later a poll by the *Los Angeles Times* (Skelton 1989, 12) showed 62 percent to be against "a constitutional amendment to ban legalized abortions." Yet consider two polls by the *New York Times*–CBS News in 1984 (Herbers 1984). One found 63 percent opposing an amendment "that would make all abortions illegal" while another found only 48 percent disapproving of an amendment that permitted abortions "only in order to save the life of the mother." This represented a shift of 15 percent toward a constitutional amendment permitting one therapeutic exception for abortion.

The latest development in the abortion policy debate involves the "abortion pill," RU-486, which pro-choice advocates hope will diffuse the controversy by making the abortion decision truly personal and confidential. In early 1993 Gallup asked its American respondents whether "you, personally, favor or oppose making this pill available in the United States by prescription" (*Gallup Poll Monthly* 1993b, 26). Fifty-four percent would, but 41 percent would not. Curiously, men (61 percent) were much more likely to approve its distribution than women (49 percent); otherwise this issue seems to cleave the body politic in ways similar to how attitudes are framed about surgical abortion. Majorities of Democrats, college graduates, and people earning more than $20,000 (but especially $50,000 or more) supported use of RU-486, whereas a majority of Republicans (56 percent) and a plurality of people without any college education (48 percent) were opposed (those earning under $20,000 split, 48 percent in favor and 47 percent against).

Interests: The Limits of Pluralism

Both the coalition-building process and the boundaries of group conflict over abortion will be examined cross-culturally by coding all the organizations that have lobbied the legislative and judicial branches in both countries. Included are all American groups that testified at any of the twenty-three congressional hearings on abortion policy from 1973 to 1988,* and in Canada by those giving testimony before the Legislative Committee on Bill C-43 of the House of Commons in 1990 (table 4.3). As an aside, note that most of the organizations that made presentations to the Legislative Committee of the House of Commons were invited back to appear before the Standing Senate Committee on Legal and Constitutional Affairs. By one count, the Senate "heard from 38 individuals and groups and, with the exception of two Tory cabinet ministers, the Law Reform Commission of Canada, and the Plymouth Brothers, none favored [Bill C-43]" (Brodie, Gavigan, and Jenson 1992, 114). Also classified for this comparative analysis are the groups that submitted briefs in eighteen U.S. Supreme Court abortion cases between 1973 and 1989† and intervenors before the Canadian Supreme Court in the trilogy of abortion cases: *Morgentaler v. The Queen* (1988), *Borowski v. Canada* (1989), and *Tremblay v. Daigle* (1989).

In the United States, single-issue groups represented 69 percent of all pro-life groups that gave congressional testimony and 53 percent of pro-life amici before the Supreme Court. Pro-choice single-issue groups were re-

---

*The hearings were listed in Congressional Information Service (CIS) *Annual Editions,* 1973–1988, 4520 East-West Highway, Bethesda, MD, 20814. This compilation excluded hearings on Health and Human Services funding (usually including the Hyde Amendment on Medicaid), District of Columbia funding, and Department of Defense funding because they also covered broad unrelated areas. The scope of these particular hearings focused on Title X of the 1970 Public Health Service Act (10), Civil Rights Restoration Act of 1987 (1), abortion clinic violence (1), antiabortion funding rider to the 1964 Civil Rights Act (1), fetal pain (1), Public Health Emergency Act (1), constitutional amendments (5), and bills dealing with life from conception (1) and adolescent pregnancies (2).

†The cases are: *Roe v. Wade,* 410 U.S. 113 (1973); *Doe v. Bolton,* 410 U.S. 179 (1973); *Bigelow v. Virginia,* 421 U.S. 809 (1975); *Connecticut v. Menillo,* 423 U.S. 9 (1975); *Planned Parenthood of Central Missouri v. Danforth,* 428 U.S. 52 (1976); *Beal v. Doe,* 432 U.S. 438 (1977); *Maher v. Roe,* 432 U.S. 464 (1977); *Poelker v. Doe,* 432 U.S. 519 (1977); *Colautti v. Franklin,* 439 U.S. 379 (1979); *Bellotti v. Baird,* 443 U.S. 622 (1979); *Harris v. McRae,* 448 U.S. 297 (1980); *Williams v. Zbaraz,* 448 U.S. 358 (1980); *H.L. v. Matheson,* 450 U.S. 398 (1981); *Akron v. Akron Center for Reproductive Health, Inc.,* 462 U.S. 416 (1983); *Simopoulos v. Virginia,* 462 U.S. 506 (1983); *Planned Parenthood Association of Kansas City, Missouri v. Ashcroft,* 462 U.S. 476 (1983); *Thornburgh v. American College of Obstetricians and Gynecologists,* 476 U.S. 747 (1986); *Webster v. Reproductive Health Services,* 109 S.Ct. 3040 (1989).

Table 4.3

Interest Groups Providing Legislative Testimony and Amicus Curiae Briefs on Abortion in the United States and Canada

Pro-Life Groups			Pro-Choice Groups	
United States	Canada	Type of Group	United States	Canada

		Classification of Groups Providing Testimony Before Committees of the United States Congress and the Canadian Parliament		
16	6	Religious	28	1
2	1	Health/Medical	19	1
—	1	Civil Liberties/Law	3	3
—	—	Family Planning	22	2
—	4	Women's Groups	33	14
46	6	Single-Issue*	16	9
—	2	State/Federal Government	3	0
—	—	Ethnic/Racial	5	—
—	—	Labor Unions	—	2
3	2	Others	10	3
67	22		139	35

		Classification of Groups Acting as Amici Before the Supreme Courts of the United States and Canada		
17	1	Religious	43	—
2	—	Health/Medical	35	—
7	—	Civil Liberties/Law	53	1
—	—	Family Planning	23	—
3	1	Women's Groups	122	1
57	3	Single—Issue	32	1
15	2	State/Federal Government	14	—
—	—	Ethnic/Racial	21	—
—	—	Labor Unions	12	—
7	—	Others	38	—
108	7		393	3

Sources: Amicus activity in the United States is based on eighteen abortion cases from *Roe v. Wade* (1973) to *Webster v. Reproductive Health Services* (1989) and in Canada on these cases: *Morgentaler v. The Queen* (1988), *Tremblay v. Daigle* (1989) and *Borowski v. Canada* (1989). Legislative testimony in Canada was on Bill C-43 (1990) in the House of Commons and in the United States during twenty-three congressional hearings in the Senate and House of Representatives between 1973 and 1988.

*Includes single-issue factions within other categories, such as Catholics for a Free Choice and Baptists for Life, which are not counted among, respectively, the pro-choice and pro-life religious groups.

spectively 12 percent and 8 percent of the U.S. totals, which affirms that narrowly focused advocatory groups are a much more important ingredient of the pro-life lobby than of the pro-choice coalition. By virtue of the number and diversity of the groups aligned in each camp, it has been argued that pro-lifers can be characterized as a lobby since their coalition-building efforts are not as widespread as what has been achieved by pro-choice advocates (Tatalovich and Daynes 1993). A listing of the groups that most frequently lobbied Congress or the Supreme Court (Tatalovich and Daynes 1993, 55) illustrates this point. Most active on the pro-life side were (frequencies indicated):

National Right to Life Committee	15
U.S. Catholic Conference	13
Americans United for Life	11
Legal Defense Fund for Unborn Children	9
American Life Lobby	6
American Citizens Concerned for Life	6
United Families Foundation	5
U.S. Coalition for Life	5
American Association of Pro Life Obstetricians and Gynecologists	5
Lawyers for Life	4
Catholic League for Religious and Civil Rights	4

It is obvious that the leading edge of the pro-life movement is the purist single-issue organizations. That does not apply to the pro-choice coalition in the United States, as these comparable data show:

Planned Parenthood Federation of America	25
American College of Obstetricians and Gynecologists	16
American Public Health Association	16
National Organization for Women	16
National Abortion Rights Action League	15
National Family Planning and Reproductive Health Association	14
Young Women's Christian Association of the USA	12
Alan Guttmacher Institute	11
American Association of University Women	11
Union of American Hebrew Congregations	10
American Jewish Congress	10

The only single-issue organization is the National Abortion Rights Action League (NARAL). Founded in 1969 as the National Association for the Repeal of Abortion Laws, NARAL in 1973 renamed itself the National Abortion Rights Action League.

The pristine pro-life single-issue group is the National Right to Life Committee, which testified at ten congressional hearings between 1975 and 1986. Americans United for Life (AUL), or its Legal Defense Fund, testified three times before committee hearings. Established in 1971, AUL is the oldest national pro-life organization. American Life Lobby is a militantly fundamentalist group whose energies are directed specifically against Planned Parenthood. In a pamphlet American Life Lobby claimed Planned Parenthood was "founded by a woman who once said: 'THE MOST MERCIFUL THING THAT A LARGE FAMILY DOES TO ONE OF ITS INFANT MEMBERS IS TO KILL IT' " (American Life Lobby 1980). There also are single-issue factions that dissent from the generally pro-abortion positions of established religious, medical, legal, and women's organizations: Doctors for Life, Lawyers for Life, American Association of Pro Life Obstetricians and Gynecologists, American Association of Pro-Life Pediatricians, Feminists for Life of America, National Association of Pro-Life Nurses, Baptists for Life, Lutherans for Life, United Church of Christ Friends for Life, and Presbyterians Pro-Life.

Canadian Physicians for Life (CPL) is the most vocal example in that country. Founded in 1975, CPL recalls the 1963 CMA code of ethics, which stated: "The induction or procuring of abortion involves the destruction of life. It is a violation of the moral code, except where there is justification for its performance. The only justification is that the continuance of pregnancy would imperil the life of the mother" (House of Commons 1990, 11). The CMA abandoned that position but the CPL still subscribes to the original. What also motivates this splinter group is unease about antidemocratic rule in the CMA. The CPL alleges that the CMA policy is not supported by its membership, based on the CMA's own polling, and in 1989 CPL undertook its own survey to prove the point. Of 10,519 doctors who responded, 65 percent agreed that CMA policies "favour abortion on request," and 47 percent agreed (45 percent disagreed) that a new law should "be stronger than the old one in terms of society's obligation to the fetus." Overall, CPL reported that 30 percent of physicians would totally legalize abortions; 39 percent would do so under certain circumstances, but only 21 percent would restrict abortions to cases in which the mother's life was threatened, and 4 percent more would ban abortions entirely.

In Canada, single-issue groups are seemingly more important to both sides of the debate, unlike in the United States, where such groups have a lesser role in the U.S. pro-choice movement. A linchpin of the pro-life network is Campaign Life Coalition, though other groups that gave testimony include Canadian Physicians for Life, Nurses for Life, and Campaign Québec-Vie. The Canadian Abortion Rights Action League (CARAL) is the counterpart of NARAL. Others who endorse pro-choice objectives include the Pro-Choice Action Network, Tories for Choice, Men for Women's Choice, Coalition for Reproductive Choice, Physicians for Choice, and Canadians for Choice. The Pro-Choice Action Network, Canadians for Choice, and CARAL are umbrella organizations that speak for other groups, most of which did not make formal presentations to Parliament. The Pro-Choice Action Network represents at least six like-minded groups across Canada, such as the British Columbia Coalition for Abortion Clinics and the Halifax Pro-Choice Action Group. Of eighteen organizations belonging to Canadians for Choice, ten gave testimony, but some very prestigious organizations are among those that did not: the Canadian Unitarian Council, the Canadian Union of Public Employees, the Canadian Federation of Business and Professional Women's Clubs, the National Council of Jewish Women, the Canadian Association of Sexual Assault Centres, the Law Union of Ontario, Grandmothers for Choice, and The Issue Is Choice.

The Canadian Abortion Rights Action League is comprised of eighty-five mainly local and provincial member groups, of which six—the Humanist Association of Canada, the Coalition for Reproductive Choice, the YWCA of Canada, the Yukon Status of Women Council, the National Association of Women and the Law, and the Coalition québecoise pour le droit à l'avortement libre et gratuit—gave formal testimony. In documentation to support its arguments, CARAL also listed twenty-nine national organizations opposed to recriminalization of abortion. Most of them had appeared at the committee hearings, but not these: Canadian Autoworkers, the Canadian Psychiatric Association, the Canadian Daycare Advocacy Association, the Communication Workers of Canada, the Disabled Women's Network: Canada, the National Organization of Immigrant and Visible Minority Women of Canada, and the Society of Obstetricians and Gynaecologists of Canada.

Looking beyond those representatives who attended the parliamentary hearings does suggest an even more extensive network of pro-choice groups. Thus, in both Canada and the United States the battle over abortion affects a relatively narrow band of interests, but the pro-life *lobbies* are virtually a single-issue phenomenon, while notable political alliances are forged within the pro-choice *coalitions*. The pro-choice movement is larger and more diverse and has prestigious national associations but still is not an all-encompassing group network. The Canadian data are a microcosm—with some differences—of the American pattern.

In the United States, the mainstays of the pro-choice coalition are women's groups, health care associations, organized religion, and family planning organizations. After *Roe* the abortion battle shifted to Congress, where pro-lifers were promoting restrictive constitutional amendments and barriers to federal funding of abortions. To meet that threat and strengthen their own lobbying, seven pro-choice organizations formed an "information exchange," which, following enactment of the Hyde Amendment, was formalized as the Abortion Information Exchange (AIE). The key organizations were the National Abortion Rights Action League, the Religious Coalition for Abortion Rights, the Planned Parenthood Federation of American, Zero Population Growth, the National Organization for Women (NOW), the National Women's Political Caucus, and the American Civil Liberties Union (ACLU). AIE grew to include over fifty organizations in 1983 (Staggenborg 1986, 378).

Four categories of groups—women's, religious, family planning, and medical/health care—accounted for most of the pro-choice organizations giving congressional testimony (73 percent), with single-issue groups accounting for another 12 percent, while in Canada women's organizations and single-issue pro-choice groups together accounted for 66 percent of the total. More than half of the eighty-five member groups in CARAL represent women's interests of one kind or another. The women's organizations that gave testimony on Bill C-43 included: the Fédération des Femmes du Québec, the National Action Committee on the Status of Women, the National Association of Women and the Law, the Canadian Federation of University Women, the YWCA of Canada, the National Council of Women of Canada, the Canadian Advisory Council on the Status of Women, and the Women's Legal Action and Education Fund.

One caveat is that—today, if not earlier—feminism seems more prominent within the ranks of the Canadian pro-choice movement, compared to its U.S. counterpart, despite the fact that women's rights were not made explicit in the *Morgentaler* (1988) ruling. The data (table 4.3) show that the largest contingent within the U.S. pro-choice coalition is comprised of groups dedicated to the social, economic, and political advancement of women. Most active politically have been some older organizations such as the Young Women's Christian Association and the American Association of University Women and feminist rivals such as NOW, though NOW did not endorse liberalized abortion laws until 1967. So the outpouring of feminist energy was a recent phenomenon triggered by the impending *Webster* decision:

> When *Roe* was decided, slightly more health and medical groups filed briefs than did women's organizations, and as late as 1983 . . . health/medical

groups were more prominently involved than were groups representing women. While health and medical associations had an obvious interest in the outcome of the 1986 *Thornburgh* [*v. American College of Obstetricians and Gynecologists*] decision, nonetheless about twice as many women's groups filed briefs in that case. By the time *Webster* reached the Supreme Court docket in 1989, more than four times as many women's groups collaborated on amicus briefs as did health and medical organizations. (Tatalovich and Daynes 1993, 56)

Some pro-choice proponents are prestigious medical associations. The American Public Health Association and the American College of Obstetricians and Gynecologists were especially active in giving testimony to Congress. Others, though less active, included the Association of Planned Parenthood Professionals, the American Medical Association, the American Psychiatric Association, the American Academy of Pediatrics, the Association of American Medical Colleges, and the American Nurses Association. Family planning groups counsel alternatives to childbirth, so they have a vested interest in the outcome of the abortion battle. No organization is quite the nemesis of pro-lifers and right-wingers for supporting sex education and birth control as well as abortion rights that the Planned Parenthood Federation of America is. Planned Parenthood was very active in lobbying Congress, having testified more than any other pro-choice group (fifteen times). It was opposed to restrictions on Medicaid funding of abortions and pro-life constitutional amendments but supported Title X family planning grants. Others included the National Family Planning and Reproductive Health Association and the Alan Guttmacher Institute, the research arm of Planned Parenthood.

The Canadian Medical Association, after Section 251 of the Criminal Code was struck down, stated "that there is no need for this section to be replaced" and adopted a new three-part statement on abortion:

- Induced abortion is the active termination of a pregnancy before fetal viability.
- The decision to perform an induced abortion is a medical one, made confidentially between the patient and her physician within the confines of existing Canadian law. The decision is made after conscientious examination of all other options.
- Induced abortion requires medical and surgical expertise and is a medical act. It should be performed only in a facility that meets approved medical standards, not necessarily a hospital. (*Canadian Medical Association Journal* 1988, 1176A)

Thus the CMA in 1988 endorsed elective abortion and apparently gave Morgentaler the go-ahead to establish other abortion clinics insofar as nonhospital abortion providers were deemed appropriate. The CMA General Council in 1988 went beyond that statement by adding other endorsements, for example, that "induced abortion should be uniformly available to all women in Canada," that "health care insurance should cover all the costs of providing all medically required services relating to abortion including counselling," and "that there should be no delay in the provision of abortion services" (*Canadian Medical Association Journal* 1988, 1176A).

Since the CMA was firmly against the recriminalization of abortion, physicians mounted a campaign against Bill C-43 by threatening to refuse to do any abortions. In the Senate hearings Justice Minister Kim Campbell accused the physicians "of 'ignorance,' of 'exploiting pregnant women by refusing their requests for abortion,' and [of] 'using the interests of women as a tactic in a political battle' " (Brodie, Gavigan, and Jenson 1992, 113). The role of organized medicine was a decisive factor in the Senate tie vote that killed the bill. "The doctors, as Campbell recognized, were playing 'hardball politics' and, judging by the Senate committee's reactions to these exchanges, they were winning" (Brodie, Gavigan, and Jenson 1992, 113). Unlike the variety of medical and health care groups that came to endorse the pro-choice position in Canada, the CMA was almost alone in its political campaign against Bill C-43. Testimony was given by Planned Parenthood of Canada, but neither the Canadian Psychiatric Association nor the Society of Obstetricians and Gynaecologists of Canada gave formal testimony at this critical time, although during the summer and fall of 1990 the latter organization surveyed its membership and announced that only 158 obstetricians and gynecologists would continue performing abortions if Bill C-43 was enacted (Brodie, Gavigan, and Jenson 1992, 112).

In sum, though organized medicine in the United States was allied with a larger number of health care associations in its abortion advocacy, even more in the 1980s than during the 1960s reforms (see chapter 1), it can be said without hesitation that the Canadian Medical Association represented both the leading edge of the political opposition to recriminalization and the dominant intellectual force in Canada's abortion debate of that decade.

In Canada abortion may be implicitly viewed by feminists as a woman's right, but in the United States it is sanctified as a right by the Supreme Court. Organizations of lawyers or civil libertarians are quite prominent in the American pro-choice coalition, and these kinds of groups have tended to focus their lobbying activities on the judiciary, not Congress (see table 4.3). Most important is the American Civil Liberties Union and its Reproductive Freedom Project. The ACLU acted as amicus in five cases and gave congressional testimony at four hearings. The Canadian Civil Liberties Union (CCLU) gave testimony to the parliamentary committee and acted as intervenor to the Canadian Supreme Court. By contrast, the Canadian Bar Association did not testify on Bill C-43, and the American Bar Association, consistent with its usual nonposition on abortion (see chapter 1), never gave congressional testimony and has not authored an amicus brief since 1973.

The groups in the final contingent of the pro-choice coalition are varied and reflect differing social characteristics of the American and Canadian societies. Few racial and ethnic groups are specifically represented in the United States, which seems ironic given the adverse consequences strict antiabortion laws portend for the minority poor. There are groups speaking for Chinese, blacks, Mexicans, and Puerto Ricans, but their level of activity is low. The NAACP Legal Defense and Education Fund testified twice and the Urban League did so once. No such racial or ethnic groups made appearances before Parliament on Bill C-43. In the United States an array of groups favor legalized abortion for ideological, lifestyle, or idiosyncratic reasons. The American Ethical Union defends freedom of conscience; Americans for Democratic Action are liberal advocates; Americans United for Separation of Church and State and also People for the American Way are against abortion policy reflecting a particular religious point of view. Other groups are the Sierra Club, alert to the impact of overpopulation on the environment; Public Citizen, a group founded by the consumer advocate Ralph Nader; and the American Library Association.

Another variation pertains to the economic sector. In the United States no business or national trade associations made public their positions on abortion, but labor unions were more involved in Canada, and their role in this debate raises an interesting question about whether old-style class politics or postmaterialist values lie at the core of their actions. Organized labor never testified before a congressional hearing on abortion, and the Teamsters and the AFL-CIO are *not* among the twelve unions that acted as amici in Supreme Court cases (see table 4.3). One was the American Federation of State, County, and Municipal Employees, a large organization, but four others were locals in New York City. The Canadian Labour Congress (CLC), Canada's counterpart to the AFL-CIO as the nation's largest union, was the only labor organization to give testimony on Bill C-43, although the pro-choice coalition also includes the Canadian Union of Public Employees, Canadian Autoworkers, and the Communication Workers of Canada.

The 17th Constitutional Convention (1988) of the Canadian Labour Congress resolved that "choice is an equality and economic issue affecting women" and proceeded to decry provincial actions that deny funding for abortions as promoting "a two-tier system of Medicare" and thus demanded "that the federal government recognize that abortions are a medically required service and therefore should be included in all provincial Medicare plans" (House of Commons 1990, issue 4). In its testimony the CLC, which represents 2.3 million members, reminded the MPs that it first endorsed a pro-choice position in 1972 and then proceeded to rhetorically ask "whether this was a labour matter," to which the "rank and file members of affiliates from coast to coast answered, in no uncertain terms, that it is" (House of Commons 1990, issue 4, appendix C-43/4, 40).

> For us, then, fundamental rights to equality, justice and fairness cannot exist in one location and not in another: nor can they be gained in one place and not in another. Our members cannot have dignity and equality in the workplace, but not in society; in the factory, but not in the streets; in the office, but not in the home. The forces which deny our rights in the workplace are the same forces which deny them elsewhere, and for the labour movement, to defend our members is to confront those forces wherever they are. (House of Commons 1990, issue 4, appendix C-43/4, 41)

And who are those forces? They are "doctors, courts, government, police and assorted third-party intervenors. As long as women's decisions about pregnancy are subordinated to decisions made by others, women in Canada are neither free nor equal, but are forced to live in servitude," the CLC declared, and after surveying the legal landscape and the problems with Bill C-43, it returned to its basic indictment: "What all of this will mean, in real terms, is *control*. By means of the blunt instrument of criminal law, women once again will have their reproductive capacity appropriated by others and managed by the coercive power of the state" (House of Commons 1990, issue 4, appendix C-43/4, 41, 51). Clearly this statement is more a manifesto of feminism than a call to arms by the working classes. It seems very unlikely that the AFL-CIO in the United States—even had it taken a public stand on abortion—would have articulated a full-blown feminist political ideology as justification for its views.

Virtually all mainstream Protestant and Jewish denominations in the United States support legalized abortion: the United Methodist Church, the Unitarian Universalist Association, the American Jewish Congress, the United Synagogues of America, the Church of the Brethren, the United Church of Christ, the American Baptist Churches (USA), the Presbyterian Church (USA), and the United Presbyterian Church of the USA. However, this solid phalanx of pro-choice churches has given way to pragmatism in recent years. Pro-life factions exist within established Protestant churches, and their opposition has forced some mainstream denominations to soften their position about abortion on demand. In 1988 the 2.5-million-member Episcopal Church amended its pro-choice position with the statement that abortion is morally acceptable only "in extreme situations" and never "as a means of birth control, family planning, sex selection or any reason of mere convenience" (*Newsweek* 1989a, 45). A rejection of abortion as a birth control device is also embodied in revised policy statements by the American (Northern) Baptist Churches, the United Methodist Church, and the newly merged Evangelical Lutheran Church in America. These shifts are explained by J. Robert Nelson, a Methodist theologian, who maintains that "there's a silent plurality of people in the congregations who have very strong reservations about the legitimacy of abortion. These people are not happy with the pro-choice resolutions passed at general conferences or with positions taken by denominational agencies in the name of the whole church" (*Newsweek* 1989a, 46). The Presbyterian Church (USA) followed suit in 1992 by moderating its nine-year-old strong pro-choice stance with new language acknowledging that government has a "limited legitimate interest" in regulating abortions and restricting them "in certain circumstances" (*New York Times* 1992b, A13).

The United Church of Canada (the largest denomination), the Presbyterian Church in Canada, and the Anglican Church of Canada are sympathetic to liberalized abortion laws but not necessarily to elective abortion. The 1977 statement (affirmed in 1988) of the Presbyterian Church in Canada declared "that the unborn has the right to life and that only a danger to the mother's health indicating the likelihood of permanent or prolonged mental or physical impairment be regarded as grounds for abortion" (Muldoon 1991, 121). Only the United Church of Canada gave testimony in 1990:

> We do not support "abortion on demand." We believe that abortion should be a personal matter between a woman and her doctor, who should earnestly consider their understanding of the particular situation permitting the woman to bring to bear her moral and religious insights into human life in reaching a decision through a free and responsive exercise of her conscience. (House of Commons 1990, issue 11)

Unique to the United States is a single-issue organization called the Religious Coalition for Abortion Rights (RCAR), which represents twenty-eight groups from fourteen denominations. RCAR was established in 1973 to prevent a constitutional amendment outlawing abortion, which it believed "would enact into civil law one particular theology—a theology that is not shared by a majority of Western denominations" (Religious Coalition for Abortion Rights 1978). RCAR gave testimony five times but filed no amicus briefs with the Supreme Court until it joined with thirty-four other religious groups as amici in a friend-of-the-court brief in the 1989 *Webster* case. There is nothing like RCAR in Canada, signifying that the abortion conflict in the United States is very much embroiled in the debate over separation of church and state as a constitutional principle and, on political grounds, in the furor over the forceful advocacy of the Roman Catholic Church. This sectarian dispute overlies the secular battle over women's rights versus traditional family values.

There is no establishment clause against an official church in the Canadian Charter of Rights and Freedoms. Instead, Section 2 lists "freedom of conscience and religion" as a "fundamental freedom" secured by the document, which presumably extends to churches' petitioning of the government. Of course, in Canada the Roman Catholic Church and pro-lifers, unlike in the United States, have not urged enactment of an amendment to the Charter disallowing abortion, although the issue had complicated the deliberations over writing the Charter (Morton 1992, 111–16).

Catholics and Church-State Relations

Though some denominations may tolerate limited therapeutic abortion, generally the churches in the United States that oppose pro-choice orthodoxy and defend the unborn are fundamentalist Protestants and evangelicals, Baptists, and Mormons, but at the forefront are the Catholics. The intimate relationship between the Roman Catholic Church and the pro-lifers causes opponents to raise the specter that church-state separation is threatened. Abortion advocates even charge that the National Right to Life Committee operates as the secular arm of the church: "There is convincing evidence that Catholics and the Catholic Church overwhelmingly dominate the RTL [right-to-life] movement. Not only do Catholics comprise the bulk of RTL rank-and-file organizations, but the Church provides the movement's financial and institutional base" (Jaffe, Lindheim, and Lee 1981, 79). The National Conference of Catholic Bishops (NCCB), its Committee for Pro-Life Activities, the U.S. Catholic Conference, and related groups such as the Knights of Columbus and the Catholic League for Religious and Civil Rights have all given testimony before Congress.

The National Committee for a Human Life Amendment is a political action committee (PAC) first created in 1974 following a legal suit by the Women's Lobby, which charged that the Catholic Church had failed to register as a lobbying organization (New York Times 1974a, 33; 1974b, 14). This counteroffensive by the pro-choice forces was matched by a much-publicized and unprecedented effort by the bishops to engage in political action. A 1975 Pastoral Plan for Pro-Life Activities (and its formal reaffirmation ten years later) was launched to aggressively promote the church's antiabortion teaching in three areas: (1) a public-information effort, (2) a pastoral effort for women with problem pregnancies, and (3) a public-policy effort to gain legal protection for the unborn (Tatalovich and Daynes 1981a, 155–57). The pastoral plan was symbolically very important, says Byrnes (1991, 60): "The significance of the bishops' opposition to abortion was not limited to its effect on Catholic voters, however. The bishops also presented themselves and their church as the center of a broad, grass-roots movement opposed to legal abortion. By 1976, 'right-to-life' was much more than a term in one of the NCCB's official statements. It was also the name of a growing social movement, supported and funded by the Catholic bishops, that was organized nationwide to engage in single-issue political action to achieve its goals."

The storm of criticism this action produced forced the bishops to issue a 1976 statement entitled "Political Responsibility: Reflections on an Election Year." The bishops did not see themselves in the middle of a conflict between church and state; to the contrary, they argued that they had a right to speak out and defend social justice and human rights in the U.S. political system. However, three years later they found it expedient to make yet another statement, this time advising Catholics to evaluate political candidates on issues other than their abortion stand. It implied that the bishops did not intend to create a religious voting bloc but again repeated the 1976 theme that the church had a responsibility to educate its membership on doctrine and to provide guidance on issues having moral and social significance. More striking was the church's ten-year legal battle against Abortion Rights Mobilization (ARM), a group that sued to deny the Roman Catholic Church its religious tax exemption because of its partisan political campaigning. Ultimately the Supreme Court let stand a lower-court ruling that ARM lacked standing to sue insofar as it could not establish how its interests had been directly injured by the church's tax exemption (Segers 1995a, 100).

In sharp contrast was the restrained, by American standards, testimony given to a parliamentary committee by the Canadian Conference of Catholic Bishops on Bill C-43:

> Catholic teaching on abortion is clear and unequivocal. Abortion is a moral evil because it involves the destruction of human life. Direct killing of an unborn child is never justified.
>
> The induced termination of a pregnancy is permissible, however, if it is the indirect result of efforts to prevent death of the mother. Examples of these situations are ectopic pregnancies and cancer of the uterus. The death of the unborn child in these cases is not commonly said to be an abortion. (House of Commons 1990, issue 3, appendix C-43/1)

However, the Canadian bishops "recognize[d] that there are strongly held views which differ from ours. This is understandable because the basic values of life and freedom are at stake. It is also part of the reality of living in a pluralistic society." What was unusual about their testimony, given the U.S. scenario where pro-choice advocates regularly accuse the Roman Catholic Church of trying to impose its abortion views on non-Catholics, is that the Canadian bishops agreed that "authentic pluralism" means "that no one group has the right to impose its particular point of view" on others and that government "has a key role to play in the formation of a collective conscience within the framework of a climate of social peace and respect for people who hold differing views" (House of Commons 1990, issue 3, appendix C-43/1).

The Bishops further argued that Parliament has a duty to legislate for the "common good," whereupon they focused on Bill C-43. First, they applauded the absence of a "gestational approach" so that the bill "accepts that human life has intrinsic value from the beginning." Second, the requirement of "grounds [for abortions] is significant because it affirms that abortion is more than a matter of choice and reinforces the state's interest in protecting the unborn child." Third, they welcomed the use of criminal law to send a "powerful message" on abortion. Beyond that, they believed that Bill C-43 was seriously flawed, and five amendments were recommended: (1) a more restrictive health criterion and elimination of social, economic, and psychological reasons as justification for abortion, (2) a requirement that medical opinions be obtained from two physicians, (3) "informed consent" requirements such as waiting periods and mandatory counseling, (4) penalties other than jail terms for women who illegally abort, and (5) a "conscience clause" to allow health care workers not to participate in abortions for religious or moral reasons.

The bishops concluded by reminding the MPs that, "as we wrote to your predecessors in 1966, Christian legislators must make their own decisions. The norm of their actions as legislators is not chiefly the good of any religious group but the good of society." All in all, this testimony was deferential in tone and did not unduly specify how Parliament should decide. Nor did the Canadian bishops retreat to a position that only imminent danger to the woman's life justified an abortion. Instead, they focused on the word *health* in the statute and gave the impression that therapeutic abortions were not outside the realm of possibility:

> The health risk must be substantial, serious, and permanent. Moreover, it should be such that it cannot be treated by any other commonly accepted medical procedure. This amendment is critical to ensure that all therapeutic alternatives are explored and that abortion is not used to remedy other problems or the stress or anxiety which may ordinarily accompany an unexpected or undesired pregnancy. (House of Commons 1990, issue 3, appendix C-43/1)

This occasion was not the first time that the Canadian Catholic hierarchy took a restrained approach to abortion; indeed, its lack of theological stridency is responsible, according to Michael Cuneo (1989), for the rise of "revivalist Catholics" who challenge both their church and their society for lax moral standards and a betrayal of the unborn. The bishops' mention of 1966 in their statement to Parliament refers to when the Canadian Catholic Conference (CCC) announced that the church would not oppose legalization of contraceptives, and its public statement following public hearings by a parliamentary committee gave its rationale, which was in part:

> The bishops, furthermore, asserted that Catholic legislators are not bound to vote only for laws that are in conformity with the teaching of the church. While responsibly acknowledging their dual obligations as members of both the church and the civil community, Catholic legislators "should not stand idly by waiting for the Church to tell [them] what to do in the political order." Matters of politics, the bishops continued, are properly the jurisdiction of the laity, and while the Catholic legislator should be cognizant of what the church teaches on a subject such as contraception, his "ultimate responsible conclusions are his own as he fulfills the task he has along with all other legislators." (Cuneo 1989, 26–27)

In 1967 the Canadian bishops returned to this same theme when Parliament considered easing the divorce laws. According to Cuneo (1989, 28), "The bishops reaffirmed the Catholic position on the indissolubility of marriage, and also acknowledged the impossibility in a pluralistic society of enforcing the Catholic marital ideal as a public norm. 'Canada is a country of many religious beliefs. Since other citizens, desiring as we do the promotion of the common good, believe that it is less injurious to the individual and to society that divorce be permitted in certain circumstances, we would not object to some revision of Canadian divorce laws that is truly directed to advancing the common good of civil society.' " It would not be long before the Canadian Catholic Conference had to cope with abortion reform, since in 1968 the Trudeau government proposed to liberalize the criminal code.

On March 5, 1968, a delegation from the Canadian Catholic Conference gave testimony before another parliamentary committee. Its spokesman, Bishop Remi De Roo of Victoria, delivered the opening statement: "We are here on your invitation to try to help with a complex and difficult question. We come therefore in a spirit of dialogue. That is, we do not feel that we have the whole answer. We do not want to impose a particular point of view" (quoted in de Valk 1974, 73). Eventually the MPs wanted to know about the relationship between morality, the law, and the common good, to which the Reverend E.J. Sheridan, another CCC delegate, responded: "It is not a question of allowing people to adopt a position or imposing our position on others or on Catholics. The Bishops are convinced . . . that a loose law in the matter of abortion is simply not for the common good. It is a bad law because it introduces an element of disorder, a fundamental disrespect for life, which we have great apprehensions is likely to grow" (quoted in de Valk 1974, 77). Nor would the bishops assume the legislative role and propose their preferred kind of bill. Bishop De Roo stated the case this way:

> The distinction may be the following one: in view of our basic stand, do we have a test to propose? The answer is no. No Bill will be proposed in view of our fundamental stand. But, on the other hand, would we object to another text which would be bound in with the problem of life? This is a different matter. We may not want to propose, but we may or may not protest. (quoted in de Valk 1974, 78)

If the bishops would not specify how to reform the law, then the question was raised whether they would criminalize all abortions. To that, Sheridan gave a decidedly nondoctrinaire answer: "No. As I understand your question, that abortion is illegal under any circumstances, no. The bishops have never been in favour of tightening the present law so as to exclude abortion. Abortion is permitted under our present Criminal Code, and certainly the bishops have never moved, do not wish to move, in the direction of tightening that. In other words, we do not believe that our moral principle must be enshrined in criminal law" (quoted in de Valk 1974, 79–80).

No such inhibitions surrounded the highly publicized 1984 debate between New York City's archbishop John H. O'Connor and nationally known pro-choice Democrats: Mario Cuomo, then governor of New York State, who was the keynote speaker at the national convention, and vice presidential candidate Geraldine Ferraro (D-New York), a member of Congress. In June of that year O'Connor bluntly had stated that he could not see "how a Catholic in conscience could vote for an individual explicitly expressing himself or herself as favoring abortion" (Byrnes 1991, 119). Subsequently O'Connor accused Ferraro of misrepresenting the official Catholic position on abortion. The purpose of these confrontations by O'Connor and other Catholic prelates, according to Byrnes (1991, 121), "was to make clear that as Catholic bishops they would not accept Catholic politicians who acquiesced in legal abortion."

The cautious demeanor by the CCC in 1968 seemingly appeased neither side of the abortion debate. "This issue," editorialized the *Globe and Mail* (quoted in de Valk 1974, 81–82), "first concerns the right of any group of citizens to violate through law the conscience of other citizens. For that is precisely what abortion laws do." The paper, which had championed the cause of abortion reform for years, then drew the distinction between law and morality and charged that "the bishops are now opposing abortion reform not because it threatens public order or the common good. They oppose it on essentially moral and theological grounds. Their imposition of Catholic morality and dogma on the rest of Canada is incompatible with their own distinction between moral and civil law."

But Alphonse de Valk, sympathetic to pro-life concerns, took offense that the bishops offered "no prophetic stand" on abortion but stood on the sidelines as the "legalization of abortion was introduced, defended and pushed through by a heavily Catholic [Liberal] party, thereby making Canada the only country in the world where Catholics bear this responsibility" (de Valk 1982, 107–8). The church had failed its mission, in de Valk's (1982, 108) opinion: "Let us ask once more: why did the Bishops withdraw their opposition to legalizing contraceptives and widening the grounds for divorce, and why did many Catholics do the same to abortion? Answer: because they had come to accept, willingly or unwillingly, consciously or unconsciously, what was being hammered into their heads by the secular media and a wide variety of spokesmen and women for the new ethic, namely, that opposition in these matters was purely theological and denominational, in short, for Catholics only."

The bishops' weak defense of church teachings on abortion, and previously on birth control and divorce, was the backdrop for a divergence of opinion between the Canadian Catholic Conference and grassroots pro-life activists. According to Cuneo (1989, 35), "by the early 1970s a pattern of mutual mistrust between the Canadian hierarchy and the [pro-life] movement as a whole was already firmly established. The majority of activists were convinced that the bishops' anti-abortion commitment was limited to what the traffic would bear, and that the future of the movement belonged to lay Catholics who would be foolish to count on the support of the church hierarchy in moments of political crunch." Thus, in Canada activist right-to-lifers were not beholden to the Canadian Catholic Conference and their views were nonnegotiable compared to those of the church hierarchy. The reverse is true in the United States, where the American bishops have been outspoken on abortion for two decades along with their single-issue allies, though "the strong pro-life stands by . . . Catholic leadership has failed to mobilize a majority of the members . . . to oppose abortion" (Cook, Jelen, and Wilcox 1992, 101).

There are other pro-life churches that are less strident in their advocacy. The Mormon Church (Church of Jesus Christ of Latter-day Saints) testified before a congressional committee only once, though its importance lies in the geographical concentration of its membership: (half of the four million Mormons live in the intermountain West. As *Christianity Today* once editorialized, "In states where they (the Mormons) exercise political clout the charge has often been made that abortion is a 'Mormon' issue" (*Christianity Today* 1976, 29). The Southern Baptist Convention is the largest non-Catholic denomination opposing abortion, with 13.4 million members, yet it does little more than issue policy statements. Agencies of the Lutheran Church (Missouri Synod) testified four times, and the only pro-life Jewish groups to do so were the Rabbinical Council of America and the American Jewish Theological Seminary. The National Association of Evangelicals and the Christian Action Council, founded by the Reverend Billy Graham, joined like-minded churches as amici in the *Webster* case.

In Canada more religious groups gave testimony against liberalized abortions than in favor (see table 4.3). In addition to the Canadian Conference of Catholic Bishops were spokespersons from the Pentecostal Church, the Salvation Army, the Evangelical Fellowship of Canada, and Plymouth Brethren. Also testifying, and categorized as a religious group, was the Société canadienne pour la défense de la Tradition, de la Famille et de la Propriété, described as a "Catholic-inspired secular organization whose purpose is to safeguard the fundamental values of Christian civilization" (House of Commons 1990, issue 11). Other pro-life churches that did not attend included the Baptist Convention of Ontario and Quebec, the Lutheran Church–Canada, and the Evangelical Lutheran Church in Canada (Muldoon 1991, 102–9).

Given that Catholics and non-Catholics do not differ all that much in their abortion attitudes, and even if lay Catholics do not follow the dictates of their church—for Canada as well as for the United States—pro-choice and pro-life activists are a self-recruited group, and religion may have a bearing on the process of self-selection. Data on American activists indicate that to be true. The archetypical pro-life woman, among other things, "is not employed in the paid labor force and is married to a small businessman or a lower-level white-collar worker; her family income is $30,000 a year. She is Catholic (and may have converted), and her religion is one of the most important aspects of her life" (Luker 1984, 197).

Granberg (1981, 158–59) similarly found that pro-lifers and pro-choice activists were not unlike each other on economic-status variables but that these groups of women activists—78 percent of the activists supporting the National Abortion Rights Action League and 63 percent of the activists aligned with the National Right to Life Committee were women—differed greatly on social traits. That is, the right-to-life activists grew up in larger families, were more likely to be married, and have more children than the NARAL activists. And religion is a key consideration insofar as Granberg estimated that seven in ten National Right to Life Committee members were

Catholics, whereas among the National Abortion Rights Action League membership Jews (17 percent) and people without any religious affiliation (40 percent) were overrepresented.

Pro-Life Extremism

If certain American pro-choice activists have crossed the line of political civility by turning the issue of church-state separation into a grudge fight with the National Catholic Conference of Bishops, certain pro-lifers seemingly have a monopoly on the use of confrontation tactics and violence, including kidnappings, bombings of abortion clinics, and even murder. To begin with, the number of Americans who admit to joining a pro-life (9 percent) or a pro-choice (4 percent) organization is not all that great (*Gallup Report* 1981b), so those pro-lifers who resort to direct action are a fraction of the minority of activists. Curiously, even though the pro-choice zealots are not linked to violent acts, a *Los Angeles Times* survey (Skelton 1989, 14) found that only 26 percent of the public held favorable impressions of pro-choice leaders, compared to 24 percent having favorable impressions of pro-life leaders.

Harris surveys from 1985 indicate nearly universal condemnation of such confrontational and violent tactics, with 81 percent viewing clinic bombings as terrorism and 83 percent seeing them as "not the American way," while 71 percent believe they "are probably being conducted by fanatics" (*Family Planning Perspectives* 1985a, 77). Also, 82 percent of the respondents to a CBS News–*New York Times* poll felt "there is absolutely no excuse for these [abortion clinic] bombings, they're the same thing as terrorism," whereas only 5 percent felt that the bombings "should be treated as a forceful kind of political protest" if nobody was killed or injured (*Family Planning Perspectives* 1985a, 77). Eighty-eight percent told an ABC News poll that attacks on clinics are "criminal acts"—only 12 percent viewed them as "civil disobedience"—and a Gallup poll that *Newsweek* commissioned found 95 percent expressing the opinion that clinic bombings hurt the antiabortion cause (*Family Planning Perspectives* 1985a, 77).

In early 1993 Gallup quizzed a subsample of pro-life sympathizers (people who believe that abortion is murder) about direct-action pro-life tactics (*Gallup Poll Monthly* 1993a, 41). When asked whether various tactics were "appropriate" or "not appropriate," there was virtual consensus that "blocking access to abortion clinics" (83 percent), "placing ads on television that contain graphic pictures of abortions" (76 percent), or "publicizing the names, addresses and phone numbers of doctors who perform abortions" (73 percent) were not appropriate. When asked about the recent shooting of a

Florida abortionist, and whether "the shooting is a direct consequence of the anti-abortion movement's confrontation tactics, or . . . simply the act of a fanatical individual acting on his own," by a margin of more than two to one they attributed that incident to one fanatic (52 percent) rather than the movement (23 percent).

In the United States direct-action tactics and civil disobedience are associated with Operation Rescue, founded in the late 1980s by Randall Terry (Wills 1989) as a militant alternative to the National Right to Life Committee, which has disavowed the use of such tactics. What kind of supporters are attracted to these very different organizations? A study by Guth, Kellstedt, Smidt, and Green (1994) tried to answer that question. First, there are many commonalities between those two antiabortion groups:

> Those supportive of both Operation Rescue and NRLC are the most extreme in their opinion on abortion, hold traditionalist moral views and think government should enforce those views, put a lower priority on other governmental functions, are adherents of fundamentalist and charismatic religious beliefs, possess a militant perspective on Christian political involvement and participate at a high level, are conservative and Republican, and exhibit traditional social and family roles in their own lives. (Guth, Kellstedt, Smidt, and Green 1994, 124)

As to what differentiates the Operation Rescue adherents from the National Right to Life Committee sympathizers, there is a strong religious component to the answer:

> Those who oppose abortion but are not obsessed with this issue, or do not share Operation Rescue's religious or political militancy, or see the political world in different ideological terms are unlikely to be converted to direct action tactics. But the fact that the beliefs and attitudes of OR [Operation Rescue] sympathizers are common among fundamentalists, Pentecostals, and charismatics suggests that the end of the abortion wars is not yet near. (Guth, Kellstedt, Smidt, and Green 1994, 126)

Newspapers are replete with accounts of demonstrations and "rescues" at abortion clinics across the country—Wichita, Buffalo, Denver, Little Rock, San Francisco, Atlanta, Houston, and other cities too numerous to mention. Case studies of individuals who engage in "rescue" work reveal that many view their personal sacrifice in religious terms (Maxwell 1994), so an escalation of conflict over abortion may occur despite newly enacted laws and judicial decisions aimed at guaranteeing access to abortion clinics and making pro-lifers legally liable for their actions (Lewin 1990, A16). Indeed, and paradoxically, Randall Terry eventually may be viewed as "moderate" alongside those antiabortion crusaders who have taken their fervor to even greater extremes.

On March 10, 1993, during a demonstration against a Pensacola, Florida, abortion clinic, pro-life zealot Michael Griffin shot and killed Dr. David Gunn, who was employed at the facility, whereupon the August 1993 edition of *Life Advocate* asked, "Who Killed the Innocent—Michael Griffin or Dr. David Gunn?" (Hill 1993). In August, Rachelle "Shelly" Shannon shot Dr. George Tiller, another abortionist, in Wichita, Kansas. On July 29, 1994, Paul J. Hill killed abortionist Dr. John Britton and his bodyguard and wounded a woman at the same Pensacola abortion clinic where Gunn had been murdered seventeen months earlier. In late December 1994 John C. Salvi III was arrested for murdering two people and injuring five others at a Brookline, Massachusetts, abortion clinic.

These shocking events affirmed the obvious—namely, that violence was a growing threat to abortion providers in the United States. The Feminist Majority Foundation, which maintains a clinic protection program, documented that 52 percent of clinics surveyed had experienced some kind of violence—death threats, bombings, blockades by protesters—during 1994, a small increase from 1993. Twenty-five percent of the facilities reported death threats against physicians or other staff (Smothers 1994).

In November 1994 a sniper fired two shots from a military assault rifle through the window of the Vancouver home of gynecologist Dr. Garson Romalis, who was seriously wounded (*New York Times* 1994). As the first such episode in Canada, it was condemned by Prime Minister Jean Chrétien, who called for stricter gun controls, and by Mike Harcourt, the British Columbia premier, who said he would consider barring protests outside abortion clinics; the British Columbia Medical Association called for legislation outlawing the stalking of abortion doctors. The other noteworthy episode occurred in 1992 when Dr. Henry Morgentaler's Toronto abortion clinic was bombed. Other than those, "anti-abortion demonstrations today are infrequent, and draw few protesters. But abortion workers and doctors across Canada say there has been a distinct increase in covert harassment—death threats, dismantled power lines and phones, and, in British Columbia, the use of license-plate numbers to search government computers for information on clinic employees" (Breckenridge 1995).

The usual tactic employed by militant antiabortion activists in Canada was to apply pressure directly to hospitals to reduce or stop the number of abortions performed, as happened at Victoria General Hospital, where the Pro Life Society of British Columbia and Physicians for Life led the lobbying effort (Grescoe 1980). Morgentaler's opening of abortion clinics in 1983 outside of Quebec, in Winnipeg, and then in Toronto provoked antiabortion demonstrations led by crusader Joe Borowski (Morton 1992, 154–66). In early 1985 Cardinal Carter joined forces with Campaign Life Coalition by announcing in the Toronto archdiocesan newsletter plans for an extensive pro-life demonstration outside the Morgentaler clinic between February 18 and 21, designed to influence the newly elected PC government of Premier Frank Miller to close the clinic (Cuneo 1989, 59). The strategy worked in the short term but ultimately backfired because a Toronto jury refused to convict Morgentaler for performing abortions in his clinic.

So Morgentaler's decision to locate clinics throughout Canada prompted a "new phase" in that country's abortion controversy, particularly after the jury trial in Ontario led to his acquittal on charges of unlawfully opening his Toronto clinic, because "the combination of Morgentaler's success with the realization that neither the majority of the population nor the political leaders can be relied on to support the prolife position has strengthened the resolve of prolifers" (*Christian Century* 1985, 924). Morgentaler's Supreme Court victory in 1988 once again "unleashed activism on both sides" as "anti-abortionists engaged in civil disobedience to shut clinics down, facing criminal charges in provincial courts and heightening hostile rhetoric on both sides" (Meyer and Staggenborg 1995, 13). During 1989 picketers assembled at an abortion clinic in Vancouver while Campaign Life Coalition Calgary protested at the huge Peter Lougheed Centre hospital in Calgary and Direct Action for Life did the same at Royal Alexandra Hospital in Edmonton. These "rescue operations" were organized by Michael Malley, the Canadian counterpart to Randall Terry, who vowed to continue despite court injunctions against him. Said Malley: "If we keep challenging trespassing charges, mischief charges and injunctions, Parliament's only solution will be to re-criminalize abortion. That is our objective" (quoted in Stewart 1989).

Summary

The contours of public opinion on abortion are fundamentally the same in Canada and the United States, though Canadians may be somewhat more liberal. Most people in both countries favor abortion under certain conditions, namely therapeutic ones, rather than elective abortion. Yet most Americans would not repeal *Roe v. Wade,* and surveys find that Canadians do not favor recriminalizing abortion. A poll commissioned by CARAL in November 1989 found that 62 percent of Canadians disagreed "with the federal government's plan to put abortion into the Criminal Code" (House of Commons 1990, issue 4), and a national poll in December 1991 showed that 66 percent were opposed (Brodie, Gavigan, and Jenson 1992, 114).

One of the early policy case studies of the U.S. abortion controversy (Tatalovich and Daynes 1981a) suggested that the pro-lifers had characteristics of a mass movement while the abortion reform agitation of the 1960s had more of an elite composition. Since the established interests that had been mobilized, almost without exception, favored legalized abortion, the single-issue group was the logical means by which pro-lifers could mobilize ordinary citizens and organize dissent inside established organizations. This characterization still applies to the pro-life lobby with equal force today, both in the United States and Canada, although single-issue groups are always utilized more prominently by Canadian pro-choice activists.

Comparing the pro-choice coalitions and the pro-life lobbies cross-nationally leads one to conclude that their similarities outweigh their differences, though there are some noteworthy caveats to that generalization. The pro-life lobby in Canada is a carbon copy of that in the United States: Catholics and evangelicals are the leading religious players, along with their single-issue allies—the National Right to Life Committee in the United States and Campaign Life Coalition in Canada. On the economic front, neither in Canada nor in the United States have major business or trade associations become involved, but while the biggest U.S. labor organizations have not aligned themselves with the pro-choice movement, some very large Canadian unions have done so.

In the United States, the battle lines over abortion indicate that two cleavages underlie the antagonists. One is secular, about the status of women and the traditional family within society (Fried 1988). The second is sectarian, reflecting deep theological differences in how Jews, Protestants, and Catholics interpret the beginning of life. Though the dominant position of women's groups in the Canadian and American pro-choice coalitions is a recent development, given that both countries' 1960s abortion reform movements were spearheaded by health care and medical professionals, my sense is that the force of feminism is greater today in Canada than in the United States. The scope of feminist ideology extends even to organized labor if the Canadian Labour Congress is taken as representative of that constituency. On the other hand, there seems to be far less sectarian conflict in the Canadian abortion debate, and there church-state separation is a non-issue. Direct-action tactics, too, seem to be a minor irritant on the Canadian scene but a major problem for abortion providers in the United States.

5

No Mandates on Abortion

Party Politics and Elections

The asymmetrical coverage of how Canadian and American electoral systems impinge on the abortion controversy gives a strong clue to why institutional differences in regimes really matter. That is the lesson of this chapter. In the United States, abortion has been thoroughly politicized by the two major parties, the electoral system, and presidential campaigns, but in Canada the issue has been politically neutralized. Let's begin first with the Canadian story.

Canadian Elections Minus Abortion

In Canadian politics, abortion seems to be almost irrelevant. The 1988 national elections continued the Progressive Conservative (PC) government under Prime Minister Brian Mulroney, which had to cope with abortion policy following the *Morgentaler* ruling that same year. But abortion was not a salient consideration in why the voters rejected the Liberal Party or endorsed the Progressive Conservatives. The dominant issue in the 1988 campaign was free trade, specifically the free trade agreement (NAFTA) with the United States. Moreover, a listing of the most important election issues in Canada since the 1974 elections does not even mention abortion policy. As Harold D. Clarke and his associates explain: "Substantial numbers [of respondents] moved from the choice of an economic issue (e.g., inflation) as most important in 1974, to a confederation issue (e.g., national unity) in 1979, and back to an economic issue (e.g., the Tory budget) in 1980." They go on to say, "In 1984 as well, the electorate's attention sud-

144

denly shifted to the problem of unemployment, mirroring this economic evil's new status as the nation's number one problem in public opinion polls. Finally, the public's shift in attention to free trade in 1988 was so total as to leave all other election issues far behind" (Clarke, LeDuc, Jenson, and Pammett 1991, 71).

A preelection national survey in 1988 showed that 89.4 percent of respondents mentioned free trade as the most important election issue that year, whereas only 0.8 percent cited abortion (Kornberg and Clarke 1992, 203). Of that tiny minority, 28 percent chose the position of the Progressive Conservatives as closest to their view on abortion, 18 percent preferred the stand of New Democratic Party, and 12 percent aligned themselves with the Liberals (10 percent chose another party and 31 percent expressed no opinion). Following the 1988 election the Canadian sample was reinterviewed, and this time 1.5 percent named abortion as the most important issue (Kay, Lambert, Brown, and Curtis 1991), not particularly impressive given the fact that the Supreme Court of Canada had recently made its highly publicized and controversial ruling in *Morgentaler* (1988).

The Campaign Life Coalition made an attempt to politicize abortion during the 1988 elections by supporting PC and Liberal candidates for Parliament based upon their pro-life inclinations. According to Pal (1991, 285), "at least 74 anti-abortion candidates were elected on November 21, 1988," and "several nomination races were contested by pro-choice and pro-life candidates, and pro-life activists targeted 30 ridings in which to mount direct mail campaigns."

A comparison of those parliamentary candidates who were formally endorsed by the Campaign Life Coalition (seventy-four Progressive Conservatives, fifty Liberals, and one New Democrat) as against those candidates who were not endorsed—and taking into account the overall partisan electoral swing in each province—concluded that "Campaign Life's endorsement during the 1988 federal election campaign did not provide a significant benefit to the group of 125 major party candidates that were identified" (Kay, Lambert, Brown, and Curtis 1991). Nor did candidates endorsed by the Canadian Abortion Rights Action League fare much better, although CARAL limited its endorsements to Ontario Province, where sixty-five of its seventy-seven endorsements went to New Democrats.

The New Democratic Party (whose party platform had supported women's freedom of choice on abortion since 1971) retained its official pro-choice position in the 1988 elections, while the only party to embrace the pro-life movement was the new Christian Heritage Party. The newly formed Reform Party, though conservative, chose not to take a formal position on abortion but rather allowed their parliamentary candidates to be guided by constituency opinion. Neither the Progressive Conservatives nor the Liberals adopted abortion planks, and Brian Mulroney stated that each Progressive Conservative MP could vote on abortion according to his or her own conscience. This posturing led Vancouver Campaign Life activist Paul Formby to call both Mulroney and John Turner (the leader of the Liberals) "gutless wonders" for not making abortion a party policy, insofar as both men were Catholics (Byfield 1988).

For the 1993 elections, the National Action Committee on the Status of Women published a voters' guide that summarized the positions of the major political parties on three questions: "Does your party commit itself not to reintroduce further anti-choice legislation? Does your party support amending the Canada Health Act to ensure that the provinces guarantee access to abortion services? What other measures would your party take to maintain a woman's rights to reproductive choice?" (Léger and Rebick 1993, 82). It was reported that the Progressive Conservatives did not respond to the first and third questions and, on the second, contended that the provinces should determine what services they will provide. The Liberals' response was that its government would not introduce a bill on abortion, although a Private Member could not be stopped from doing so, since there was no party position on abortion. The Liberals would consider amending the Canada Health Act to include abortion as a "medical service" and, moreover, advocated sex education and family planning. Most pro-choice was the New Democratic Party statement that no new legislation would be introduced, that they would increase access (without specifying how), that the NDP had no position on the Canada Health Act, and that NDP member of Parliament Dawn Black had proposed increased funding for Planned Parenthood to conduct research and education efforts on sexually transmitted diseases and safe and effective contraception.

Apparently the Liberals under John Turner had contemplated using abortion as a tactical ploy to gain a political edge over Mulroney. During the campaign, in August, Mulroney said that abortion should be permitted in cases of rape, incest, and "certain personal situations," and his advisers implied that the prime minister would say more on the subject during his televised debate, later in the campaign, with Turner and NDP leader Ed Broadbent. For his part, Turner refused even to indicate how he might counsel his own daughter on abortion, saying it was "such a personal question," but news agencies learned that his handlers were reconsidering their decision to refrain from debating abortion, given the stream of media criticism against Turner. Then the press reported that the Liberals were working on a tactical shift, which Turner might reveal during the debates. Said one unidentified Liberal staffer: "Maybe we should not be cowed by the reaction of a small interest group" (Janigan, Mackenzie, Clark, and Laver 1988, 16).

The heads of the major political parties debated on October 24 and 25, but there were no spectacular abortion revelations by Turner or anyone else. The confrontation mainly focused on NAFTA plus the scandals and patronage appointments that plagued the Mulroney government. A week earlier Turner's chief of staff, Peter Connolly, had confided to some reporters that the Liberal leader planned to startle his opponents during one of the TV debates by openly advocating elective abortion during the first twenty-two weeks of a woman's pregnancy and, furthermore, that Turner would act without the approval of other party officials. Since the Liberal Party has been divided by its own pro-life and pro-choice contingents, other high-ranking party officials quickly issued a series of public denials, Connolly subsequently apologized for the furor, and ultimately John Turner made no such comments during either of his televised debates (*Facts on File World News Digest* 1988, 795).

So the Canadian voters were offered a choice—of sorts—on abortion, but apparently single-issue voting was no more obvious in 1993 than it was in 1988, although the electoral outcomes were dramatically different. The relationships between party affiliation and abortion attitudes and between abortion attitudes and candidate choice for 1993 and 1988 (table 5.1) show *no* linkages; compare this to the situation in the United States (see tables 5.2 and 5.3), where statistically significant albeit *weak* linkages were found, especially in recent presidential elections.

In 1988 a plurality of people who identified with the Progressive Conservatives held pro-choice views (46 percent), and the same applied to most Liberals (46 percent) and a majority of New Democrats (59 percent). By 1993 people self-identifying with those three parties *all* shifted toward the pro-choice position, which now was embraced by 56 percent of Liberals, 60 percent of Progressive Conservatives, and 66 percent of New Democrats. This poll also included respondents who identified themselves as being affiliated with the Reform Party—more conservative than Progressive Conservative—and the French Catholic bloc of the Parti Québecois in Quebec Province. While the largest contingent of pro-lifers identified with the Reform Party, they made up (at 13.6 percent) less than one-third of the number of Reform partisans who called themselves pro-choice on abortion. And even 68 percent of respondents who identified with the Parti Québecois expressed pro-choice views.

In other words, the center of political gravity on abortion shifted to the left in Canada between 1988 and 1993, which partly may explain why abortion did not surface as a campaign issue in the most recent Canadian

Table 5.1

Canadian Abortion Attitudes by Party Affiliation and Relationship Between Abortion Attitudes and Candidate Choice, 1988 and 1993 National Elections
(percentages based on weighted responses)

	1988 Party Identification		
	Conservative	Liberal	New Democrat
1988 Abortion Attititude*			
Pro-Life	11.0	12.5	8.6
Moderate	43.3	41.7	32.9
Pro-Choice	45.8	45.8	58.5

Lambda = .00000

	1993 Party Identification				
	Conservative	Liberal	New Democrat	Reform	Parti Québecois
1993 Abortion Attitude*					
Pro-Life	5.3	10.1	8.1	13.6	4.1
Moderate	34.7	33.6	25.6	43.6	28.2
Pro-Choice	59.9	56.3	66.2	42.8	67.7

Lambda = .00146

	1988 Abortion Attitude*		
	Pro-Life	Moderate	Pro-Choice
1988 Candidate Choice			
Reform	2.5	2.2	1.7
Conservative	47.5	48.3	46.8
Liberal	27.8	30.0	27.7
New Democrat	15.8	17.1	21.2
Other	6.5	2.4	2.6

Lambda = .00000

	1993 Abortion Attitude*		
	Pro-Life	Moderate	Pro-Choice
1993 Candidate Choice			
Reform	21.2	24.6	17.4
Conservative	10.5	12.6	16.1
Liberal	53.2	44.5	42.6
New Democrat	5.5	5.4	7.5
Parti Québecois	9.7	12.8	16.4

Lambda = .00000

(continued)

Table 5.1 *(continued)*

Sources: 1988 data from Richard Johnston et al., *Canadian National Election Study, 1988* (computer file). Ann Arbor, MI: Inter-university Consortium for Political and Social Research (distributor), 1990. 1993 data from Richard Johnston, Andre Blais, Henry Brady, Elisabeth Gidengil, and Neil Nevitte, *Canadian National Election Study, 1993: Incorporating the 1992 Referendum Survey on the Charlottetown Accord* (computer file). Ann Arbor, MI: Inter-university Consortium for Political and Social Research (distributor), 1995.

[*]The 1988 question was: "According to the Supreme Court, the Charter of Rights says that governments cannot make abortions absolutely illegal. Now we would like to get your views on abortion. We know that this is a sensitive question. Of the following three positions, which is closest to your own opinion: one, abortion should NEVER be permitted, two, should be permitted only after need has been established by a doctor or three, should be a matter of the woman's personal choice?" The three options were coded "Pro-Life," "Moderate," and "Pro-Choice" in this table. The 1993 question was: "Now we would like to get your views on abortion. Of the following three positions, which is closest to your own opinion: One: abortion should NEVER be performed, Two: should be permitted only after NEED has been established by a doctor, OR Three: should be a matter of the woman's PERSONAL CHOICE?" The three options were coded "Pro-Life," "Moderate," and "Pro-Choice" in this table.

---

national elections. However, the wording of the Canadian National Election Study questions (table 5.1), when compared to the language of the American National Election Study questions (tables 5.2 and 5.3), seems to invite a more liberal response. The moderate option between the pro-life and pro-choice extremes allows Canadians to select a more permissive criteria for abortions ("need"), whereas Americans who hold moderate views have to choose between limiting abortions only to cases of life endangerment and rape or else permitting them for reasons other than rape, incest, or life endangerment where "need" has been established. But even allowing for this possible source of polling bias, people who hold an absolute pro-life position on abortion are a small segment of the Canadian electorate, even among Progressive Conservatives, so there is less political incentive in Canada for any political party to embrace the pro-life agenda.

To avoid taking sides in the abortion debate would seem to be an optimal strategy in Canada, since these aggregate statistics indicate that abortion attitudes seemingly had *no* effect on the overall electoral outcome in 1988, when the Progressive Conservatives won in a landslide, and in 1993, when Progressive Conservatives were literally eliminated as a viable parliamentary party. In 1988, 48 percent of pro-life respondents and moderates and 47 percent of pro-choice respondents gave their votes to reelecting the PC government of Prime Minister Brian Mulroney. In 1992 even *more* pro-lifers (53 percent) than moderates (45 percent) or pro-choice respondents (43 percent) voted Liberal. Despite their national setback, the Progressive Conservatives under Mike Harris took control of the Ontario provincial government in a mid-1995 election. While Harris supported a woman's right to abortion, he added one more plank to his election platform: no new free-standing abortion clinics (Brown 1995).

The 1993 national elections transformed the Canadian party system. Both the Reform Party and the Parti Québecois showed tremendous strength at the polls, while the Progressive Conservatives and the New Democratic Party suffered precipitous declines. Yet again, the outcome hinged on economic considerations—the NAFTA trade accord with the United States and Mexico, for example, coupled with Mulroney's reputation as the most unpopular prime minister in recent Canadian history. Abortion played little if any role in that major partisan shakeup. The Canadian electorate shifted to the right in 1988 and back to the left in 1993 irrespective of their views (at least in the aggregate) on abortion policy.

However, this left-to-right imagery ought not to be exaggerated at the expense of regional politics. Because the 1988 election was essentially a referendum on NAFTA, that debate caused gas-exporting Alberta Province to unite with electricity-exporting Quebec Province. But in 1993 that geographical coalition dissolved—and destroyed the Progressive Conservatives in the process—with the rise of regional political parties, the Reform Party in Alberta and the Parti Québecois in Quebec. Meanwhile, a familiar scenario is unfolding for the 1996 presidential elections in the United States.

Abortion Politics in the United States

In the United States, abortion has been stubbornly resistant to a political settlement because of the intense partisanship that has enveloped the issue in recent years. Yet the blame for this situation must be laid directly on political elites, not the citizenry. Most Americans and Canadians hold centrist views on abortion, and that moderation extends to most voters regardless of party loyalty. More important, the vast majority of Americans show virtually no proclivity for single-issue voting on abortion when evaluating the presidential candidates. The evidence consistently points to the polarization of abortion politics as a top-down rather than a bottom-up phenomenon, which means that deliberate choices have been made by American (but not Canadian) politicians to sustain abortion as a burning controversy. The ultimate question, with all its normative implications, is why?

Partisan Attitudes

Attitudes among Republicans and Democrats are virtually a carbon copy of those among the general population; at most, there may have been marginal polarization after 1980. Gallup polls asking whether abortions should be legal "under any circumstances," "under only certain circumstances," or "in all circumstances" show tremendous stability among partisans and the general population. Gallup polls taken between 1975 and 1988 (*Gallup Report* 1975; 1979; 1983; 1989) do not suggest that self-identified Republicans or Democrats view abortion very differently. The strong pro-choice category included 18 percent to 23 percent of Republicans and 19 percent to 23 percent of Democrats, and the absolute pro-life view was expressed by 14 percent to 25 percent of Republicans and 17 percent to 26 percent of Democrats. The highs were recorded for both groups of partisans in 1975, but, as more recent polls show, there has been a slight decline in the number of Republicans and Democrats with pro-life views and a corresponding rise in the percentages favoring abortions under any circumstances. Clearly the majority of Republicans and Democrats always have agreed with the moderate view that abortions are justified under certain (though unspecified) conditions.

The same conclusion can be drawn from American National Election Studies over the past six presidential elections (table 5.2). Four gradations in abortion attitudes are cross-tabulated with party identification. The plurality of Republicans, Democrats, and independents fall into the second-most-restrictive category, allowing abortions only to protect the mother's life and in cases of rape, for the elections of 1972–1980, but some shifting has occurred since then, with gains recorded by the pro-choice option among all three party groups. In 1984, 33 percent of Republicans, 38 percent of independents, and 39 percent of Democrats expressed opinions favoring the strongest pro-choice position; in 1988 the statistics showed retrenchment mainly by Democrats; but by 1992 the gap between Republicans and *both* independents and Democrats had widened considerably. In that election year 52 percent of Democrats and 49 percent of independents but only 39 percent of Republicans chose the strongest pro-choice position as their own.

In other words, the strongest pro-life position garners the support of one in ten Republicans or Democrats, whereas the strongest pro-choice view was held by roughly one-third of Republicans and by four or five of ten Democrats. While these patterns imply that the Democratic Party ought not to pursue the pro-choice agenda so ardently that a sizable minority of Democratic voters may be alienated, more compelling is the conclusion that pro-life stridency by the Republican Party cannot be attributed to, and in fact misrepresents, the rank-and-file GOP.

Polarized Activism

Why do the two parties diverge so dramatically on abortion if, in fact, ordinary Republicans and Democrats are closer than not in their opinions? First, candidates are nominated in primaries that attract lower turnouts than

Table 5.2

U.S. Abortion Attitudes by Party Affiliation

	Republicans	Independents	Democrats	
Pro-Life	9.1%	11.6%	13.5%	
Life/Rape	45.7	48.0	50.2	Gamma = −.128
Other Reasons	18.7	17.1	16.0	(.01 significant)
Pro-Choice	26.5	23.4	20.3	
1972: N =	889 (100%)	346 (100%)	1,054 (100%)	
Pro-Life	9.0	8.9	14.6	
Life/Rape	46.0	44.2	48.6	Gamma = −.118
Other Reasons	17.9	18.6	13.9	(.01 significant)
Pro-Choice	27.0	28.3	22.9	
1976: N =	630 (100%)	258 (100%)	699 (100%)	
Pro-Life	9.0	9.3	10.4	
Life/Rape	46.9	42.4	46.6	Gamma = −.016
Other Reasons	19.3	16.3	17.3	(insignificant)
Pro-Choice	24.8	32.0	25.7	
1980: N =	467 (100%)	172 (100%)	537 (100%)	
Pro-Life	13.3	17.9	11.5	
Life/Rape	31.8	31.4	30.5	Gamma = +.068
Other Reasons	22.1	13.1	18.7	(.01 significant)
Pro-Choice	32.8	37.6	39.4	
1984: N =	856 (100%)	229 (100%)	803 (100%)	
Pro-Life	12.0	9.9	14.4	
Life/Rape	35.3	32.1	33.9	Gamma = −.014
Other Reasons	19.3	19.3	18.1	(insignificant)
Pro-Choice	33.4	38.7	33.7	
1988: N =	814 (100%)	212 (100%)	703 (100%)	
Pro-Life	11.9	8.9	10.1	
Life/Rape	33.9	25.2	24.3	Gamma = +.165
Other Reasons	15.6	16.7	13.5	(.001 significant)
Pro-Choice	38.6	49.3	52.0	
1992: N =	898 (100%)	270 (100%)	859 (100%)	

Source: American National Election Studies, 1972–1992. The 1984, 1988, and 1992 question was: "There has been some discussion about abortion during recent years. Which of the opinions on this page best agrees with your view? (1) By law, abortion should never be permitted. (2) The law should permit abortion only in case of rape, incest or when the woman's life is in danger. (3) The law should permit abortion for reasons other than rape, incest, or danger to the woman's life but only after the need for the abortion has been clearly established. (4) By law, a woman should always be able to obtain an abortion as a matter of personal choice."

These variations in wording were used in 1972, 1976, and 1980: "(1) Abortion should never be permitted. (2) Abortion should be permitted only if the life and health of the woman is in danger. (3) Abortion should be permitted if, due to personal reasons, the woman would have difficulty in caring for the child. (4) Abortion should never be forbidden, since one should not require a woman to have a child she doesn't want."

general elections, so possibly Republican and Democratic primary voters are more divided than the parties' rank-and-file identifiers. Second, delegates to the national conventions and other party activists are more issue-oriented and thus may represent more-extreme positions on abortion. Third, the presidential candidates need money, and PACs supply campaign funds precisely to influence the writing of party platforms and the policy views of the nominees. Looking at 1988 ANES data convinced Wilcox (1995, 69) that "primary election voters are no more extreme on the abortion issue than other partisans" and, moreover, "what is striking is the similarity between Democratic and Republican primary voters."

His analysis of the views of party delegates to the 1988 national conventions similarly did not validate the polarity hypothesis (Wilcox 1995, 69), but on this matter other research draws different conclusions. Plissner and Mitofsky's (1988) examination of the views of the 1988 convention delegates showed that on government funding for abortion, 22 percent of Democratic delegates but 62 percent of Republican delegates were opposed when, to the contrary, rank-and-file Republicans (62 percent opposed) and Democrats (56 percent opposed) held similar views on the question. These findings, and others, led to a situation "of Democratic elites being decidedly more liberal and Republican elites more conservative than ordinary, garden-variety adherents of their respective parties." Similarly, a 1988 *New York Times* survey revealed that 72 percent of Democratic delegates versus 29 percent of Republican delegates to their national conventions agreed that "abortion should be legal, as it is now." But among the general public, that viewpoint was held by 40 percent of the adults polled, which closely matched the opinion expressed by Democratic voters (43 percent) and Republican voters (39 percent) (Oreskes 1988). In other words, the delegates who nominated Michael Dukakis much more closely mirrored the position of pro-choice advocates than they did that of Democratic voters as a whole, while the delegates who nominated George Bush reflected the pro-life position more accurately than they did the views of the GOP voter constituency.

Outside the conventions are political action committees, whose contributions weigh heavily in the political campaigns. A study by Wilcox (1989, 16) of PAC spending during the 1980, 1982, and 1984 elections found that "pro-choice PACs contribute heavily to Democrats, while pro-life PACs give mainly to Republicans."

Abortion Campaigning

Even before *Roe* was decided, President Nixon first marked abortion as a political issue by repudiating his own President's Commission on Population Growth, whose report favored abortions on demand, and publicly siding with Terence Cardinal Cooke of New York City, who led efforts to repeal New York State's elective abortion law. But the abortion issue was not mentioned in the Democratic or Republican platforms for 1972, though the National Women's Political Caucus had urged adoption of a Democratic Party plank supporting the right to abortion. The 1972 Democratic presidential candidate was George McGovern, who, though against the Vietnam War and very liberal, argued both that abortion was a "private matter" between the woman and her physician and that states should have "sole jurisdiction" over abortion policy (Daynes and Tatalovich 1992, 546).

By 1976 partisanship over abortion was beginning. The Democratic Party platform now stated that while "we fully recognize the religious and ethical nature of the concerns which many Americans have . . . it is undesirable to attempt to amend the U.S. Constitution to overturn the Supreme Court decision in this area." And the GOP favored "a continuance of the public dialogue on abortion and supports the efforts of those who seek enactment of a constitutional amendment to restore protection of the right to life for unborn children" (quoted in Daynes and Tatalovich 1992, 546–47). This pro-life plank resulted because convention delegates backing President Ford acceded to the demands of Ronald Reagan, his challenger for the nomination, that the party endorse a pro-life constitutional amendment. Ford opposed abortion on demand and *Roe* but would not support a constitutional ban, citing the mother's health, rape, and "other unfortunate things" that might warrant an abortion (Daynes and Tatalovich 1992, 547).

In 1976 the many contradictory statements by Jimmy Carter caused him so many difficulties during the primary and general election campaigns that ultimately the Democratic nominee asked for a meeting with the Catholic bishops. But his strategy to reach an accommodation with the bishops backfired when, after the much-publicized meeting, they announced that they were still "disappointed" with Carter's views. After a subsequent session with Gerald Ford, however, their prepared statement was more upbeat, indicating that the bishops were "encouraged that the President agrees on the need for a constitutional amendment. We urged him to support an amendment that will give the maximum protection possible to the unborn" (Byrnes 1991, 74–77). In their October presidential debate, Gerald Ford reiterated his support for a constitutional amendment that "would turn over to the States the individual right of the voters in those States the chance to make a decision by public referendum," whereas once again Jimmy Carter tried to placate both sides to the controversy: "I am strongly against abortion. I think abortion is wrong. I don't think the Government ought to do anything to encourage abortion, but I don't favor a constitutional amendment on the subject." Instead, he promised to "do everything I can to minimize the need for abortions with better sex education, family planning, with better adoptive procedures," and he expressed opposition to federally financed abortions (quoted in Daynes and Tatalovich 1992, 548).

By 1980 the ambiguous policies and rhetoric of the Carter administration had satisfied neither side of the abortion dispute, and the National Organization for Women refused to endorse his reelection. Ronald Reagan, who had called *Roe v. Wade* "an abuse of power as bad as the transgressions of Watergate and the bribery on Capital Hill" (cited in Daynes and Tatalovich 1992, 549), had strong pro-life backing, and the Republican platform reciprocated.

The GOP supported "a Constitutional amendment to restore protection of the right to life for unborn children . . . [and] Congressional efforts to restrict the use of taxpayers' dollars for abortion," and GOP conservatives affirmed their pro-life commitment by adding a very controversial plank to the platform calling for "the appointment of judges at all levels of the judiciary who respect traditional family values and the sanctity of innocent human life" (Daynes and Tatalovich 1992, 549). (All GOP platforms since have contained that pledge.) Meanwhile, more problems plagued President Carter on abortion, because the Democratic Party's liberal wing, led by Senator Edward Kennedy (D-Massachusetts) forced the Carter supporters at the Democratic convention to accept several "minority" planks. One was this strong pro-choice statement: "We fully recognize the religious and ethical concerns which many Americans have about abortion. We also recognize the belief of many Americans that a woman has a right to choose whether and when to have a child. . . . The Democratic Party supports the 1973 Supreme Court decision on abortion rights as the law of the land and opposes any constitutional amendment to restrict or overturn that decision" (quoted in Daynes and Tatalovich 1992, 549–50).

The high (or low) point of this rhetorical partisanship came in 1984, when the Republicans wrote a platform statement on abortion that rebutted virtually every position taken by the Democratic Party (Daynes and Tatalovich 1992, 550). The Democrats recognized "reproductive freedom as a fundamental human right" and thus opposed "government interference in the reproductive decisions of Americans, especially government interference which denies poor Americans their right to privacy by funding or advocating one or a limited number of reproductive choices only." They also supported the *Roe* decision "as the law of the land" and opposed "any constitutional amendment to restrict or overturn that decision." Moreover, the plank took notice that abortion clinics were under siege: "We deplore violence and harassment against health providers and women seeking services, and will work to end such acts." The Republicans, in turn, covered all the pro-life bases they could:

> The unborn child has a fundamental individual right to life which cannot be infringed. We therefore reaffirm our support for a human life amendment to the Constitution, and we endorse legislation to make clear that the Fourteenth Amendment's protections apply to unborn children. We oppose the use of public revenues for abortion and will eliminate funding for organizations which advocate or support abortions. We commend the efforts of those individuals and religious and private organizations that are providing positive alternatives to abortion by meeting the physical, emotional, and financial needs of pregnant women and offering adoption services where needed. (quoted in Daynes and Tatalovich 1992, 550)

President Reagan received the endorsement of the National Right to Life Committee, just as he had in 1980, and Democrat Walter Mondale was nominated with the support of the National Abortion Rights Action League. Mondale also sought to pacify feminist delegates to the national party convention, who threatened to nominate Representative Geraldine Ferraro (D-New York) unless he selected a woman as his running mate. Mondale selected Ferraro, but the representative, a Catholic with a strong pro-choice voting record, provoked a sharp confrontation with Archbishop John H. O'Connor of New York City over a letter she had once signed saying, "The Catholic position on abortion is not monolithic and . . . there can be a range of personal and political responses to it" (Byrnes 1991, 120). The furor made clear that "abortion was still the first priority of a major segment of the American Catholic hierarchy," which, of course, was perceived as "damaging the campaign of the Democratic candidate for vice-president of the United States" (Byrnes 1991, 121). The partisan conflict over abortion also surfaced during the October 7, 1984, presidential debate between Reagan and Mondale. Reagan asserted that the unborn was protected by the constitutional guarantees of life, liberty, and the pursuit of happiness to all of us, and Mondale, in response, criticized the Reagan-supported constitutional amendment that would prohibit abortion even in case of rape or incest (Daynes and Tatalovich 1992, 551).

In 1988 Vice President George Bush, the Republican candidate, carried the pro-life mantle for his party, and Massachusetts governor Michael Dukakis, in the end, became committed to the pro-choice position. At first Dukakis tried to unify the party around broad principles devoid of specific policy commitments, and nowhere in the 1988 Democratic platform was the word *abortion* used. Rather, the Democratic opposition to restrictions on federal funding of abortions was couched in the euphemism "that the fundamental right of reproductive choice should be guaranteed regardless of ability to pay." Again the GOP platform wasted few words:

The unborn child has a fundamental individual right to life which cannot be infringed. We therefore reaffirm our support for a human life amendment to the Constitution, and we endorse legislation to make clear that the 14th Amendment's protections apply to unborn children. We oppose the use of public revenues for abortion and will eliminate funding for organizations which advocate or support abortion. (quoted in Daynes and Tatalovich 1992, 552–53)

Over the course of his political career Bush had flip-flopped on his abortion views, and during the campaign, when asked about his differences of opinion with other Republicans on abortion, he replied, "Nobody in our party takes a litmus test that says that everybody has to agree on every issue. I expect the Democrats could say the same thing" (quoted in Daynes and Tatalovich 1992, 553). However, his voice of moderation contrasted sharply with other language of the 1988 GOP platform, in which pro-lifers, as they had in 1980 and 1984 (and would do again in 1992; see below), demanded that judicial nominees be evaluated according to their abortion views.

Questions about abortion were asked of both candidates in their televised debates of September 26 and October 15. Though Bush and Dukakis held dissimilar views on abortion, the debates were noteworthy for the lack of political stridency by either candidate. Both agreed that abortion was distasteful, as have all presidential contenders over the years. Bush made references to the unborn as living beings, something Dukakis never did, while abortion was framed by Michael Dukakis as a difficult personal decision for the woman, though he never asserted a constitutional right to abortion. However, this tone changed in the final days of the campaign, when Dukakis, on October 30, told a rally that he was a liberal in the tradition of Roosevelt, Truman, and Kennedy and, on the following day, dramatized the threat to legalized abortion should a new Republican administration be elected: "I believe that a choice that personal must be made by the woman in the exercise of her own conscience and religious beliefs. And that's one of the reasons why we don't want George Bush and Dan Quayle appointing new Justices to the Supreme Court of the United States" (quoted in Daynes and Tatalovich 1992, 555).

George Bush was elected president, and he generally sustained the pro-life policies of his predecessor. However, on January 22, 1990—the anniversary of the *Roe v. Wade* decision—President Bush delivered a message to the antiabortion protestors rallying at the Supreme Court, the very same day White House press secretary Marlin Fitzwater told reporters that Bush's views are "a personal choice of conscience" and added: "We all feel there is room within the party for varying points of view."

Lee Atwater, then Republican national chairman, also spoke briefly to pro-choice Republicans rallying at party headquarters and repeated the comments he had made to the Republican National Committee the prior week, emphasizing his commitment to an "umbrella party" that would tolerate both sides of the abortion issue. Atwater's speech followed the defeats of GOP gubernatorial candidates in hotly contested elections in Virginia and New Jersey; both losses were attributed to some crossover voting for the Democrats by suburban Republican women (Daynes and Tatalovich 1992, 558). Just how small the GOP tent on abortion would become was vividly illustrated during the Bush-Clinton election campaign of 1992.

Some GOP liberals thought it inevitable that the 1988 antiabortion language would be softened by 1992, but that was not to be. Not only did both parties reaffirm their differences of opinion, but George Bush, in a strategic blunder, allowed the right wing free reign at the national convention. In contrast, the Democratic convention was now under control of the "new" Democrat Bill Clinton, who chose softer but no less ambiguous language supporting abortion. Here are the Republican and Democratic platform planks for 1992, side by side (*New York Times* 1992a):

Republican Plank	*Democratic Plank*
We believe the unborn child has a fundamental individual right to life which cannot be infringed. We therefore reaffirm our support for a human life amendment to the Constitution, and we endorse legislation to make clear that the Fourteenth Amendment protections apply to unborn children. We oppose using public revenues for abortion and will not fund organizations which advocate it. We commend those who provide alternatives to abortion by meeting the needs of mothers and offering adoption services. We reaffirm our support for appointment of judges who respect traditional family values and the sanctity of innocent human life.	Democrats stand behind the right of every woman to choose, consistent with *Roe v. Wade,* regardless of ability to pay, and support a national law to protect that right. It is a fundamental constitutional liberty that individual Americans—not government—can best take responsibility for making the most difficult and intensely personal decisions regarding reproduction. The goal of our nation must be to make abortion less necessary, not more difficult or dangerous. We pledge to support contraceptive research, family planning, comprehensive family life education and policies that support healthy childbearing and enable parents to care more effectively for their children.

Abortion Voting

America's political parties have drawn the line on abortion, so conditions would seem ripe for the "rational voter" model to operate. This model stipulates that once people correctly perceive how an issue divides the major political parties, they would vote for the party whose position is closest to their own on that particular issue. But the evidence makes clear that, for *most* voters in *all* presidential elections to date, the choice between Republican and Democratic candidates has not been dictated by single-issue calculations (table 5.3).

According to the American National Election Study (ANES) for 1972, there was a statistically significant, albeit slight, tendency for pro-life supporters to cast more votes for Richard Nixon than for George McGovern. However, in that landslide election Nixon won upward of three-fifths of the vote, irrespective of whether people were strictly pro-life, favored risk to the life of mother and rape as exceptions, would expand therapeutic abortions for other reasons, or expressed a pro-choice viewpoint.

In 1976 voters were probably confused in trying to untangle the policy differences on abortion between Gerald Ford and Jimmy Carter, and the study data show no statistical relationship between abortion attitudes and candidate choice that year. A *New York Times*–CBS News survey in September revealed that while 47 percent of people supporting an amendment to ban abortions planned to vote for Carter, Carter was also getting votes from 45 percent of those who were opposed to that constitutional ban. Among those favoring the amendment, 30 percent were backing President Ford, although he was also supported by 35 percent of the people opposed to that amendment (Daynes and Tatalovich 1992, 555). Similarly, Vinovskis (1980b, 199–201) found that voters favoring abortion were more likely to support Carter, but the issue hardly mattered, since less than one-tenth of 1 percent of respondents to the postelection survey cited abortion as important.

Things began to change by 1980, according to another *New York Times*–CBS News poll: 17 percent named abortion as one of the three most important issues in that campaign (Granberg and Burlison 1983, 232, 236). However, the backers of independent candidate John Anderson in 1980 were "considerably more liberal" in their abortion views than those who preferred Reagan or Carter, and so Granberg and Burlison (1983, 232, 236) concluded that Reagan and Carter supporters "were not divided over abortion, that the abortion issue was hardly salient in the minds of most voters, and that although the major parties and candidates held quite distinct positions on abortion in 1980, by and large these distinctions were not very

Table 5.3

Bivariates Between Abortion Attitudes and Candidate Choice in U.S. Presidential Elections, 1972–1992

Year	Pro-Life	Life/Rape	Other Reasons	Pro-Choice
1972				
Republican	62.6	68.8	61.7	59.0
Democrat	37.4	31.2	38.3	41.0
Gamma = .111[†]				
1976				
Republican	42.5	51.1	52.9	46.8
Democrat	57.5	48.9	47.1	53.2
Gamma = -.001				
1980				
Republican	55.0	56.0	66.7	51.3
Democrat	45.0	44.0	33.3	48.7
Gamma = .017[‡]				
1984				
Republican	64.0	63.2	61.7	50.4
Democrat	36.0	36.8	38.3	49.6
Gamma = .179[*]				
1988				
Republican	53.8	61.4	53.8	44.8
Democrat	46.2	38.6	46.3	55.2
Gamma = .179[*]				
1992				
Republican	54.1	55.0	51.8	27.7
Democrat	45.9	45.0	48.2	72.3
Gamma = .397[*]				

Source: National Election Studies, 1972–1992. The 1984, 1988, and 1992 question was: "There has been some discussion about abortion during recent years. Which of the opinions on this page best agrees with your view? (1) By law, abortion should never be permitted. (2) The law should permit abortion only in case of rape, incest or when the woman's life is in danger. (3) The law should permit abortion for reasons other than rape, incest, or danger to the woman's life but only after the need for the abortion has been clearly established. (4) By law, a woman should always be able to obtain an abortion as a matter of personal choice." These variations in wording were used in 1972, 1976, and 1980: "(1) Abortion should never be permitted. (2) Abortion should be permitted only if the life and health of the woman is in danger. (3) Abortion should be permitted if, due to personal reasons, the woman would have difficulty in caring for the child. (4) Abortion should never be forbidden, since one should not require a woman to have a child she doesn't want."

Note: Gammas are significant at [*].001 or [†].01 or [‡].05 level.

apparent to the electorate." In a similar vein Bolce (1988) drew the conclusion that "while substantial ignorance and misperception persists, the public's ability to recognize correctly the stands of the two major parties (and their presidential candidates in 1980) on the issue increased significantly between 1976 and 1980." The 1980 ANES analysis (Table 5.2) does show that Jimmy Carter did best with pro-choice voters, yet Republican Ronald Reagan, a pro-life conservative, won the majority of votes regardless of the view on abortion expressed by voters.

For 1984 Granberg (1987) found that Reagan voters were significantly more likely to oppose abortion than Mondale voters, though very few people considered abortion to be a salient issue. Only 1 percent mentioned abortion to be among the three most important problems facing the nation (0.4 percent picked abortion as *the* critical problem). The ANES data confirm that Reagan obtained a larger share of the vote from people whose views on abortion shifted from pro-choice to pro-life, and the reverse relationship applied to Democratic candidate Walter Mondale. Clearly other factors caused this victory of historic proportions for President Reagan; he won the majority of votes in each opinion category, including those of people who subscribed to the pro-choice position.

In 1988 the GOP was victorious by a substantial margin. A *New York Times*–CBS News survey found that 53 percent of Dukakis supporters believed that "abortion should be legal as it is now," compared to the 33 percent of Bush supporters who held that opinion (Daynes and Tatalovich 1992, 555). The American National Election Study data show that Dukakis won 55 percent of the votes of people with the strongest pro-choice opinions, while Bush carried the majority among those who expressed a pro-life, narrowly therapeutic, or expanded therapeutic view of abortion.

To date the most pronounced cleavage over abortion has surfaced during the 1992 election. President Bush decisively won the votes of pro-lifers and people who would limit abortions to cases of endangerment to the mother's life and rape and narrowly won the support of the majority of people who tolerated "other" reasons for abortion, but Clinton captured 72 percent of the voters classified as strongly pro-choice. Exit polling indicated to Pomper (1992, 150) that the "president [Bush] also gained, surprisingly, on the abortion issue. Although a strong 2–1 majority favored the 'right-to-choice' position, the pro-Bush minority favoring 'right-to-life' was more likely to cast ballots on the basis of this issue."

Abramowitz (1995) might demur, since his analysis of ANES results found that abortion attitude had a stronger impact on Republicans than Democrats; among "voters who were aware of the candidates' positions on abortion, and especially among those for whom abortion was a salient issue, abortion attitudes were strongly related to candidate preference in the expected direction—voters who supported abortion rights were much more likely to vote for Clinton than those who opposed abortion rights" (Abramowitz 1995, 183). Abramowitz also took note that "despite the fact that the two major parties have taken well-publicized and sharply contrasting positions on abortion since 1980, only 51 percent of all survey respondents, and only 59 percent of those who actually voted, knew what those positions were" (Abramowitz 1995, 180).

Wilcox (1995, 73) concluded that the American National Election Study bivariates show "that the public has gradually aligned its partisanship with the positions of the presidential parties on abortion. The correlation between abortion attitudes and partisanship in the 1970s was essentially 0. By 1984, the correlation had grown to .05. . . . In the 1992 NES data, the correlation between party identification and abortion attitudes was .12, more than twice as high as in 1984." But we cannot overstate the case, because those values are still modest; more important, a slight partisan realignment in mass opinion may not translate into voter choice during a presidential campaign.

That abortion attitudes by Republicans and Democrats do not translate into votes for pro-life Republican candidates versus pro-choice Democratic candidates is suggested by a simple comparison of the statistical relationships (gammas) found between (1) abortion attitude and party affiliation in table 5.2 and (2) abortion attitude and candidate choice in table 5.3. In 1972 the negative relationship between party and attitude (meaning that more Republicans were liberal on abortion than Democrats) was reversed by the time votes were actually cast, because more-liberal Democrats gave a proportionately greater number of votes to George McGovern. Similarly in 1976, the negative gamma means that proportionately fewer Democrats had liberal views on abortion compared to Republicans, but that relationship fell apart when voters of both parties cast their ballots. In 1980 no relationship between party and attitude is indicated, but a barely significant gamma suggests that, in voting, there was a noticeable tendency for conservatives on abortion to give more votes to Reagan and for those with more-liberal views to shift some votes to Carter.

For 1984, 1988, and 1992, each statistically significant gamma indicates some effect of "rational voting" insofar as people with liberal abortion opinions more often voted Democratic and those with conservative views more often voted Republican. But the connection between party affiliation and abortion attitude was marginal in 1984 (though in the correct direction) and statistically insignificant in 1988, showing the strongest positive relationship in 1992. In other words, barely in 1984 but especially in 1992 both relationships operated as they should *if* party affiliation was a source for voter attitudes on abortion and *when* voters chose between presidential candidates based on their "rational" assessment of party positions on abortion.

The fact that four elections (1972, 1984, 1988, and 1992) showed, as hypothesized, some degree of "rational" linkage between abortion attitude and voting behavior—despite contrary or weaker relationships between party affiliation and abortion opinion—would indicate that partisan campaigning serves to highlight policy differences and thereby strengthens the linkage between attitude and voting behavior. Of course, this logic assumes that, for ideological reasons, Republicans are supposed to be pro-life and Democrats are inclined to be pro-choice. It also makes a big assumption that abortion will play a more important role in voter calculations than other kinds of election stimuli, and this assumption is not warranted based on recent multivariate analysis.

Wattier, Daynes, and Tatalovich (1996) analyzed the ANES data for all six presidential elections from 1972 to 1992 to evaluate the impact of issue voting on abortion as compared to party affiliation, candidate image, and incumbent popularity (or retrospective voting). While the strongest predictor was candidate image, with retrospective voting a close second in 1992, in every regression model the variables for party, candidate, and incumbent popularity were statistically significant, but abortion attitude had no impact on candidate choice *except* in 1992. And even for the Clinton-Bush-Perot contest, abortion attitude was far less important than candidate image, party, and incumbent popularity. Overall, these findings show quite conclusively that the electorate has *not* been choosing between presidential candidates from a single-issue perspective on abortion.

Why did abortion attitude surface as a predictor in 1992, albeit a weak one? Does this suggest a delayed issue evolution of the kind suggested by Greg Adams (1992)? He shows how increasing party polarization in congressional votes on abortion bills had a causal relationship to the increasing partisanship on abortion in mass opinion since 1980. As Adams concluded:

> Evidence supports the claim that an issue evolution is underway with respect to abortion. Parties in Congress and the masses have changed on abortion, and there is at least cursory evidence that abortion is becoming one of the defining issues for the two parties.... These results suggest that partisan cues, given through Congress and the executive branch, are a necessary precursor for action at the mass level. (Adams 1992, 15)

The polarization between Republican and Democratic grassroots opinion, which increased in the 1992 presidential election, may be a result of

Supreme Court retrenchments since 1989, insofar as *Webster* encouraged the pro-choice movement to renew its grassroots organizing and commitment to electioneering. So findings of a linkage between abortion attitude and presidential choice in the 1992 election may reflect a resurgence of pro-choice activism. If that is true, then a realignment on abortion may be taking place, but one grounded in gender rather than in political party. Whether Adams is right or wrong about his prognosis of realignment, he is essentially correct that abortion has polarized party elites much more than the party rank and file, unlike what has happened in Canada.

Summary

At various times the abortion controversy has spawned pro-life insurgency candidacies in both the national Republican and Democratic parties. The 1996 nonstarter GOP primary campaign by Alan Keyes, a conservative African-American, was based almost entirely on pro-life advocacy, making him purer of purpose than even his fellow conservatives columnist Patrick Buchanan and U.S. senator Phil Gramm (R-Texas). Two decades earlier, in the wake of *Roe v. Wade,* pro-lifers were developing political muscle, and they first targeted the Democratic Party. In New York State a Right to Life Party was founded and nominated Ellen McCormack as its presidential candidate. McCormack "ran an avowedly single-issue campaign" in contesting the Democratic primary of 1976, winning 238,000 votes in eighteen primary states and capturing twenty-two convention delegates; four years later she appeared on the ballot in three states, garnering a total of only 32,327 votes (Spitzer 1987, 58–61). By running McCormack in 1980, the New York party split with the National Right to Life Committee, which had endorsed Ronald Reagan, and in 1984 the New York party refused to endorse anybody because, as McCormack put it, "Reagan is for therapeutic abortion . . . to protect the physical and mental health of the mother. . . . We don't condone abortion under any circumstances" (quoted in Spitzer 1987, 62).

Nor are the effects of the abortion controversy limited to presidential campaigns, since the issue permeates other national and statewide elections. Its impact may vary from state to state and across time, but analysts have documented that abortion attitude can affect vote choice in races for the U.S. Senate (Cook, Jelen, and Wilcox 1994b; Hershey and West 1983), governor (Cook, Jelen, and Wilcox 1994a; Howell and Sims 1993), and lieutenant governor (Cook, Hartwig, and Wilcox 1992). What accounts for this contagion of abortion politics at all levels of American electoral behavior?

The weakness of American political parties makes them subject to infiltration by pro-choice and especially pro-life single-issue activists. At the national level the widespread use of primaries to choose presidential nominees, with party conventions simply ratifying the collective result of the primary contests, makes the parties vulnerable to policy activists who volunteer their efforts on behalf of the candidates with the purest views on abortion, who control disproportionate numbers of votes in the primaries and party caucuses, and who organize political action committees to channel campaign funds directly to those candidates without going through the party organizations. So thoroughly have primaries democratized the process by which Americans recruit their presidential candidates that the Democratic and Republican leaderships no longer monopolize the nomination process and consequently cannot screen out policy zealots or political mavericks who are beholden to single-issue causes. The fact that pro-lifer Patrick Buchanan—a columnist who has never held elective office—won an upset victory over Senator Robert Dole—a seasoned politician and the favorite of the GOP political establishment—in the 1996 New Hampshire GOP primary illustrates once again that weak political parties are subject to "capture" by strongly organized single-issue groups.

In Canada there are powerful disincentives for a backbencher to betray the party organization and seek the backing of single-issue activists; a politician who does that risks not being appointed to the cabinet should his or her party win control of the government. The fate of longtime Liberal MP John Nunciata of Ontario is illustrative. Despite his considerable seniority and probably because of his strong pro-life views, he was not included by Prime Minister Chrétien in his cabinet or given any other significant party leadership position. Indeed, during the 1993 federal election campaign in Ontario, Liberal party officials (presumably with Chrétien's tacit approval) intervened in several ridings to prevent pro-life candidates from securing the nomination in place of party regulars.* This kind of intervention by the party establishment to guarantee that their partisans are nominated is rare in American politics, and presidents (given the disastrous results of Franklin D. Roosevelt's failed "purge" of southern conservatives in 1938) especially avoid getting involved in intraparty fights for the nomination of congressional candidates.

What is happening in the United States gives poignant testimony to the validity of the party consensus model, as represented by Herbert Agar. Agar (1950), and others of an earlier generation of party theorists, argued that secession and the Civil War were largely caused by the breakdown of

---

*This observation about the 1993 Canadian elections was provided to me by Professor F.L. Morton of the University of Calgary, who reviewed the first draft of this manuscript for M.E. Sharpe, Inc.

political consensus after the two major parties adopted sharply partisan stands on the slavery question. Some commentators today have drawn the comparison between the abortion debate and the historic debate over slavery, given the scope, intensity, persistence, and volatility of both issues. The Civil War analogy may be excessive, but the kind of political strife over abortion that has affected state government and all three branches of the federal government seems also to be excessive given the standards of contemporary political life. If it continues unabated, that kind of combat may pose dangers to U.S. norms of democratic behavior, the legitimacy of governmental institutions, and political stability. In sum, the failure to date of the American two-party system to pursue a consensus-building strategy contrasts sharply with the experiences in Canada.

6

Two Models of Executive Politics

Politicized America and Depoliticized Canada

This chapter should be dedicated to the memory of Woodrow Wilson—as political scientist, that is, since he anticipated the Progressive Era with his clarion call for a "politics-administration" dichotomy (Wilson 1887). What he meant was that politicians should make policy but administrators ought to implement it, and by establishing a professionalized public administration insulated from party politics, Wilson hoped to displace patronage and create a career government service based on merit selection so that individuals with talent, honesty, and objectivity could be recruited. Wilson, an Anglophile, nurtured his ideas from the British.

Canadian political science has not developed a homegrown version of the politics-administration debate, probably because the problem is obviated by its parliamentary government. Deep within the system is a logic that recognizes that the politics-administration division is meaningless and, therefore, the appropriate means for resolving the politics-versus-administration issue is to keep political agents accountable for everything that occurs within the policy-making and administrative realms. Thus parliamentary government gives rise to what S.L. Sutherland calls the "blaming cycle"[*] (Americanists refer to this as "retrospective" voting by the electorate)—defeating the government is compensation for the inability of Canadians to designate separate roles for administrators and politicians in the decision-making process.

---

[*]Professor Sutherland, who shared this concept with me during an electronic interview in December of 1995, develops this thesis at length with regard to "dirty hands" (corruption) in both the Canadian and American regimes. See Sutherland (1995a).

In the United States, however, party politics was not the only threat to professionalization of government service, because the ethos of Jacksonian democracy, steeped in the spoils system, gave way to more-contemporary notions about "representative" bureaucracy—the idea that those who serve in the public sector should resemble their agency's clients sociologically and, more important, even attitudinally. The American bureaucracy is supposed to be accountable to the public opinion and specialized publics. So while nobody accuses the federal government of being a dumping ground for Republican or Democratic hacks, a more fundamental concern is that public agencies have been "captured" by private interests rather than acting in ways to promote the general welfare.

There is yet another way that the government bureaucracy in the United States has been politicized in ways that are truly foreign to the Canadian experience, and here modern political science is partly to blame. With the growth of the modern welfare state and a huge state apparatus, the budget of the federal government in 1995 was $1.6 trillion, and big government means permanent government or bureaucratic government. If Americans are more individualistic than Canadians and if private enterprise is held in greater esteem in the United States than in Canada, the corresponding result is that Americans depreciate the value of public-sector employment more so than Canadians. *Bureaucracy* is a term laden with connotations of pathology: waste, inefficiency, resistance to change, arrogance, and self-aggrandizement.

Self-aggrandizement—meaning that bureaucrats have strong survival instincts and will do whatever is necessary to protect (and expand) their programs, budget, and personnel—has caused recent presidents, notably but not exclusively Republicans, to try to assert direct control over line operations in the federal bureaucracy or, alternatively, to shift more functions away from the departments to the executive branch. This issue is debated among academics, some arguing that such intrusion weakens the civil service system and destroys the ideal of the "neutral-competent" bureaucracy (Heclo 1977, 1975), while others argue that the permanent government must be "politicized" by the administration in order to keep bureaucrats ultimately accountable to the electorate (Moe 1985; Nathan 1983). By focusing on abortion policy implementation in Canada and the United States, this chapter offers a novel way to assess the benefits and disadvantages of neutral competence versus politicization in governmental bureaucracies. The argument is that abortion has fully politicized the federal bureaucracy in the United States but has barely made a mark on the Canadian permanent government.

United States: Abortion Versus Bureaucracy

Abortion has intruded on the workings of the American federal bureaucracy because key decision makers and agencies have been subjected to political pressure from the White House (for the most part during the Reagan and Bush administrations) and/or from the Congress to defend or promote a particular policy (in most instances the pro-life agenda). Those actions resulted because pro-life spokespersons were appointed to sensitive administrative positions, or rules and regulations were promulgated by political appointees sympathetic to that cause, or bureaucratic activities were monitored by pro-life activists. For its part, Congress gets involved by trying to micromanage the scope of bureaucratic activities regarding abortion, most typically by proscribing certain kinds of behavior. In this bureaucratic struggle, particularly during periods of divided government, an agency or official under attack from pro-lifers and a Republican administration sometimes can gain allies among liberal congressional Democrats or pro-choice advocacy groups. That scenario is rare; more frequently both the legislative and executive branches join forces to bring pressure on a recalcitrant agency or administrator (the U.S. Civil Rights Commission is the best example). The bureaucratic landscape affected by abortion politics may be circumscribed by listing the key appointees and agencies whose jurisdiction explicitly or implicitly has been implicated in the abortion debate. Here are the leading bureaucratic actors:

Department of Justice
    Attorney General
    Solicitor General
Department of Health and Human
    Services (HHS)
        Secretary of Health and Human
            Services
        Office of Population Affairs
        National Center for Family
            Planning Services
National Institutes of Health
Food and Drug Administration (FDA)
Surgeon General of the United States
Legal Services Corporation (LSC)
General Accounting Office (GAO)
U.S. Customs Service
Office of Personnel Management (OPM)

Federal Bureau of Investigation (FBI)
Bureau of Alcohol, Tobacco, and
    Firearms (BATF)
Health Care Financing Administration
    (HCFA)
Centers for Disease Control (CDC)
U.S. Civil Rights Commission
Consumer Product Safety Commission
    (CPSC)
Department of State
    Agency for International
        Development (AID)
    Peace Corps
United States Supreme Court
Federal Communications Commission
    (FCC)
United States Marshals Service

Department of Justice

The attorney general is one of four members of the so-called inner cabinet, because the Justice Department is charged with enforcing federal laws and does not represent any specific clientele interests. Unfortunately, however, the attorney general is apt to be a personal confidant and political adviser to the president, and his or her instincts are honed as much for electoral considerations as legal niceties. President Reagan's first attorney general was William French Smith, whose relationship with the president went back to California, when Reagan was governor, but it was Smith's successor, Edwin Meese, another Reagan intimate, who after his appointment in 1985 promptly began to attack the Supreme Court for its overzealous efforts to "incorporate" (that is, apply) the Bill of Rights to state governments.

During 1985 the Justice Department announced that it would not utilize civil rights laws to prosecute protesters who harassed women at abortion clinics unless the protesters happened to be employees of local, state, or federal governments. By its interpretation, confrontations between women seeking access to abortion clinics and demonstrators should be managed under the Fourteenth Amendment rather than through civil rights laws (Tofani 1985). Such a narrow view of civil rights reflected the antiabortion attitudes of the Reagan administration, critics charged. Moreover, pro-choice advocates would have preferred that the FBI, rather than the BATF, conduct investigations of clinic bombings (Marcus and Pichirallo 1985). President Reagan did not want the high-profile FBI to be involved, and William Webster, then FBI director, agreed that FBI involvement would have escalated the meaning of clinic bombings to a national terrorist conspiracy when most federal officials believed that these violent acts were the work of individual extremists (*Washington Post* 1985). To its credit, the BATF made arrests in twenty of the thirty-one abortion clinic bombings during a two-year period (Weil and Churchville 1985).

However logical the Reagan policy to avoid FBI involvement was in the mid-1980s, it was abandoned when Democrat Bill Clinton chose Janet Reno as his attorney general. Within hours of taking the oath of office, Reno said, "I want to look at the laws on the books now to see if there is any remedy that we might undertake in response [to protesters who interfere with women who seek clinic abortions]"; she also said, "Just as there should be a Federal remedy for racial discrimination and for gender discrimination, I think in this instance somehow or another there has got to be a Federal response to interference through physical conduct which restrains access to a woman's right to choose" (quoted in Johnston 1993). Following the second murder of a doctor at a Pensacola, Florida, abortion clinic, the Justice

Department announced the formation of an interagency group to pool the efforts of domestic terrorism experts from the FBI, BATF, and United States Marshals Service. Also, U.S. marshals were dispatched to a dozen locations across the nation to help protect abortion clinics and, more important politically, to show a federal law-enforcement presence. Abortion rights leaders have long been unhappy about the tepid response by federal authorities to clinic violence, and apparently Attorney General Reno too had second thoughts about the scope of federal involvement. Paul J. Hill, the assailant in the second Pensacola clinic killing, theoretically could have been charged with the federal crime of violating the newly enacted Freedom of Access to Clinic Entrances Act of 1993, but the Justice Department was not enthusiastic about doing so, at least not before state charges were filed. In the view of James Wagoner, executive vice president of NARAL: "They seem to be tentative and hesitant about getting in the middle of this so-called 'abortion fight,' but that's outrageous because what we are talking about here are domestic terrorists who are using murder and mayhem to impose their political beliefs" (quoted in Johnston 1994b).

Just one day after the fatal shooting of the abortionist and his bodyguard in Pensacola, however, it was reported that the FBI would abandon its long-standing posture of not getting involved with abortion-related violence and would begin a broad investigation into accusations that the violence directed against abortion clinics is the work of a conspiracy of antiabortion militants. "We believe there is a nationwide conspiracy," said NOW executive vice president Kim A. Gandy. "The Justice Department and the FBI do not have a handle on it yet. They don't know the extent of the problem" (Johnston 1994a). Apparently the FBI was pressured by the Justice Department to take this initiative, and newly installed FBI director Louis J. Freeh welcomed the opportunity to gain more visibility for his agency, but senior officials within the FBI resisted on the grounds that there is a gray area between legitimate political protest and criminality and, more important, that the agency might suffer at the hands of a future administration with pro-life sympathies (Johnston 1994a).

Under President Bush the attorney general was Richard Thornburgh (a former governor of Pennsylvania, during whose tenure an important abortion case reached the Supreme Court). Though not as strident as Meese, Thornburgh approved of plans to use the pending Supreme Court case of *Webster* to overturn *Roe*. But his actions provoked a mild rebellion by some two hundred government attorneys in his department, who filed a petition stating their opposition to the administration's interference with a woman's right to choose an abortion (Biskupic 1989). As one of the dissident lawyers put it: "It was difficult for us to discover any motive other than that they just wanted to identify the department with the political agenda of the far right" (quoted in Wines 1989). When Thornburgh resigned to make an unsuccessful bid for a U.S. Senate seat, his successor was William P. Barr, who told the Senate Judiciary Committee that he opposed the *Roe v. Wade* ruling on abortion. The committee was impressed by Barr's candor but, as liberal Democratic senator Joseph R. Biden (D-Delaware) said, "I'm for you for Attorney General, but don't come up for the Court" (quoted in Berke 1991).

The actual filing of an amicus brief for the U.S. government before the Supreme Court is the responsibility of the solicitor general. The brief that accompanied the *Webster* case was written by Solicitor General Charles Fried. It argued that the high court should reverse its ruling that there is a constitutional right to abortion and allow the states to define the limits of legal abortions. It is pretty much agreed that before the onset of the Reagan and Bush presidencies, the solicitor general was solidly professional and virtually a tenth member of the Supreme Court, given the high court's reliance on the solicitor general's legal opinions and judgment (Caplan 1987). But appointees under Reagan and Bush began using a litigation strategy to promote those administrations' social agendas, so much so that the solicitor general's office became a political extension of the president (Witt 1986a).

The first Reagan appointee was Rex Lee, but he moved cautiously to avoid jeopardizing the status of his office. According to Lee, on various issues it was a question of whether one should "blow the bugle," as President Reagan preferred, or "win the war" (Witt 1985, 1463), which explains why Reagan's administration, said Lee, wanted to "stand up and be counted" (Witt 1986b). Then came Charles Fried, who even submitted amicus briefs in cases where the U.S. government had no direct interest, but eventually he also had a change of heart about such advocacy. When conservatives criticized him for becoming too restrained, Fried responded: "I think that what accounts for [the conservative criticism] is that some of these folks are like Trotskyites in New York in the 30s. . . . They are somehow more interested in ferreting out heresy and deviance in their own midst than in accomplishing a generally shared vision. I think it is a pathology" (quoted in Kamen 1989). In September 1989 Kenneth Starr was appointed solicitor general by President Bush, and he continued with the litigation strategy of his predecessors. In his amicus brief accompanying the 1990 *Hodgson v. Minnesota* case involving parental notification, Starr defended the state regulation but did not issue a broadside against a woman's right to choose.

Surgeon General

The office of surgeon general was another position that historically had resisted being politicized, but recently nominees of Republican and Democratic presidents have been individuals of less than stellar medical credentials who were chosen to make a political statement. Under Reagan the position was held by Dr. C. Everett Koop, initially a favorite among pro-life activists since he had coauthored a book (Koop and Schaeffer 1983) that examined the negative health effects of abortions. Koop held those views until 1987, when Reagan asked him to update the earlier study. Some $200,000 was appropriated by HHS to the project, but to the chagrin of pro-lifers, the summary report in 1989 determined that abortions had only minimal physical or psychological effects on women. Such findings, which irritated conservatives, caused Koop to soften his views; he remained personally opposed to abortion but acknowledged that the scientific evidence was inconclusive (Tolchin 1989).

Koop served through both Reagan terms, after which President Bush chose Dr. Antonia Novello, a native Puerto Rican, as surgeon general. She too opposed abortion, in line with Bush's own views. But before Novello was chosen, apparently Dr. Burton Lee, who was the White House physician, withdrew his name from consideration for the post of surgeon general because, he said, "I feel very strongly that anyone who takes that job should be able to support the president's position on abortion, and on this issue we differ" (quoted in *Congressional Quarterly Almanac* 1989, 305). Following Bush's defeat by Bill Clinton, the Clinton administration reversed several pro-life initiatives from the Reagan-Bush years and began appointing pro-choice defenders to sensitive positions, including that of surgeon general. Clinton's first choice became a public-relations disaster for the administration. Dr. Joycelyn Elders, an African-American pediatrician whom Clinton, as governor, had appointed director of the Arkansas Health Department, minced no words in talking about condom distribution in schools, early sex education, government funding of abortions, supplying Norplant (a contraceptive device) to drug-addicted prostitutes at no charge, and childhood masturbation (for which she was later pressured to resign). Conservatives, the Roman Catholic Church, and the Christian right opposed her nomination, but she was confirmed by a 65–34 vote (Wines 1993).

President Clinton's next choice for surgeon general, Dr. Henry W. Foster Jr., was a respected African-American obstetrician from Tennessee, and by all accounts a decent and compassionate person. But his nomination was sidetracked by revelations by the National Right to Life Committee (Gray 1995) that he had performed abortions (and though he had done relatively few during his many years of delivering babies, the fact that Foster kept changing his recollections of how many abortions he had actually performed raised questions about his truthfulness) and, later on, charges that he had knowingly participated in the infamous Tuskegee experiments in which four hundred poor black men were denied treatment for syphilis in order to assess the progress of that disease (Lewis 1995). A dozen medical organizations, including the AMA, the Tennessee Medical Association, the largely black National Medical Association, the American College of Physicians, and the prestigious American College of Obstetricians and Gynecologists, rallied to his defense, but the Foster nomination got bogged down in presidential politics as pro-lifers led by Senator Phil Gramm (R-Texas), a rival to Senator Robert Dole (R-Kansas) for the 1996 presidential nomination, pressured Dole, as majority leader, not to schedule a vote on the confirmation. Dole outmaneuvered Gramm, as well as Clinton, by agreeing to call for a vote only if sixty senators first voted to end a Republican-led filibuster. The effort came up short, 57 to 43 (Clines 1995).

NIH

The director of the National Institutes of Health, who oversees fourteen institutes that investigate the causes of and treatments for diseases such as cancer and heart disease, has become increasingly politicized since the mid-1980s. In October 1989 two candidates for the directorship withdrew from consideration because they were asked questions about abortion. White House spokesperson Alixe Glen replied that candidates were queried about "issues such as abortion and many other health-policy issues. It is important that these people be willing to support the president's position and articulate his strategy, but that is not a litmus test." Reportedly Dr. William Danforth (who was then chancellor of Washington University) was asked two questions: "What are your views on abortion? And what are your views on fetal research?" (*Congressional Quarterly Almanac* 1989, 305).

It was not until September 1990 that Dr. Bernadine P. Healy, a Cleveland cardiologist, was selected by HHS secretary Louis W. Sullivan to head the National Institutes of Health. Almost immediately the National Right to Life Committee refused to endorse Healy because, based on her past statements, "what comes across is someone not at all sympathetic to the pro-life point of view," said National Right to Life Committee legislative director Douglas Johnson (quoted in Hilts 1990). For one thing, Healy was on the advisory panel of experts that had voted to support federal grants for the use of fetal tissue from abortions in medical research, which the National Right to Life Committee (and Secretary Sullivan) opposed. In the opinion of

Congressman Henry A. Waxman (D-California), the very liberal chair of the House Subcommittee on Health and the Environment, the continued vacancy in the directorship was "a disgrace" because Bush's term was already half over. "In attempts to cater to the extremists of the anti-abortion lobby, the White House has used candidates' positions on abortion and fetal research as a litmus test for any appointments. I don't know whether Dr. Healy was subjected to such a litmus test. I don't know if she passed the test. I just hope that they've picked someone who knows biomedical research, who can defend such research in the face of budget cuts" (quoted in Hilts 1990).

The ban on research on the use of fetal tissue for transplants to cure disease was first imposed on NIH by HHS secretary Dr. Otis Bowen in March 1988. Shortly thereafter NIH proceeded to establish an Ethical Advisory Board to assess whether research proposals on in vitro fertilization should be funded. In September an executive order, which would have banned all uses of fetal tissue in research, was proposed by Gary Bauer, assistant to the president for policy development, and forwarded to Secretary Bowen (Boffey 1988b). But the White House backed off when Reagan's press secretary, Marlin Fitzwater, denied that such a proposal reflected administration policy, although President Reagan did request added protections for the "unborn or newborn children from experimentation, research, and organ transplantation" unless the child benefited from them (Boffey 1988a). Then a week later the newly created Ethical Advisory Board recommended that human fetal tissue obtained from legal abortions should be utilized for medical therapy as well as research (Leary 1988). During FY89 (October 1, 1988, through September 31, 1989) the NIH had funded some one hundred research projects using fetal tissue, at a cost of $8.3 million (Kolata 1989).

Eventually Congress got involved in this controversy by enacting the National Organ Transplant Act of 1988, which Reagan signed into law, prohibiting the sale of fetal tissue and organs and providing a $50,000 fine and a possible five-year prison term for violations (Lewin 1988a). So despite the recommendations of at least two advisory committees to the NIH, the ban on funding research using fetal tissue that commenced in March of 1988 under Reagan was renewed by Bush's HHS secretary, Dr. Sullivan, in November 1989. Under President Bush, Dr. Bernadine Healy, newly confirmed as head of the National Institutes of Health, expressed opposition to the ban on fetal tissue research, but said she would defer to her superiors on the matter. Representative Waxman introduced legislation to end the ban. "We cannot sit by as these people's [medical] needs are ignored and as ideologues overrule scientists about research," he said (quoted in Hilts

1991). Legislation lifting the ban passed the House of Representatives in 1991 (though it was a dozen votes shy of the two-thirds needed to override the expected presidential veto), and in May 1992 the Senate voted 87–10 to do the same. To head off this political confrontation, the Bush administration in May 1992 authorized the federal government to establish storage banks for fetal tissue from miscarriages and tubal pregnancies for experimentation, while keeping the ban on the use of tissue from aborted fetuses. Critics responded that too little fetal tissue would be obtained from those sources and that the Senate had rejected such an idea the previous month. A "Dear Colleague" letter from a group of representatives and senators, including abortion foes Senators Strom Thurmond (R-South Carolina) and Alan K. Simpson (R-Wyoming), stated: "If you care about research to treat Parkinson's disease, Alzheimer's disease, diabetes and birth defects, you should not be persuaded by any arguments that tissue from spontaneous abortions, miscarriages, ectopic pregnancies, or tubal pregnancies will do enough" (Leary 1992). As expected, President Bush vetoed the legislation lifting the ban on use of fetal tissue, and contrary to optimistic predictions, it was not overridden by Congress. It's repeal was delayed until January 20, 1993, when President Bill Clinton signed five abortion-related memoranda to reverse executive restrictions dating back to the Reagan administration.

One of these memoranda rescinded the ban on fetal tissue research, which Clinton defended by saying: "This moratorium has significantly hampered the development of possible treatments for individuals afflicted with serious diseases and disorders, such as Parkinson's disease, Alzheimer's disease, diabetes and leukemia" (quoted in Toner 1993). The others would allow women in the armed forces to obtain abortions at military hospitals so long as they paid for them, directed the FDA to reassess whether the abortion pill RU-486 should be permitted into the country, lifted a 1988 prohibition on the ability of family planning clinics that get federal funds to counsel women on abortions, and (pending legislative approval) would have restored funding to United Nations programs that provide abortions or abortion counseling. Each of these actions involved distinct elements of the bureaucracy, but two were especially important. RU-486 is under the jurisdiction of the Food and Drug Administration, and the gag order on abortion clinics involved the Office of Population Affairs in the Department of Health and Human Services.

Health and Human Services

This department is a natural for pro-lifers to try to penetrate. In 1987 JoAnn Gasper, then deputy assistant secretary, on her own initiative, refused to renew two grants to Planned Parenthood, contrary to instructions from HHS secretary Otis R. Bowen, and she was dismissed (Pear 1987c). Bowen also was personally opposed to abortion but did not believe that HHS, without statutory authorization, could prevent Planned Parenthood from obtaining grant monies. Then President Reagan indicated that the secretary was "fully supportive of my position on abortion" (quoted in Greenhouse 1987). Gasper's successor was Nabers Cabaniss, who also had strong pro-life beliefs (Pear 1987a). When George Bush assumed the presidency, he had to choose his cabinet, including the HHS secretary. His nominee, Dr. Louis W. Sullivan, did not have a crystal clear position on abortion and eventually had to clarify his views on the subject. Sullivan met with the Bush transition team as well as Senator Orrin G. Hatch (R-Utah) and Representative Vin Weber (R-Minnesota), both pro-lifers. They left the meeting convinced that Sullivan would likely attract "strong pro-life people in the department" (quoted in Toner 1988). At first the National Right to Life Committee was opposed to Sullivan and told the White House: "Nomination of a Secretary of H.H.S. who does not have solid pro-life credentials would produce severe and longstanding disappointment among hundreds of thousands of pro-life activists who worked hard for the Bush/Quayle ticket" (quoted in Boyd 1988).

HHS assistant secretaries also had to overcome a litmus test regarding their views on abortion-related issues. Robert Fulton, Oklahoma's secretary of social services and Sullivan's pick to be an assistant secretary, withdrew his name after antiabortion groups accused him of helping to cover up a number of incidents in which doctors at an Oklahoma hospital denied medical care to some newborns with severe birth defects. On the other hand, those people who opposed abortion encountered little resistance. Kay James, HHS assistant secretary for public affairs, was previously affiliated with the National Right to Life Committee, and HHS assistant secretary for health Dr. James Mason, according to the committee's sources, "is said to be sympathetic to the president's position on abortion" (*Congressional Quarterly Almanac* 1989, 305). White House press secretary Marlin Fitzwater defended their screening of prospective nominees, saying: "You can call it whatever you want—but the fact is, yes, anybody who is coming into a policy-making position, we'll ask what their beliefs are and whether they can support our policy" (quoted in Rovner 1989). HHS secretary Sullivan agreed with respect to the assistant secretaries but demurred when positions such as the directorship of NIH or that of the Centers for Disease Control were at stake, arguing that managerial and scientific expertise were needed and that to do otherwise would politicize those positions (Hilts 1989).

The "Gag" Rule on Family Planning Clinics

The programmatic thrust of HHS dates back to 1970, when President Nixon established the Office of Population Affairs and the National Center for Family Planning Services. The purpose was to provide family planning services, but to satisfy concerns of the United States Catholic Conference, the Senate made authorization contingent on preventing the use of abortion as a method of family planning. President Nixon never gave direction to the Department of Health, Education, and Welfare on that specific question (Littlewood 1977, 55). These actions followed enactment of Public Law 91-572 (Family Planning Services and Population Research Act of 1970), and since 1972 the Code of Federal Regulations has included an absolute ban on the use of funds under this program for abortion. Under Title X of the law, grants are made to public and private nonprofit organizations that operate voluntary family planning projects and clinics.

A 1982 report by the General Accounting Office—Congress's watchdog agency—found no evidence that Title X monies were used directly for abortions or to advise clients to get an abortion (Report by the Comptroller General of the United States 1982). However, the GAO did advise Congress about questionable practices due to ambiguous HHS and Office of Management and Budget (OMB) guidelines. This investigation was requested by Senator Orrin Hatch (R-Utah), a well-known pro-life spokesperson, and Senator Jeremiah Denton (R-Alabama), but the GAO findings did not assuage the pro-lifers. At the end of 1985, as the FY86 budget was being debated, Senator Hatch and Representative Jack Kemp (R-New York) collaborated on amendments to further restrict discretion under Title X so that no such funds could be used for abortion referral or counseling except where the mother's life was endangered and, furthermore, so that no Title X funds could be awarded by grant or contract to any organization involved with abortions. Their antiabortion measure remained buried in a House committee through 1986, but in August of the following year the Reagan administration moved to achieve that objective by administrative fiat (Pear 1987b).

An ardent conservative was Edwin Meese, who became attorney general in Reagan's second term. The Justice Department under Meese urged a change in long-standing policy by the Department of Health and Human Services, which allowed women to receive abortion counseling and referrals at family planning clinics that received federal monies. In 1987 the Justice Department rendered an interpretation of the Family Planning and Population Services Act of 1970 to the effect that any counseling and referrals on abortion inevitably promote abortion because a woman might choose to abort after being counseled on abortions as an option. Thus if a public hospital had received HHS funds and that hospital offered both abortion-related services and family planning counseling, the two programs would have to be entirely separate and could not share facilities, receptionists, or even telephone systems (Pear 1987b).

Title X of the Family Planning and Population Services Act established the federal government's family planning program, which remains the major source of funds for family planning clinics, most managed by Planned Parenthood, but the law prohibits funding such projects if they utilize abortions as a method of family planning. However, for seventeen years after the enactment of the bill in 1970 these family planning clinics could provide abortion information and referrals to women interested in considering an abortion.

Planned Parenthood depended upon those Title X funds, since in 1987 it ran 769 family planning clinics and received about $30 million of federal funds to operate them each year (Roberts 1987). Planned Parenthood is on the pro-life enemies list, so much so that conservatives tried to eliminate family planning funding for the organization. When Thomas R. Burke, chief of staff to HHS secretary Bowen, refused to deny Planned Parenthood those government monies, conservatives pushed for his resignation. Burke was a Catholic and personally opposed to family planning, but his understanding of the law did not preclude Planned Parenthood's right to obtain family planning grants (Rich 1987).

The so-called gag rule implemented by the Reagan and Bush administrations to prohibit abortion counseling by family planning clinics that received Title X grants pursuant to the 1970 act was quickly challenged in several lawsuits. The states of New York, Massachusetts, and California, joined by the City of New York as well as family planning groups in California, Missouri, Pennsylvania, and Colorado, went to court, primarily charging that the restrictions were detrimental to the well-being of pregnant women and risked undermining the business operations of the clinics (Lewin 1988c). In Colorado, Judge Zita L. Weinshienk found the regulations unconstitutional because they were an "unduly burdensome interference with a woman's freedom to decide whether to terminate her pregnancy" and also imposed "an uncomfortable straight-jacket" on her physician (quoted in Pear 1988b).

A federal district judge in Boston went further, issuing an injunction permanently prohibiting the HHS secretary from enforcing the decree "anywhere within the United States" because the regulations were not constitutional (Pear 1988a), and in May 1989 the U.S. Court of Appeals for the First Circuit agreed, ruling that HHS had "gone beyond a mere refusal to fund and has interfered with the decisional process by dictating what information a woman may receive and by intruding into her relationship with her physician" (quoted in Barringer 1989). There was a contrary ruling, however, in July 1988 when New York federal district judge Louis L. Stanton upheld the regulations' constitutionality, saying the restrictions did not "prohibit or compel speech" but rather granted monies to support one viewpoint over another (Lewin 1988b), and in November 1989 the U.S. Court of Appeals for the Second Circuit upheld the HHS regulations (Brozan 1989). With conflicting signals from the lower federal bench, the stage was cast for review by the Supreme Court.

Meanwhile, Democrats in Congress failed in their attempt to enact legislation allowing federally funded family planning clinics to discuss abortion with their patients. In 1991 both the House of Representatives and the Senate approved such legislation, which was vetoed by President Bush, but then the House came up twelve votes short in its attempt to override. The bill fractured party loyalties, as 222 Democrats and 53 Republicans voted to override while 43 Democrats and 113 Republicans voted to sustain the veto. The outcome was a major defeat for the Democratic leadership, notably Speaker Thomas S. Foley, who could not rally enough rank-and-file Democrats despite openly making it a party issue (Clymer 1991).

Back in the judicial arena, New York's challenge to the gag rule, which federal district and appellate courts had upheld, involved Dr. Irving Rust, a physician who worked at a clinic that received Title X funding. He brought the suit against HHS secretary Louis Sullivan, but after being rebuffed by two lower federal courts, he petitioned for a hearing before the Supreme Court. Certiorari was granted, and *Rust v. Sullivan* (1991) was eventually decided in favor of the Bush administration (see table 2.2). Chief Justice Rehnquist, joined by Justices Kennedy, Scalia, Souter, and White, argued that the language of Title X was ambiguous as to whether Congress intended to prohibit funds for abortion counseling, and in the absence of clear statutory intent, the federal judiciary should defer to the executive branch's interpretation of the law. Justices Blackmun, Marshall, Stevens, and O'Connor dissented for various reasons. O'Connor felt Congress should decide the question; Blackmun upheld free speech and freedom of choice arguments; Stevens believed that, in fact, Congress had expressed its approval for funding such counseling activities given its long history of providing appropriations for the Title X program. Thus the gag rule remained in force until eliminated by President Clinton in January 1993.

The FDA and RU-486

The political implications of developing an abortion pill are enormous. It would mean that a woman would be able to obtain an abortion in a physician's office without going through a surgical procedure at a clinic or hospital. Though not 100 percent risk-free or entirely effective in every case, a medicinal abortifacient would ensure that the decision to terminate a pregnancy is a wholly personal one and not within the public purview. Pro-lifers who are unalterably opposed to marketing such a pill in the United States say that killing the unborn is murder whatever the means.

That is the story of RU-486, developed in France in 1982 by the pharmaceutical firm of Roussel-Uclaf, a subsidiary of its German parent company, Hoechst AG. Eight years later, in June 1980, the American Medical Association endorsed the testing of RU-486 in the United States (*New York Times* 1990), which began in 1996 because the Clinton administration is sympathetic. Pro-lifers call RU-486 the "death pill" and a "chemical time bomb" even though preliminary research in other countries suggests that the drug also can be used to treat Cushing's syndrome, glaucoma, and certain cancers in addition to enhancing fertility (*Scientific American* 1986). A 1986 study found RU-486 to be "an effective and safe method for termination of very early pregnancy but that it should be used only under close medical supervision" (Couzinet et al. 1986, 1565). The FDA must give its approval to drugs, certifying that they are safe and efficacious, before they can be marketed. In 1988 the FDA promulgated regulations allowing unapproved drugs to enter the country if used to treat "life-threatening conditions," but on September 26, 1988, the FDA ruled that those new regulations did not apply to RU-486 (Kolata 1988).

The cost of researching contraceptive drugs, not to mention something like RU-486, is very high, and product liability laws pose additional obstacles. C. Bardin, of the Population Council, indicated that the controversial nature of this research is driving companies out of the field. In 1970 there were twenty companies involved in contraceptive research and family planning techniques, but by 1988 only one remained. The Population Council was the only research organization devoted to studying contraceptives, and Ortho Pharmaceuticals was the only company still conducting research on birth control pills and spermicide (Kolata 1988). Another complication is the history of women's advocacy aimed at getting more strict FDA regulations on such products. Continuing lawsuits against the manufacturer of the Dalkon Shield IUD explain why product liability insurance is high and, more important, why the FDA approval process takes so long. Other drugs (not necessarily RU-486) that are designed to cause second-trimester abortions may require five to seven years of testing, cost in the neighborhood of $30–$70 million, and ultimately take perhaps seventeen years before appearing on the market (Fraser 1988).

But the biggest roadblock to the marketing of RU-486 in the United

States, even today, is the reluctance of U.S. drug companies to become involved with this product mainly because pro-life activists have threatened to mount an extensive boycott against any company that supplies it. For nearly two decades the Upjohn Pharmaceutical Company of Michigan has been boycotted by the National Right to Life Committee for marketing two FDA-approved drugs (prostaglandins) that bring about second-trimester abortions (Kolata 1988). And there has been political opposition in Congress, though primarily from the Reagan and Bush administrations. Pro-life representative Robert Dornan (R-California) unsuccessfully offered an amendment on June 14, 1988, as a rider to the 1988 HHS appropriations bill, to prohibit the FDA from ever using appropriated funds to test RU-486 (*Congressional Record* 1988).

Pro-choice advocates tried to make an end run around the FDA by appealing to the judiciary. In 1992 Leona Benten was arrested at Kennedy International Airport in New York City for bringing RU-486 pills into the country. Benten, who was in the early stages of pregnancy and wanted an abortion, had been recruited for this by Abortion Rights Mobilization. The objective of contriving a test case challenging the FDA regulations was devised by Lawrence Lader, one of the foremost abortion activists during the 1960s and the president of Abortion Rights Mobilization. Federal district judge Charles P. Sifton (a Carter appointee) ruled against the FDA, which is authorized by law to confiscate unapproved drugs entering the country, declaring: "The record before this court, reveals a history of political and bureaucratic timidity mixed with well-intentioned blundering in dealing with two of the most charged and significant issues of our time: AIDS and abortion." Moreover, he said, "In the face of political outcry, a retreat was ordered by the FDA, again without the investigation, notice, or [public] comment required by law" (quoted in Hilts 1992b, A13). In other words, the refusal by the FDA to include RU-486 in its list of exceptions for unapproved drugs was not accomplished according to established procedure, and so Sifton ordered the drugs returned to Benten, though he declined to invalidate the FDA policy.

The Bush administration quickly appealed to a three-judge panel (all Reagan or Bush appointees) of the Second Circuit Court of Appeals, which stayed the order. Then Benten and her allies petitioned the Supreme Court for an expedited review, asking for a stay of the order by the appellate court, but the high court voted 7–2 (Justices Blackmun and Stevens dissented) to deny the stay and not to review the merits of the case, *Benten v. Kessler* (1992). As a spokesperson for the FDA reacted: "The agency is pleased with the decision because it says this is a medical issue to be decided by the doctors and scientists at the agency. It means the court supports our discretionary import policy" (quoted in Hilts 1992a).

A breakthrough of sorts in the bureaucratic impasse came in early 1993 after President Clinton directed HHS secretary Donna E. Shalala (liberal and pro-choice, she had been chancellor of the University of Wisconsin) to review the FDA ban on RU-486. A month later FDA commissioner David A. Kessler met with the head of Roussel-Uclaf, Edouard Sakiz, and the company agreed to discuss how to arrange an agreement under which RU-486 could be marketed in the United States by another company or research institution. The drug is available in government clinics in France, Britain, and Sweden, and about 120,000 women have used the drug so far. Said Kessler: "I told Mr. Sakiz that if there is a safe and effective alternative to a surgical procedure for abortion, American women should have access to that alternative. I reiterated the F.D.A. position that a new drug application should be submitted. Mr. Sakiz agreed that RU-486 should be made available in the United States, but he emphasized the importance of achieving that without the involvement of Roussel-Uclaf" directly in the U.S. market (quoted in Hilts 1993). It was not until May 1994 that an accord was reached whereby Roussel-Uclaf would give the patent rights to RU-486 and all related technology free to the Population Council, a nonprofit contraceptive research organization in New York City, which in turn would seek a U.S. company to produce the drug. By giving up its patent rights, the French manufacturer hoped to avoid product liability suits and any boycott by pro-life groups. The agreement "concludes months of complex negotiations," said HHS secretary Shalala, "and reflects the Clinton Administration's repeated urging to bring the process to fruition" (quoted in Seelye 1994).

The big imponderable in the agreement, however, is how to find an American pharmaceutical company willing to resist boycott threats from the pro-lifers and actually manufacture the drug for a wide market. Besides that, the political landscape tilted dramatically toward the pro-life side when the 1994 elections gave the Republicans control of both houses of Congress. In March 1995 Americans United for Life filed a citizens' petition with the FDA, demanding that the strictest possible criteria be used in evaluating RU-486 and that data from foreign studies not be relied upon. Among those who reportedly signed the petition were Representative Thomas J. Bliley Jr. (R-Virginia) and eighteen other GOP representatives, Senator Dan Coats (R-Indiana), and three Democratic representatives (Hilts 1995). Meanwhile, medical researchers were studying how the use of two widely available prescription drugs, in sequence, could bring about an abortion. The use of methotrexate interferes with cell growth and division, and the subsequent administering of misoprostol, an ulcer drug that causes uterine contractions, reportedly produces abortion during the first nine weeks of a pregnancy. Such a technique could revolutionize the delivery of abortion services, since it could be prescribed by general practitioners without the involvement of surgeons or gynecologists (Brody 1995).

While members of Parliament regularly question the Canadian prime minister and his/her cabinet about public policy and administrative failures, it is rare indeed for the legislative branch to intervene directly in the implementation process. But Congress is not Parliament, and its oversight authority allows and encourages legislators to give close scrutiny to administrative agencies. It is not unusual to find, therefore, that Congress also has intervened on behalf of the pro-life agenda to curb pro-choice advocacy by federal agencies. Two illustrations, the Legal Services Corporation and the U.S. Commission on Civil Rights, will serve to make this point.

Congressional Micromanagement

A July 25, 1974, act of Congress, which President Nixon signed, transferred the legal services program from the Office of Economic Opportunity (OEO) to an independent corporation, the Legal Services Corporation (LSC), managed by an eleven-member board of directors. This reorganization followed three years of troubled negotiations between the Democratic-controlled Congress and the White House, because throughout the LSC's history (since President Johnson established his War on Poverty in 1964) conservatives have charged it with being is an activist liberal agency that has sued local governments and agencies on behalf of the poor. One amendment included in this reorganization statute (PL 93-355) was offered by pro-life representative Lawrence J. Hogan (R-Maryland) to prohibit "legal assistance with respect to any proceeding or litigation relating to abortion." His absolute ban was modified by a substitute amendment from Representative Harold V. Froehlich (R-Wisconsin) that proscribed activities regarding nontherapeutic abortions only, which was accepted by a 316–53 margin, after which the House of Representatives passed the modified Hogan Amendment on a lopsided 301–68 roll call. Hogan's action was prompted by OEO reports in which officials said that—despite Congress's 1970 ban on family planning grants for abortion—legal services attorneys in community-action agencies should help their clients obtain abortions and, moreover, should oppose state laws that restricted abortions (*Congressional Quarterly Almanac* 1973, 581–85). The final language of the Legal Service Corporation Act of 1974 reads as follows:

> No funds made available by the Corporation under this subchapter, either by grant or contract, may be used ... to provide legal assistance with respect to

any proceeding or litigation which seeks to procure a nontherapeutic abortion or to compel any individual or institution to perform an abortion, or assist in the performance of an abortion, or provide facilities for the performance of an abortion, contrary to the religious beliefs or moral convictions of such individual or institution.

Although this language looks tightly written, pro-life legislators complained that the law was being circumvented. In 1980 Senate conservatives Jesse Helms (R-North Carolina), Strom Thurmond (R-South Carolina), and Gordon J. Humphrey (R-New Hampshire) alleged that LSC attorneys were illegally lobbying for abortions, with the result that the Senate passed restrictions to prohibit the LSC from taking on nontherapeutic abortion cases (Cohodas 1980). After Ronald Reagan was inaugurated as president, his preference was to kill the LSC outright and fund such programs from discretionary block grants to the states. Senator Hatch, who supported this move, charged, "Though I have supported legal services in the vain hope they will concentrate on really helping the poor, personally I have come to the conclusion that they will never do that." He also alleged that legal-aid lawyers spent "millions of dollars in what we call lawyer activism for liberal social programs instead of working for the common needs of the poor" (quoted in Cohodas 1981, 529). However, the prestigious American Bar Association rallied to support the beleaguered LSC, and even some GOP representatives refused to gut its funding entirely. Four years later Congress did add an amendment to an appropriations bill for the Departments of Commerce, Justice, and State as well as the federal judiciary that prohibited the LSC from using its funds for any abortion litigation whatsoever (Pagel 1989).

The U.S. Civil Rights Commission was created by the Civil Rights Act of 1957 to be a watchdog for civil rights progress in the country, and presidents have appointed to the commission liberal-leaning members who sometimes have been quite outspoken in their civil rights advocacy. In 1978 Congress approved Public Law 95-444, which in addition to extending the life of the commission, forbade it from collecting and analyzing abortion laws and policies of government. The antiabortion rider offered by Representative David C. Treen (R-Louisiana) stated: "Nothing in this or any other Act shall be construed as authorizing the Commission, its Advisory Committees, or any person under its supervision or control to appraise, or to study and collect information about, laws and policies of the Federal Government, or any other government authority in the United States, with respect to abortion."

What triggered the congressional backlash was an April 1975 report by the commission entitled "Constitutional Aspects of the Right to Limit

Childbearing." Although this was the only study on abortion the commission conducted in its twenty-one-year existence, nonetheless opponents argued that the commission had overreached its jurisdiction in dealing with this subject. The viewpoint of the commission was that because minority women very often are poor, abortion directly involves their rights to equal protection under the Constitution. Representative Treen was unimpressed, countering that abortion "is not a civil rights matter" and, furthermore, that "no one denies that, unfortunately, minorities are disproportionately represented among the poor. But that analysis surely does not authorize the commission to appraise every law . . . that may impact poor persons." He also charged that the commission "does not have the mission of advising Congress that it must spend public funds on services of one sort or another for the poor, because not to do so denies 'equal protection' to racial and ethnic minorities" (*Congressional Record* 1978). His arguments carried the day. The House of Representatives approved his amendment 234–131, and given the strength of that margin, House conferees told the Senate that no final legislation would be enacted unless this antiabortion rider was upheld. It was.

The commission ran into trouble again in 1989, this time because of conservative advocacy by members who had been appointed by Presidents Reagan and Bush. Through his appointments of African-Americans Clarence Pendleton, the first chairman under Reagan, and later William B. Allen, Reagan fundamentally moved the commission away from its historical mission. Reagan's appointees, especially the outspoken Pendleton, were opposed to affirmative action, comparable worth pay equity for women, and abortion. On this occasion, during the Bush administration, Representative Edwards (D-California), a liberal, tried to bar Allen from investigating allegations of abusive behavior by police officers who had to constrain antiabortion demonstrators.

Canada: Abortion and Bureaucracy

Abortion has not tainted the workings of the Canadian bureaucracy because there public administration is more removed from political intrusions. Yet there also may be a normative agenda for the Canadian bureaucracy more important than single issues such as abortion: For example, there has been heightened concern to attract more francophones to enter the civil service (Jackson and Jackson 1994, 393–94), undoubtedly as another method of dealing with the perennial problem of national unity, just as both prime ministers who have led Canada since 1984 (Brian Mulroney and Jean Chrétien) resided in Quebec Province (though Kim Campbell, who succeeded Mulroney from June to November 1993 so that Campbell could head the Progressive Conservatives during their reelection campaign, was from British Columbia). Also, there might well be an ideological agenda among careerists in the Canadian bureaucracy insofar as the Liberal Party held power for all except about seven years between 1935 and 1984; in addition, federal civil servants in 1966 created a Public Service Alliance of Canada (Hodgetts 1973, 325), which, as one of the largest unions in the country, has enrolled the majority of Canadian civil servants as members.

The collective responsibility of the cabinet to the prime minister in a parliamentary government does extend to the permanent government, and though the political appointments available to the prime minister seem substantial, there are constraints on those appointment powers.

> The most significant for policy are of course the cabinet minister jobs with department portfolios. The Prime Minister also appoints ministers' top public service counterparts, the deputy heads and associate deputy heads of departments and important agencies. But it can be noted that the short list for the deputy head jobs is normally heavily dominated if not exclusively made up of career civil servants who have made their whole careers in the merit public service regulated under the Public Service Employment Act. To make these appointments, the Prime Minister is advised by the Clerk of the Privy Council, who is deputy head of the Privy Council Office, which is effectively the cabinet secretariat. This Office is designated as a department, with the Prime Minister as the responsible minister. (The Prime Minister appoints the Clerk, but not the establishment of this organisation, nor the officials of the other central support agencies—only the personnel of the Prime Minister's Office and ministers' offices are party workers.) (Sutherland 1995b, 10)

Total appointments by the prime minister are about three thousand, a large number even in comparison to the United States, but, says Sutherland (1995b, 11), "the thing that is striking is that the appointments are concentrated in two locations: the peak leadership provided by political appointments in policy roles, and a great mass of patronage appointments in the quasi-legal and quasi-business areas, *well outside the policy-making centre of government*" (emphasis ended).

Canadian prime ministers' efforts to control the civil service are not unique, of course. President Nixon ranked the bureaucracy at the top of his enemies list, and evidence suggests that he inherited a civil service whose public policy views reflected years of liberal and Democratic Party control (Aberbach and Rockman 1995). Thus Nixon launched his "administrative presidency" strategy (Nathan 1975), which emphasized formal reorganization of governmental apparatus. Much more effective was Ronald Reagan's strategy of appointing ideologically pure "Reaganites" to policymaking positions (Nathan 1983). Indeed, Savoie calls our attention to how the Republicans under Reagan, the British Tories under Margaret Thatcher, and Mulroney's Progressive Conservatives all tried to take charge of the state cadre, but in somewhat different ways:

> The politics-administration dichotomy also pressed home the belief that career civil servants should not be involved with policy. All three leaders took concrete steps to weaken the policy role traditionally played by career officials. Thatcher sought to centralize policy advice in her own office; Reagan went further than any president in fifty years in making sure that appointees and even senior career officials shared his political views; and Mulroney appointed political and policy "commissars" to all ministerial offices. Officials in the three countries report that, particularly in their first years in office, Thatcher, Reagan, and Mulroney made clear that the officials' policy roles and advice were not welcomed. (Savoie 1994, 297)

Moving beyond such generalized strategies for penetrating the state apparatus, the specific focus here is to assess what impact the Mulroney government—as compared to the Reagan administration—had on abortion policy specifically. A point of comparison is the operations of the National Action Committee on the Status of Women (NAC), Canada's most visible and prestigious group advocate of women's rights in Canada, and the Canadian Advisory Council on the Status of Women (CACSW). Here a case study is offered to assess the role of NAC and CACSW as abortion advocates during a time when the government was controlled first by the Liberals, then by Progressive Conservatives, and today again by the Liberals. Specifically, the question is whether the Mulroney government tried to politicize the CACSW and extend its reach to the NAC in ways comparable to what President Reagan did regarding the U.S. Civil Rights Commission and other agencies with liberal clientele groups.

In the United States women do not have a special advocate to monitor equal rights for women and the equity relationships between women and men. The Equal Employment Opportunity Commission (EEOC) receives complaints about bias in the workplace against women and other minorities but is not an advocacy group exclusively devoted to the feminist agenda. The Legal Services Corporation is charged with providing attorney services to the poor, not poor women specifically, which leaves the U.S. Civil Rights Commission as a potentially strong advocate for women's rights except that it, too, has a larger mandate than gender-specific violations of civil rights. All three of these agencies were moved to the right by Reagan appointees (conservative Supreme Court justice Clarence Thomas, whose sexual harassment of Anita Hill was alleged during his emotionally charged confirmation hearings, had previously been appointed director of the EEOC by President Reagan). Beyond that, as already shown, conservatives in Congress also acted to limit abortion advocacy by the LSC and the U.S. Civil Rights Commission.

In Canada, the beginnings of NAC go back to 1967, when two groups of professional and business women, the Canadian Federation of University Women and the Federation of Business and Professional Women's Clubs—worked alongside the only woman member of the Liberal cabinet, Judy LaMarsh, to lobby for creation of the Royal Commission on the Status of Women, which "moved the liberal feminist project beyond its own theory and firmly entrenched a focus among anglophone Canadian groups on the federal government as the protector of their interests" (Phillips 1991, 763). Its 1970 report made several recommendations, including the creation of a watchdog umbrella organization, the National Action Committee on the Status of Women, which came into being in 1972—to oversee progress on implementing the Royal Commission's 167 recommendations. NAC is the largest and most diverse coalition of women's groups.

In 1973 another recommendation from the Royal Commission was implemented, the establishment of the Canadian Advisory Council on the Status of Women "as an independent organization funded by the federal government" and granted "legal status" to pursue its mandate, namely "(a) to bring before the government and the public matters of interest and concern to women; and (b) to advise the Minister on such matters relating to the status of women as the Minister may refer to the Council for its consideration or as the Council may deem appropriate." The CACSW is composed of no more than thirty members appointed by the federal cabinet, of which twenty-seven are part-time members appointed for three-year terms to collectively "represent the regional, cultural, racial, and ethnic diversity of Canada as well as both official languages" plus a full-time president and two vice presidents (Canadian Advisory Council on the Status of Women 1992–1993, 4). In other words, a mechanism to defend women's interests was created through a quasi-public interest group (which receives federal funds) and a governmental entity appointed by and responsible to the government. How has the abortion debate impinged upon the workings of these two organizations since the early 1970s?

Canadian Advisory Council on the Status of Women

CACSW does not regard abortion as a legitimate means of family planning, but since 1973 it has expressed its concern about the "responsibility of women to decide whether and when to have children" and has "formally recommended to the [Liberal] Government that abortion be removed from the Criminal Code" insofar as "the current law on abortion is not working, is unjust, and must be changed" (National Advisory Council on the Status of Women 1975–1976, 17). It was not alone in voicing that complaint, because Dr. Bette Stephenson, president of the Canadian Medical Association charged in January 1975 that Justice Minister Otto Lang should be removed from office for allowing his personal views to affect his ministry's stand on abortion. Lang had applied a strict interpretation to the language of the 1969 abortion law, whereas organized medicine had adopted a more liberal stance. According to Stephenson, "We have [recommended], and [will] continue to recommend major changes in the law, but to no avail. The federal government consistently refuses the long promised parliamentary review and a frequently promised parliamentary debate on abortion" (*Facts on File World News Digest* 1975, 28B1).

The Trudeau government took action, and the CACSW was pleased with the 1977 Badgley Committee investigation of abortion implementation because its "findings coincided with CACSW's belief that Canadian women do not have equal access to therapeutic abortion" (National Advisory Council on the Status of Women 1976–1977, 6). In the year before the Liberals lost power, CACSW took notice of prosecutorial efforts to prevent Morgentaler from opening abortion clinics. It urged "provincial Ministers of Health and the Minister of National Health and Welfare, responsible for the Yukon and the Northwest Territories, to approve publicly-funded free-standing reproductive health clinics for the purposes of section 251 of the Criminal Code of Canada" and, furthermore, found "unacceptable the criminal prosecution of individual staff members of reproductive health clinics in Winnipeg and Toronto" (National Advisory Council on the Status of Women 1983–1984, 15–16).

In March 1988, after the Canadian Supreme Court vindicated Morgentaler, the CACSW adopted a far-reaching resolution. After noting that the Supreme Court of Canada had struck down Section 251 of the Criminal Code on January 28, 1988, and that "access to reproductive health services, including abortion, is inequitable across the country," the CACSW advocated a set of "reproductive health principles" that declared:

> 1. Reproductive choice is an equality issue. In our society, women become pregnant, and bear and raise children under conditions of inequality. Partial remedies for these inequities include: increased child care facilities; economic self-sufficiency for women; research to develop safe methods of contraception; access to a full range of reproductive health services; development of information, resources and services to support family planning and birth control; sex education; and access to abortion.

2. *A pregnant woman has the right to determine the best medical treatment for herself or the foetus she is carrying, in consultation with advisers of her choice and without intervention or obstruction.* No woman should be penalized for making a decision which she believes furthers her physical and mental health, the health of her children, the health of her family as a whole, or the health of any foetus she is carrying.

3. A pregnant woman who has made the decision to have an abortion should have access to abortion services at the earliest opportunity, and should not be forced into a late term abortion or denied access altogether by reason of obstructive diagnostic procedures and practices, financial impediments, geographical location or legal or quasi-legal proceedings. Reproductive health services and abortion must be available to women equitably throughout Canada, and funded completely by provincial health insurance plans, in keeping with the principles of universality, accessibility and comprehensiveness as stated in the Canada Health Act.

4. The Criminal Code and provincial regulation of medical standards and practitioners continue to provide adequate protection against malpractice and unqualified practitioners, and to ensure that the best medical practice under the circumstances is observed. *No further legislation is necessary or warranted.* (Canadian Advisory Council on the Status of Women 1987–1988, 20; emphasis added)

This statement, which couched the abortion decision in purely "medical" and "health" terms, demanded that access be provided under the Canada Health Act. No references were made to a right to choose abortion *independent* of health care considerations for the woman, her family, and the fetus, so obviously CACSW was promoting abortion services as an equity issue rather than as symbolic of feminism. It was a reasonable approach given the dominance of medicalized rhetoric over abortion policy, but the fact that the CACSW warned that no new abortion legislation was needed would mean that these Mulroney appointees would have to make a judgment when the government introduced Bill C-43.

CACSW made its views known to the House of Commons and the Canadian Senate. To Parliament, it repeated its opinion that abortion was a health issue and that women must be allowed to make informed and rational decisions about their health, that abortions ought to be covered by the Canada Health Act, that additional legislation was not necessary, and that because reproductive choice was an equality issue such services must be available to women equitably throughout the country (Canadian Advisory Council on the Status of Women 1988–1989, 22; 1989–1990, 23). When Bill C-43 cleared the House of Commons, CACSW focused on the Senate deliberations. Here the council echoed similar themes—that pending legislation reflected a lack of respect for women, that women ought to have the right to make decisions about their own bodies, and that no criminal legislation was necessary. It also commissioned an outside, independent counsel to provide a legal opinion, which argued that Bill C-43 was unconstitutional and infringed on the freedom of women and their physicians and, in addition, that the letter sent by Attorney General Kim Campbell to physicians (aimed at reassuring the doctors) had, in fact, misrepresented and downplayed the negative impacts of recriminalizing abortion. To the contrary, the legal opinion led CACSW to argue that Bill C-43 would permit criminal suits against women and their physicians. At base, however, CACSW emphasized that abortion was a health issue, not a legal issue (Canadian Advisory Council on the Status of Women 1990–1991, 40).

The fact that CACSW reported to and was accountable to the government did not prevent it from taking a strong and unequivocal stand against the government position. Such an action would have been highly improbable in the United States had a like scenario developed during the Reagan administration. At the outset, without much doubt, President Reagan would have replaced avowedly pro-choice or feminist members with his own kindred spirits. The ultimate irony is that the CACSW, while lasting through the Mulroney era without compromising its firm advocacy of abortion, did not survive the beginning of the newly elected Liberal government under Prime Minister Jean Chrétien. Shortly after his election, Chrétien reduced the status of the women's portfolio by designating Sheila Finestone as secretary of state for the status of women, rather than attaching this portfolio to a cabinet minister, as had been the custom—meaning that Finestone could not automatically attend cabinet meetings but had to request permission to do so. Then on March 14, 1994, Finestone announced several organizational changes, including abolishing CACSW and shifting its research and information functions to an existing agency, Status of Women Canada (O'Neil and Sutherland 1996).

National Action Committee on the Status of Women

The decision by Secretary of State Sheila Finestone to terminate CACSW came less than a week after International Women's Day, and women's groups immediately protested the action. "Many of NAC's supporters were among those who called for the creation of a Council to monitor and advise the government," said NAC president Sunerea Thobani, "and we continue to support it." NAC was concerned about the loss of CACSW's research and monitoring capabilities and warned that "as a result of the decision to fold the Council into Status of Women Canada, responsibility for ensuring that women's rights are safeguarded is now in the hands of the very people whose government's policies endanger those rights" (*Action Now!* 1995a). NAC also raised the alarm about Liberal cutbacks of $7 billion over three years in social spending and the elimination of 45,000 public sector jobs (*Action Now!* 1995b). These actions must have been shocking, since NAC had complained regularly that too few federal dollars were being allocated to women's advocacy groups.

In opposition to NAC, a group called R.E.A.L. Women was founded in 1983. It was pro-life and pro-family and thus was not interconnected with Canadian feminist groups (Phillips 1991, 765). Its focus on traditional values and distance from feminist orthodoxy explain why NAC and its allies were so opposed to the Mulroney government's allocation of funds to it through the Women's Program under the secretary of state for the status of women. This program was established in 1973 to fund groups that work for the equality of women.

In 1985 the Campaign Life Coalition asked that this funding program be disbanded, reportedly because *"a careful analysis of these grants indicates that the latter has resulted in a network across the country of women's centres and other radical feminist organizations, which serve as 'agents for change' to further the pro-abortion, anti-family, radical feminist philosophy and goals"* (*Action Bulletin Action* 1985). A year later the opposition changed its tactics. A House of Commons Standing Committee was authorized to report on the programs of the women's portfolio, including the Women's Program. During the annual lobbying by R.E.A.L. Women in Ottawa before the major parties in December 1986, a spokesperson said that "we have grave doubts of the largess of Secretary of State. That money should be going to people who need it more than we do" but "if the government funds then we would like to have an *equal* share" (*Action* 1987). Then NAC made an appearance before the standing committee to explain why R.E.A.L. Women's request for funding was opposed by most women's organizations (*Action* 1987). In 1991 NAC charged that "in our meetings with Tory Ministers and backbenchers we have experienced blatant attempts to single out NAC and to encourage other groups to separate themselves from NAC in order to secure their own funding." Reacting to a $75 million cutback in public funding for "public interest" groups in the upcoming federal budget, NAC recalled that, "as opposed to last year, when cuts to women's and aboriginal groups were at least made public in the budget, this one is being drawn out over several months in private negotiations. This process is fully intended to divide and conquer public interest and advocacy groups" (*Action Now!* 1991).

Federal funds had been the primary source of operating revenues for NAC since its establishment in 1972. In 1984 NAC had about 280 affiliated groups, and by 1986 the federal government accounted for three-fifths of its $680,000 annual budget (Vickers, Rankin, and Appelle 1993, 139, 141). When Mulroney was reelected in 1988, NAC claimed to represent 586 organizations whose membership totaled five million (though such a two-tiered system means that the views of NAC leaders might not necessarily represent every member of those affiliated groups). Yet funding was not increased. In fact, NAC's dependence on government largesse, unlike in the United States where interest groups are funded by their memberships, made the organization vulnerable to political leverage. Says Bashevkin (1994, 280), "The Canadian federal government therefore possessed a direct means of limiting feminist policy advocacy that was not available to national governments in the United States or Britain. The Mulroney government exercised this option in a series of budgetary decisions that reduced NAC's federal funding by 50 percent between 1988 and 1992" (see also Bashevkin 1989).

If the purpose behind the Mulroney government's cutbacks was to silence NAC, the tactic certainly did not work with respect to abortion advocacy. NAC's 1990 testimony before Parliament on Bill C-43 (House of Commons 1990) was stridently feminist. It began by declaring that "NAC believes that every woman has the fundamental right to control her own body, free from the coercion of government and courts, employer, doctor, church, family, or lover. The decision of whether or not to bear a child has a unique and profound impact on a woman's life. Women's control of their reproduction is intimately connected with their control of their lives. *Without the fundamental democratic right to decide if and when to have children, women will never achieve equality"* (emphasis in original) (House of Commons 1990, issue 5, appendix 43/6). NAC proceeded to argue that abortion symbolized the essence of feminism and thus was nonnegotiable:

> The battle over abortion rights has become the cutting edge in the movement for women's equality. Although most of the forces opposed to abortion claim that their primary concern is protection of the foetus, the effect of their agenda will be to turn the clock back to the days when women were barefoot, pregnant and in the kitchen. In fact, many of the same groups who oppose abortion also oppose most birth control measures and sex education. On this issue, there is no compromise. Women will never turn back from our long march to freedom and equality. That is why NAC sees the abortion issue as central to our very existence as a national feminist organization. (House of Commons 1990, issue 5, appendix 43/6)

Then began a point-by-point rebuttal of the legislation: that Bill C-43 would make women criminals, that it would deny abortions to healthy women, that it would further erode access to abortion services, that it would provide for choice for doctors but not for women, and that the proposed law was no compromise. Its argument concluded with its recommendations for public policy. A nationwide abortion policy would "compel reluctant provincial governments to provide adequate abortion services"; accessibility to abortions should be "standardized across the country"; and given the reality that in many places hospitals cannot meet the demand for abortion services, "free-standing, publicly-funded clinics should be established."

RU-486 in Canada

During the late 1980s, when the French manufacturer of RU-486 suspended distribution of the drug in France because of mounting protests by antiabortion organizations, the French government intervened and ordered Roussel-Uclaf to resume production "in the interest of public health"; the company agreed to do so (Wickens 1988). At that time RU-486 was not available in Canada because the manufacturer had not applied to federal authorities for a license. In mid-1992, to expedite the matter, according to Ontario health minister Frances Lankin, provincial health ministers asked the federal health minister, Benoît Bouchard, to contact Roussel-Uclaf and "encourage it to seek permission to distribute the drug in Canada." A spokesperson for Bouchard responded by saying that so far they had "not received an application by the company to begin approval testing of the pill" and further "stressed that RU-486 would have to follow the same approvals procedure as that required for all drugs entering the Canadian market," which could take "18 months to two years before studies could be completed and the pill could be marketed" (*Abortion Report* 1992). To "ease the company's fears," said Lankin, the government could "assure the company that in this country there are no criminal laws . . . with respect to abortion and that it is an issue of delivery of health care and that every province is in the business of delivering safe, effective abortions in this country." A key consideration, according to Lankin, was that RU-486 "could help hard-pressed provincial health ministries save money" because using the drug is "less expensive than an abortion procedure by a doctor in either a hospital or a free-standing clinic" (*Abortion Report* 1992).

Britain already had approved RU-486 for domestic use, and a promising development (though one of limited impact) was announced there in early 1994. The Marie Stopes Health Clinic in London gained permission from the British government to provide RU-486 to nonresident women, including

Canadians. Canadian abortion rights advocates praised the decision. "This is wonderful news," said Bonnie Johnson, executive director of the Planned Parenthood Federation of Canada, which had been urging the French manufacturer to seek approval in Canada. "The Canadian government isn't the problem here, it's Roussel-Uclaf. The fact that Canadian women can now obtain it in Britain is really going to open things up." In response, a Department of Health spokesperson, JoAnne Ford, said that Ottawa would not stop women from traveling abroad for treatment with RU-486. "If Canadians seek treatment outside the country," she said, "that's up to them" (*Maclean's* 1994, 33).

Summary

A recent study of the administrations of British prime minister Margaret Thatcher, U.S. president Ronald Reagan, and Canadian prime minister Brian Mulroney generally argues that Mulroney was least successful among the three in applying an administrative strategy to achieve neoconservative objectives (Savoie 1994), meaning that the Canadian permanent government was able to withstand politicization better than its English or American counterparts. Why so? Because "political will works. More than anything else, political will works in reforming the civil service. Thatcher had it, Reagan had some at least early on, and Mulroney had not much" (Savoie 1994, 326). Mulroney's failure was a failure of his game plan:

> The Mulroney government was also very active, unveiling one reform measure after another, virtually from the day it assumed office. The government . . . added a new senior level (a partisan policy position in each ministerial office), reorganized the economic-development departments, scrapped the government's budget-making process, established a series of new cabinet committees and SOAs [special operating agencies], unveiled PS 2000 [Public Service 2000, a reform initiative], and introduced the shared-management agenda approach that appears to be designed to improve relations between line departments and central agencies. Despite the appearance of activity, however, Mulroney's reforms have not been successful, nor have they lived up to expectations. (Savoie 1994, 238)

Tied to political will is another consideration—that Mulroney may have been less effective precisely because Thatcher and Reagan were ideologues when, in fact, Brian Mulroney was a "broker" politician looking to cut deals. Usually political brokers are not enthralled with the zero-sum, non-negotiable aspects of policymaking associated with the abortion conflict. Nor can we forget that the 1988 *Morgentaler* ruling forced abortion onto the Canadian government's agenda, whereas President Reagan carried into office a sustained antipathy to legalized abortion generally and the *Roe* (1973) decision specifically. Bashevkin sees major differences in the Reagan and Mulroney policy agendas:

> By way of contrast, Canadian neo-conservatism under Brian Mulroney was less socially driven than its US variant in the same period. The Mulroney government drew in many diverse players.... Compared with the Reagan coalition in the Republican Party, the Mulroney organization contained a relatively weak anti-feminist presence, in part because this phenomenon was less widespread in Canada than the United States. Mulroney's internal party coalition required a pragmatic approach to governing; as a brokerage politician, he tended to place greater emphasis on questions of "national unity" and "continental cooperation," where caucus consensus could be gained, than on issues of social policy like abortion where internal division was virtually assured. (Bashevkin 1994, 279)

To illustrate, until the 1980s only two women occupied high positions in any Canadian government, but in 1988 under Mulroney "women were 23 percent of all deputy ministers—for seven individuals. In fact, the increase in the numbers of elite women represents an exercise in political will, because these are Order-In-Council [patronage] appointments" (O'Neil and Sutherland 1996). Since members of CACSW were appointed by the Mulroney government, and given that the record shows CACSW did not relent on its strong pro-choice advocacy, one can only conclude that the prime minister did not seek to implement a pro-life agenda. The fact that Mulroney reduced funding for the NAC and began granting a public subsidy to antifeminist groups (Bashevkin 1994, 291), while criticized at the time, retrospectively can be partly attributed to the fiscal crisis of the state as much as political animus, given that CACSW was eliminated in late 1993 due to fiscal retrenchment by Liberal prime minister Chrétien.

In the United States, the impact of Reagan's administrative strategy across policy areas was uneven and depended as much upon circumstance as managerial fortitude. A detailed study of a relatively low-profile area of policy administration—public lands management—shows that dysfunctional consequences resulted from the competing and contradictory goals that the Reagan administration wished to achieve (Durant 1992). Even the most salient domain, macroeconomic policymaking, ultimately revealed the inherent contradictions of Reaganomics insofar as domestic budget cuts, military expansion, and deep reductions in income taxes did not achieve balanced budgets but instead generated triple-digit deficits (Frendreis and Tatalovich 1994). On his social agenda—certainly on abortion—this assessment suggests that the political penetration of the bureaucracy by Reagan appointees and the Reagan White House showed few deviations from the pro-life agenda. Where Reagan has been faulted by conservatives was his failure to include social causes in his *legislative* agenda rather than focusing so much on fiscal and budgetary priorities. It appears, however, that President Reagan used administrative (and judicial) arenas to promote his anti-abortion agenda (and other social priorities such as fighting crime and pornography) in order to satisfy conservatives and his pro-life constituency.

As a final thought, a clue to understanding why the United States allowed the abortion debate to degenerate into moral conflict may relate to the arrested development of the welfare bureaucracy under the Department of Health and Human Services. This thesis by Silverberg (1990) argues that in Western Europe medical professionals and health care ministries were able to co-opt abortion as a medical problem rather than let it evolve into a moral issue, and thus these countries were able to integrate abortion services into their existing systems of universal health benefits. That line of inquiry logically can be extended to Canada, and deserves closer scrutiny than can be attempted here, though my summary of the assertive pro-choice advocacy by feminist interests, through publicly sponsored CACSW (in league with the pressure group NAC), would imply indirectly that there was probably even less penetration of the federal health care apparatus by the Mulroney government. And by default, the specialized nature of health care delivery systems (coupled with strong support for legalized abortion by the Canadian Medical Association; see chapter 4) within a system where universal health care is widely expected to be an entitlement (although it is not legally one; see Dossetor 1994) means that bureaucratic decision making at the federal (though not necessarily at the provincial) level would lean heavily toward accepting abortions as a medical procedure.

7

Federalism and the Implementation Problem

The implementation of abortion policy depends upon the health care community, largely private in the United States but more public in Canada, and upon subnational authorities through the funding powers of states and provinces in addition to whatever medical regulations those jurisdictions can impose on the abortion procedure. There has been comparative research on state abortion policies and implementation effects in the United States, but with one notable exception (Brodie 1994), Canadian academics have not focused on the implementation problem. Research on that aspect has been done mainly by official governmental bodies, reform groups, or feminist organizations seeking to show how unfair and uneven existing abortion policy has been. This chapter offers a departure. First it reviews the research on implementation in the United States, then gives a statistical comparison of abortion rates and services in the United States and Canada, and finally discusses the legal resistance by states that culminated in the *Webster* (1989) ruling and the policy reaction of provinces to the *Morgentaler* (1988) decision.

Implementation Studies of U.S. Abortion Policy

There was no national policy on abortion in the United States until 1973, when the Supreme Court nullified both the original and reformed abortion laws in forty-six states and thus constitutionalized a right of abortion during the first trimester of pregnancy. However, the *Roe v. Wade* ruling left many unanswered questions about the extent of state regulation, whether abortion funding was mandatory, and how economic and political forces might structure the delivery system for abortion services. Some of these legal issues were addressed in subsequent litigation before the Supreme Court (see chapter 2), but the problem of access to abortion services has been left to the marketplace.

The effect of *Roe* on access to abortion services is complicated because potential implementers are not required to make abortion services available. *Roe* created choices: a constitutional right for women to choose abortion in the first trimester of pregnancy and a choice for doctors and hospitals to offer these services. But *Roe* and its progeny do *not* require that health care professionals perform abortions against their will; indeed, various federal and state laws safeguard a "right to conscience" by health care providers *not* to perform abortions. Thus hospitals and doctors can comply with *Roe* by accepting the decision as the law of the land yet still refuse to provide abortions. *Roe* does not provide an implementation strategy, leaving questions of compliance to hospitals and physicians. More than two decades after *Roe,* therefore, wide variations still exist in abortion rates and the availability of abortion services across the United States.

The logical way to provide abortions would be for hospitals to offer that service. Abortion services would utilize maternity facilities in hospitals, and many obstetrics-gynecology residency programs offer (though most do not require) training in abortion techniques. In 1985 it was determined that 72.2 percent of U.S. residency programs in obstetrics and gynecology included first-trimester abortion techniques, although only 22.6 percent made it routine training, whereas 49.6 percent made it optional. Moreover, the 27.8 percent of residency programs that offered no abortion training represented nearly a fourfold increase since 1976 in the percentage of hospital residency programs that declined to provide abortion training (Darney, Landy, MacPherson, and Sweet 1987, 160). Also, polls in 1985 reported that more than eight in ten obstetricians and gynecologists favored abortion under certain conditions, a percentage that was unchanged since 1971 (*Family Planning Perspectives* 1985b, 275). The fact that so many hospitals do not provide abortions signals that political factors are intruding.

Within one year of *Roe* a study by Brady and Kemp (1976; also Kemp, Carp, and Brady 1978) of hospitals in Harris County, Texas (the Houston Metropolitan area), found a movement toward implementation; policy changes were linked to occupancy rates and staff-bed ratios as well as to decision makers' attitudes about the Supreme Court and its abortion ruling. Similarly, Bond and Johnson (1982; also Johnson and Bond 1982; 1980) assessed the impact of *Roe* in 1979 based on a sample of hospitals in 150 randomly selected U.S. counties. They determined that "79.5% of the hospitals in communities perceived to favor abortion provide some type of abortion service, and 78.6% of hospitals in communities perceived to oppose abortion do not provide any type of abortion service" (Johnson and Bond 1982, 395). Thus community sentiment exerted an influence, albeit more indirect than direct, on decision-making processes by hospital authorities.

In retrospect, the finding by Brady and Kemp of a post-*Roe* liberalization of abortion policy was not representative of Texas or the nation, since it was based on hospitals in one of the country's largest metropolitan areas. Twelve years later Tatalovich and Daynes (1989, 83) found that 66.7 percent of hospitals in Houston with the capacity to do abortions did so, as against only 20.9 percent for the entire state of Texas, exemplifying the fact that there is an urban bias to the delivery of abortion services in the United States (see table 7.6).

Others have identified socioeconomic variables that may account for the differences in abortion rates over time and across states. For 1976 Hansen (1980) found that the strongest variables to predict the percentage of hospital abortion providers across the fifty states were the pre-*Roe* state abortion laws, Medicaid reimbursements for abortions done on indigent women, and a measure of legislative support in each state. The factors that best explained state abortion rates were metropolitanism and Medicaid reimbursements; legislative support and the pre-*Roe* state laws had minimal effects. Abortion rates depend upon abortion services, and recent analyses have affirmed that service delivery variables are key predictors of state abortion rates.

In her reanalysis for 1988, Hansen (1993b, 241) observes that "abortion rates are largely a function of urbanization and the availability of medical services." Wolpert and Rosenberg (1990, 14) found that "a one unit increase in the number of abortions performed by non-hospitals relative to the number of abortions performed by hospitals is associated with a 3.68 rise in the abortion rate," while Albritton and Wetstein (1991, 18) determined that "for every 1 percent increase in the proportion of hospitals offering abortion services, there is an increase of 3.46 in the number of abortions per 1000 live births." A geographical study of abortion rates for 1988 (Gober 1994) used supply variables, demand factors, and political conditions to assess their interactive effects. Overall, supply variables had the strongest impact on abortion rates, and because demand factors linked to "demographic attributes will change only slowly in the future," the "potential for more dramatic change lies in the two supply conditions of [Medicaid] FUNDING and [restrictive state] LAWS" (Gober 1994, 247). However, Gober used "supply" measures of abortion services, which did not account for actual abortion providers in each state.

Tatalovich and Strickland (1995) evaluated alternative delivery systems using political and environmental variables and found "that delivery system variables have greater impact on abortion rates than the pre-*Roe* legal codes, state regulations on abortions, or the socio-economic milieu of the states." What mattered most was the percentage of hospitals with the capacity to perform abortions that did indeed do them; they argued that this particular variable "operates as an indirect measure of the post-*Roe* political context of each state," which "is probably gauging the degree of public acceptance and political support for legalized abortions in each state." As to what explains the proportions of those hospitals in each state, the pre-*Roe* state abortion laws were a stronger predictor than socioeconomic conditions, suggesting that "the other 32 states with anti-abortion statutes at the time of *Roe* have yet to accommodate the high court by fostering a political environment where abortion providers are sufficient to meet the unmet demand for abortions in those areas."

Comparisons Between Canada and the United States

This analysis focuses on the period that followed a major policy change liberalizing access to abortion in both countries—the 1969 reforms in Canada and the 1973 landmark decision in the United States—and before a second phase that promised even greater access in Canada, due to the *Morgentaler* (1988) ruling, but more restrictive policies in the United States, given that the Supreme Court in *Webster* (1989) paved the way for greater state regulation of abortion.

Past statistics on abortion rates and abortion providers indicate unlike developments in the two countries, but by the end of the 1980s there was greater convergence. Trend data on total abortions and abortion rates show the patterns for both nations (table 7.1). Just two years after *Roe* the number of abortions performed yearly in the United States reached the 1 million mark, and this figure has stabilized at about 1.5 million since 1980. In Canada the number has yet to reach one-fifteenth of the U.S. total, although Canada has roughly one-tenth the population of the United States. This disparity is shown by the abortion rate, which as late as 1988 was close to two and a half times greater in the United States compared to Canada.

Canadian law originally mandated that abortions be done only in hospitals, but given the refusal of earlier juries to convict Morgentaler for his clinic operations in Quebec, he was able to operate freely since 1976, and Quebec reported those clinic abortions beginning in 1978. For 1988, the U.S. abortion rate of 27.3 per 1,000 women ages 15–44 was more than double the Canadian rate of 12.6, but a substantial jump in the Canadian rate occurred in 1990 (to 14.6) following the *Morgentaler* (1988) case, which reflects the opening of other clinics across the country. The total of

Table 7.1

Abortions and Abortion Rates in the United States and Canada

| | Canada | | | | United States | | | |
| | Hospital | | Nonhospital | | Hospital | | Nonhospital | |
Year	Number	%	%	Rate*	Number (in thousands)	%	%	Rate*
1970	11,152†	100		6.6				
1971	37,232	100		9.9				
1972	45,426	100		10.4				
1973	48,720	100		10.8	744.6	52	48	16.3
1974	52,435	100		10.4	898.6	47	53	19.3
1975	53,705	100		11.2	1,034.2	40	60	21.7
1976	58,712	100		11.4	1,179.3	35	65	24.2
1977	59,864	100		11.8	1,316.7	30	70	26.4
1978	66,710	96	3.9‡	12.3	1,409.6	25	75	27.7
1979	69,745	95	5.2	12.3	1,497.7	23	77	28.8
1980	72,099	94	6.5	12.2	1,553.9	22	78	29.3
1981	71,911	94	5.9	12.3	1,577.3	19	81	29.3
1982	75,071	94	6.0	11.6	1,573.9	18	82	28.8
1983	69,368	95	5.2	11.4	—			
1984	69,449	95	5.1	11.4	1,577.2	14	88	28.1
1985	69,216	95	5.4	11.3	1,588.6	13	87	28.0
1986	69,572	96.2	3.8	11.2	—			
1987	70,023	94.7	5.3	11.3	1,559.1	11	89	26.8
1988	72,693	93.6	6.4	11.6	1,590.8	10	90	27.3
1989	79,315	91.1	8.9	12.6	—			
1990	92,901	78.2	21.8	14.6	—			
1991	95,059	75.4	24.6	14.7	1,556.5	7	93	26.3
1992	100,497	70.6	29.4	14.9	1,528.9	7	93	25.9

Sources: Reprinted, with permission, from Donley T. Studlar and Raymond Tatalovich, "Abortion Policy in the United States and Canada: Do Institutions Matter?" in Marianne Githens and Dorothy McBride Stetson, eds., *Abortion Politics: Public Policy in Cross Cultural Perspective* (New York: Routledge, 1996). *Data for Canada:* Statistics Canada, *Therapeutic Abortions, 1992,* p. 15, table 10. *Data for the United States:* Total number of abortions: Stanley K. Henshaw and Jennifer Van Vort, "Abortion Services in the United States, 1991 and 1992," *Family Planning Perspectives* 26 (May/June 1994), p. 101, table 1; Distributions between hospitals/nonhospitals: for 1973–1982, Maureen Muldoon, *The Abortion Debate in the United States and Canada: A Source Book* (New York: Garland Publishing, 1991), p. 12, table 4; for 1983–1986, Stanley K. Henshaw and Jennifer Van Vort, eds., *Abortion Factbook, 1992 Edition* (New York: Alan Guttmacher Institute, 1992), table 6; for 1991 and 1992, directly from Alan Guttmacher Institute.

*The number of abortions per 1,000 females ages 15–44 years.

†Based on the total number of abortions, the percentage done in clinics was derived and the remainder was attributed to hospitals, although a number of abortions were done on Canadian residents in the United States with no indication how many were clinic or hospital procedures. The number of abortions done on Canadian women in the United States was over 6,000 in 1971 but generally fell since then; fewer than 3,000 were reported in 13 of the 22 years.

‡For 1981–1989 only Quebec reported clinic abortions; later data reflect clinic abortions in Newfoundland, Nova Scotia, Quebec, Ontario, Manitoba, and British Columbia (for 1990) and also Alberta (for 1991 and 1992).

21,443 clinic abortions for 1990 was distributed among six provinces (Statistics Canada 1991, 28): Newfoundland (63), Nova Scotia (81), Quebec (8,919), Ontario (10,200), Manitoba (1,051), and British Columbia (1,129).

The greater access to abortion clinics, particularly in Ontario, has caused the abortion rate to increase, and those nonhospital services also brought about a shift in the delivery system. In 1990 clinics accounted for 22 percent of total abortions, up from only 9 percent in 1989. These trends, if they continue, would mean that the demand for abortions and the supply of abortion services will begin approximating the situation in the United States.

Has the unequal distribution of abortion services across the fifty U.S. states—where, according to pro-choice critics, "responsible response has not been forthcoming from the mainstream of American medicine in the years since the Court's [*Roe*] ruling" (Jaffe, Lindheim, and Lee 1981, 31–32)—been experienced in Canada? In the United States nonhospital providers have long accounted for the vast majority of abortions. In 1992 hospitals represented 36 percent of abortion providers but performed only 7 percent of all abortions (Henshaw and Van Vort 1994, 106); specialized abortion clinics (19 percent of providers) performed 69 percent of all abortions, other clinics (19 percent of providers) did 20 percent, and 4 percent of all pregnancies were terminated in physicians' offices (which accounted for 27 percent of all providers). With one in six U.S. hospitals doing abortions in 1992, as compared to nearly one in four in Canada (table 7.2), and with a record high of 84 percent of U.S. counties having *no* abortion provider (Henshaw and Van Vort 1994, 105), lack of ready access to those services would suggest that the unmet demand for abortions in the United States may not be satisfied for years to come.

Morgentaler brought to the attention of the Canadian justices the fact that the 1969 law failed to provide access to abortion services. But this situation was not new. A decade earlier the Committee on the Operation of the Abortion Law (1977, 27), appointed by the Privy Council on September 29, 1975, "to determine whether the procedure provided in the Criminal Code for obtaining therapeutic abortions is operating equitably across Canada," issued a five hundred-page report. Its analysis of the distribution and availability of services led the committee to conclude "that the procedure provided in the Criminal Code for obtaining therapeutic abortion is in practice illusory for many Canadian women" (Committee on the Operation of the Abortion Law 1977, 141). It explained:

> Coupled with the personal decisions of obstetrician-gynaecologists, half of whom (48.9 percent) in eight provinces did not do the abortion procedure in 1974–75, the combined effects of the distribution of eligible hospitals, the

Table 7.2

Percentage of U.S. and Canadian Hospitals with Abortion Capacity that Provide Abortion Services, 1971–1992

Year	United States			Canada		
	Abortion Capacity (N)	Abortion Services		Abortion Capacity (N)	Abortion Services	
		N	%		N	%
1971				862	143	16.6
1972				861	247	28.7
1973				867	261	30.1
1974				862	259	30.1
1975	5875	1629	27.7	862	274	31.8
1976	5857	1695	31.4	861	271	31.5
1977	5881	1654	28.1	855	265	31.0
1978	5851	1626	27.8	856	261	30.5
1979	5842	1526	26.1	863	270	31.3
1980	5830	1504	25.8	862	269	31.2
1981	5813	NA		861	267	31.0
1982	5801	1405	24.2	860	261	30.4
1983	5783	NA		846*	257	30.0
1984	5759	NA		846*	249	29.4
1985	5732	1191	20.8	846*	250	29.6
1986	5678	NA		843*	254	30.0
1987	5611	NA		843*	NA	
1988	5533	1040	18.8	840*	NA	
1989	5455	NA		840*	NA	
1990	5384	NA		835*	191†	22.9
1991	5342	NA		842*	NA	
1992	5292	855	16.2	833*	NA	

Sources: Reproduced, with permission, from Donley T. Studlar and Raymond Tatalovich, "Abortion Policy in the United States and Canada: Do Institutions Matter?" in Marianne Githens and Dorothy McBride Stetson, eds., *Abortion Politics: Public Policy in Cross Cultural Perspective* (New York: Routledge, 1996). *Data for U.S. Abortion Capacity:* American Hospital Association, *American Hospital Association Hospital Statistics, 1993–94 Edition* (Chicago: American Hospital Association, 1993), table 1, p. 7. This statistic, used by the Alan Guttmacher Institute as the universe of hospitals with capacity to do abortions, is based on those reporting to the AHA that they are "community hospitals," which includes all nongovernmental, not-for-profit, and investor-owned hospitals, as well as state and local government hospitals.

Data for U.S. Abortion Services: Alan Guttmacher Institute, New York City. The number of hospitals is based on its survey of known abortion providers. The surveys were done irregularly after 1980, so this statistic is not available for 1981, 1983, 1984, 1986, 1987, 1988, 1990, and 1991.

(continued)

Table 7.2 *(continued)*

Data for Canadian Abortion Capacity and Abortion Services: Statistics Canada, Institutional Care Statistics Section, *Some Facts About Therapeutic Abortions in Canada, 1970–1982* (October 1984), p. 20. The statistics since 1983 (*) were obtained directly from Statistics Canada and reflect the fiscal year (April 1 to March 31) rather than the calendar year. Hospitals performing abortions are those reporting therapeutic abortion committees and those with "capacity" are "public general hospitals" and include voluntary, provincial, and municipal (not-for-profit) hospitals that usually have obstetrics-gynecology and medical-surgical units. Incomplete 1990 (†) data were collected by this author directly from provinces or territories (see table 7.4). The 1990 statistic *assumes* the same number of hospitals as 1986 for Northwest Territories (1) and Newfoundland (5), since neither jurisdiction responded to our request for updated information.

location of hospitals with therapeutic abortion committees, the use of residency and patient quota requirements, the provincial distribution of obstetrician-gynaecologists, and the fact that the abortion procedure was done primarily by this medical specialty resulted in sharp regional disparities in the accessibility of the abortion procedure. (Committee on the Operation of the Abortion Law 1977, 140)

Appointment of the Committee on the Operation of the Abortion Law had been recommended by an ad hoc organization of family planning physicians. In 1975 Doctors for Repeal of the Abortion Law (DRAL) petitioned Parliament to remove abortion from the criminal code. It noted that "as early as 1971 the Canadian Medical Association declared that law to be unworkable," but because "reliable information on how the law is working has been almost totally lacking," DRAL undertook a study of how the hospital TACs were operating (Doctors for Repeal of the Abortion Law 1975, cover letter).

From the 1973 *Canadian Hospital Directory,* DRAL determined how many "general" hospitals with more than ten beds existed in each province and compared that list with the hospitals reporting to Statistics Canada that they, as the law required, had established a TAC. My replication analysis for 1986 (table 7.3) shows a pattern similar to what both DRAL and the Committee on the Operation of the Abortion Law (1977) found, despite the sixteen years that have passed since enactment of the Canadian law.*

Since DRAL measured abortion capacity in terms of hospitals with ob-

---

*Of 559 hospitals with abortion capacity in 1976, 271 (or 48.5 percent) established therapeutic abortion committees according to the Committee on the Operation of the Abortion Law (1977, 107, footnote 2). But the committee did not derive the percent of "eligible" hospitals for each province.

Table 7.3

Canadian Hospitals with Abortion Capacity that Established TACs and Abortion Rates in 1975 and 1986 by Province

| | 1975 DRAL Study | | 1986 Replication Study | | | |
| | TACs[a] | Rate[b] | TACs[c] | Rate[b] | TACs[d] | TACs[e] |
Province	(OB-GYN and/or Med.-Surg.)		(OB-GYN and/or Med.-Surg.)		(OB-GYN only)	(Med.-Surg. only)
Newfoundland	22.2%	1.5	16.1%	2.5	27.8%	0%
Prince Edward Island	28.5	3.2	14.3	0.4	20.0	0
Nova Scotia	34.3	5.8	24.4	8.0	37.9	0
New Brunswick	22.5	2.6	23.3	2.0	28.6	11.1
Quebec	23.0	3.8	29.6	7.5	35.8	18.2
Ontario	56.8	13.4	46.1	12.1	53.4	18.6
Manitoba	14.0	6.0	10.3	10.2	14.8	0
Saskatchewan	10.1	7.0	6.2	4.6	9.4	0
Alberta	20.1	10.6	17.9	10.5	19.1	11.1
British Columbia	56.5	18.6	55.1	16.5	64.0	26.1
Yukon	50.0	14.8	50.0	18.9	50.0	0
Northwest Terr.	0	10.3	16.7	19.2	20.0	0
Total, Canada	32.9	9.6	28.4[f]	10.2	35.0	10.5

Sources:

[a]Doctors for Repeal of the Abortion Law, *Survey of Hospital Abortion Committees in Canada* (December 4, 1975), Library of Parliament, Ottawa, Canada.

[b]Statistics Canada, Canadian Centre for Health Information, *Health Reports*, Supplement No. 9, 1991, volume 3, no. 4, pp. 18–19.

[c]Calculated by author. These hospitals had obstetrics-gynecology and/or medical-surgical units.

[d]Calculated by author. These hospitals had obstetrics-gynecology services.

[e]Calculated by author. These hospitals had medical-surgical services but not obstetrics-gynecology services.

[f]Four hospitals with therapeutic abortion committees (TACs) in 1986 were not listed in *Canadian Hospital Directory,* vol. 39, September 1991. If they are counted, the statistic would be 28.8.

stetrics-gynecology and/or medical-surgical units, the same calculation was made for 1986 (table 7.3). Also shown is abortion capacity measured in terms of hospitals with obstetrics-gynecology services only and those with medical-surgical services only. While the figure based on obstetrics-gynecology services only is a more conservative estimate of abortion capacity, that measure had been derived for hospital-based abortion services in the United States for 1986 (Tatalovich and Daynes 1989) and will be employed here for comparative purposes.

Table 7.4

Number of Canadian Hospitals that Performed Abortions by Province in 1970, 1974, 1986, and 1990

	1970	1974	1986	1990
Newfoundland	4	6	5	5*
Prince Edward Island	2	2	1	0
Nova Scotia	6	12	12	11
New Brunswick	7	8	8	4
Quebec	16	27	38	22
Ontario	48	110	95	77
Manitoba	4	9	8	6
Saskatchewan	8	10	8	8
Alberta	18	25	22	17
British Columbia	29	54	55	39
Yukon	1	1	1	1.
Northwest Territories	0	1	1	1*
Totals	143	265	254	191

Source: Data for 1970 and 1974 from Commmittee on the Operation of the Abortion Law, *Report of the Committee on the Operation of the Abortion Law* (Ottawa: Ministry of Supply and Services Canada, 1977), p. 446. Data for 1986 provided to author by Statistics Canada. Data for 1990 collected by author directly from the provincial authorities.

*In July 1992 all twelve jurisdictions were contacted for this information, but Newfoundland and Northwest Territories did not respond. Thus the 1990 statistics for Northwest Territories and Newfoundland *assume* the same number of hospitals performed abortions in 1990 as did so in 1986.

The last year for which Statistics Canada collected abortion data was 1986, before the *Morgentaler* case (1988). To assess whether that decision encouraged other hospitals to provide abortion services, each provincial and territorial authority was contacted to determine which hospitals did abortions in 1990. The results (table 7.4) indicate that the number of Canadian hospitals doing abortions has *declined* further. Even though the *Morgentaler* case did not affect hospitals directly, its declaration, coupled with the failure of Parliament to enact new regulations, presumably would send a welcome signal to the health care community that—legally at least—they could safely perform abortions. In the United States the number of hospital providers has steadily declined since shortly after *Roe* was announced, and apparently this pattern is also taking hold in Canada. If this trend continues there, it will mean, as has happened in the United States, that clinics will *displace* hospitals as the primary providers of abortion services.

Except for New Brunswick and Quebec, the percentage of hospitals with capacity that established therapeutic abortion committees *declined* between 1975 and 1986 (table 7.3). In both years the majority of British Columbia hospitals with obstetrics or surgical units had established TACs. Then comes Ontario, though its 1975 figure of 56.8 percent dropped markedly, to 46.1 percent, by 1986. And in Quebec, where 23.0 percent of eligible hospitals had TACs in 1975, the increase to 29.6 percent by 1986 ranks this French-dominant (80 percent of the population, according to the 1987 census) province third, behind British Columbia and Ontario.

The showing of Quebec casts doubt on the simplistic view that resistance to legalized abortion is tied to Catholicism. There may be socioeconomic-status and cultural forces at work. For the four maritime provinces (New Brunswick, Newfoundland, Nova Scotia, and Prince Edward Island) the average percentage of hospitals with capacity that established TACs is 19.5 percent; that for the three prairie provinces (Alberta, Saskatchewan, and Manitoba) is lower (11.5 percent). Both those areas of Canada have fewer people and are generally less prosperous than are British Columbia, Ontario, and Quebec.[*]

These data comport with information Brodie (1994, 132–34) supplies to argue that three distinct abortion delivery systems operate in Canada. Most liberal is Quebec, where presently nineteen of the thirty clinics in Canada are found; fifteen are units within the provincial health care system, so abortions performed there are publicly funded. The elections in 1990 and 1991, which brought the New Democratic Party (NDP) to power in British Columbia, Saskatchewan, and Ontario (in 1995 the NDP was defeated for reelection in Ontario), had resulted in more access to abortion services. British Columbia introduced regulations within its Health Act to require certain hospitals within each region of the province to provide abortion services, and Ontario is the only provincial government that fully funds abortions by either hospitals or freestanding clinics. The third tier of abortion services elsewhere in Canada means that

> in the prairie provinces, access is largely confined to one clinic and a handful of urban hospitals, some of which enforce local residency requirements. In the Atlantic provinces, provincial governments have taken an active role in regulating abortion. In New Brunswick, for example, there are no free-standing clinics and the government is against their introduction. Prince Edward

---

[*]Here are the provinces ranked by median family income according to the 1987 census: (1) Ontario, $36,978; (2) Alberta, $36,091; (3) British Columbia, $33,774; (4) Manitoba, $31,464; (5) Nova Scotia, $32,938; (6) Quebec, $30,774; (7) Saskatchewan, $30,382; (8) New Brunswick, $26,880; (9) Prince Edward Island, $26,386; (10) Newfoundland, $24,458.

Island has passed legislation opposing the procedure and only funds out-of-province abortions when they are performed in a hospital and are first approved by a five-doctor panel. Similar restrictions apply in Newfoundland, where access is limited to one hospital and approval from a gynecologist, a psychiatrist and a social worker is required. (Brodie 1994, 132, 134)

At base, if the U.S. definition of hospitals with abortion capacity (obstetrics-gynecology facilities) is applied to Canada, then the percentage for Canada in 1986 would be virtually identical to the figure derived by Tatalovich and Daynes (1989) for the United States (see table 7.5). By that criterion 35.0 percent of Canadian hospitals and 34.5 percent of U.S. hospitals were providing abortion services, which means that the 1969 parliamentary decision in Canada did not induce swifter or more widespread implementation of legalized abortion than did the 1973 ruling in *Roe v. Wade*.

Using that more conservative index of capacity (obstetrics-gynecology units), how do the regional variations in Canada compare to those in the United States? Comparative statistics (Tatalovich and Studlar 1995) show that in both countries abortion facilities are most available along the Pacific coast (in the states of California, Oregon, and Washington, and in the province of British Columbia) and most restrictive as you move eastward (among the provinces of Saskatchewan, Alberta, and Manitoba, and in the thirteen American states spanning the territory between California and the Midwest). The rate of abortion implementation among the seven midwestern states, as a group, is as restrictive as the thirteen mountain states, but to the north, the rate of implementation in Ontario was more than double the overall rate for Michigan, Wisconsin, Illinois, Indiana, Iowa, Minnesota, and Ohio. What some would expect to be the outliers—Quebec, and the group of thirteen border and Deep South states—roughly fall in the middle of the distribution on abortion service availability. The variability in abortion services among the fifty U.S. states and the ten Canadian provinces points to the same conclusion. For the United States in 1986 (Tatalovich and Daynes 1989, 83) the percentage of hospitals with obstetrics-gynecology capacity ranged from a high of 75.0 percent in Hawaii to a low of 2.5 percent in South Dakota; among the Canadian provinces, there was a high of 64.0 percent in British Columbia and a low of 9.4 percent in Saskatchewan. Thus in both countries there are substantial variations in abortion services between regions and across states or provinces.

The type of hospitals that—to a degree—have implemented abortion policy is quite parallel in both societies (table 7.5) despite their unlike health care systems. This unexpected finding contradicts the view of some scholars—at least with respect to abortion—that Canadians have a more

Table 7.5

Types of U.S. and Canadian Hospitals with Obstetrics Capacity that Offered Abortion Services in 1986

	United States			Canada		
	With Capacity	Provide Services	%	With Capacity	Provide Services	%
Government*	1,112	305	27.4	310	69	22.3
Nongovernment/ Nonreligious†	1,874	838	44.7	262	149	56.9
Religious‡	476	30	6.3	71	7	9.9
For-profit	289	123	42.6	0	0	0
Osteopathic	1	0	0	0	0	0
Totals	3,752	1,296	34.5	643	225	35.0

Sources: The U.S. data are taken from Raymond Tatalovich and Byron W. Daynes, "The Geographical Distribution of U.S. Hospitals with Abortion Facilities," *Family Planning Perspectives* (March/April 1989), p. 82, table 1. The number of Canadian hospitals with therapeutic abortion committees was supplied to the author by the Therapeutic Abortions Unit, Vital Statistics and Health Status, Statistics Canada, and hospitals with obstetrics capacity were tabulated by the author from Canadian Hospital Association, *Canadian Hospital Directory*, vol. 39 (September 1991).

*For the United States, includes hospitals under federal, state, county, city, city-county, or hospital district control; for Canada, includes hospitals under the control of municipal government, provincial government, or federal government.

†For the United States, includes nongovernment and not-for-profit hospitals; for Canada, includes all "public" hospitals, which are defined as "a voluntary corporation, association or society which operates on a non-profit, non-religious, non-governmental basis."

‡For the United States, includes church-operated not-for-profit hospitals; for Canada, includes hospitals "owned and controlled by a church or one of its branches, a religious order, or by a corporation, association, or society with religious objectives" as well as hospitals under a joint control arrangement such as religious-public, religious-private, and religious-provincial government.

Note: The U.S. categories are defined by the American Hospital Association; the Canadian, by Statistics Canada.

communal ethos and are more deferential to political authority than Americans. Although hospitals controlled by public authorities represent 29.6 percent of U.S. hospitals but 48.2 percent of Canadian hospitals, it was determined that only 22.3 percent of government-managed hospitals in Canada, compared to 27.4 percent in the United States, had provided abortion services in 1986. One suspects that the governing boards of hospitals that are accountable to political elites, and indirectly to the electorate, would be alert to community preferences with respect to abortion policy. On the other hand, more (56.7 percent) Canadian hospitals that were both nongovernmental and not affiliated with a religious denomination had established TACs in 1986, as compared to the 44.7 percent of U.S. private-sector hospitals with abortion capacity that offered abortion services in that year. One would think that a higher proportion of Canadian public *and* private hospitals would offer abortion services compared to the United States *if* its collective political ethos were to extend to the provision of abortion services.

The closest linkage seemingly would influence the policies of church-affiliated hospitals. They are a small component of the potential abortion delivery system (13 percent of U.S. and 11 percent of Canadian hospitals with capacity), and table 7.5 shows that 9.9 percent actually do abortions in Canada, compared to 6.3 percent in the United States. The reason for this disparity is not obvious, though one possibility may be that proportionately more of the religiously affiliated hospitals in the United States are controlled by the Roman Catholic Church. Within months of the *Roe v. Wade* decision, the United States Catholic Conference lobbied Congress to include in the Public Health Service Act of 1973 a "right of conscience" provision so that no Catholic hospitals, physicians, or nurses could be required to perform abortions (Segers 1995b, 97). As a consequence, of the 610 Catholic hospitals in the United States in 1986, none reported doing abortions.* In Canada, seven religiously affiliated hospitals had TACs; three were located in Quebec, two in Newfoundland, and one each in Ontario and Alberta.

There are also for-profit hospitals in the United States (nearly 8 percent of all hospitals with abortion capacity), though none exist in Canada. If the for-profit hospitals were combined with the nongovernmental-nonreligious hospital sector, together they would account for 58 percent of the total with abortion capacity in the United States, of which 74 percent offered abortion services in 1986.

To summarize, the most extensive implementation of abortion services in the United States has been among the nonprofit and proprietary hospitals—the *private* sector—whereas those hospitals directly controlled by governmental authorities were less compliant in Canada than in the United States. Even in Canada, the rate of abortion implementation among nongovernment and nonreligious hospitals was more than double the rate among govern-

---

*Of the 610 Catholic hospitals in 1986, 424 provided only obstetrics-gynecology services, another 142 provided neither abortions nor obstetrics-gynecology services, and no data were available for 44 hospitals. This calculation was made based on the information in these sources: *AHA Guide,* 1986 edition (Chicago: American Hospital Association, 1987) and *1987 Guidebook for Catholic Health Care Association* (St. Louis, MO: Catholic Health Care Association of the United States, 1987).

mentally controlled hospitals. Certainly this finding must shake one's faith in "democratic" socialism as compared to the economic marketplace. The bottom line, of course, is that overall, 65 percent of U.S. and Canadian hospitals chose *not* to provide abortion services, a significant and unexpected finding given that abortion services are funded by most provincial authorities whereas only around one-tenth of U.S. abortions are covered under the Medicaid program.

A 1992 Alan Guttmacher Institute survey (Henshaw and Van Vort 1994, 103) found that 94 percent of nonmetropolitan counties and 51 percent of metropolitan counties had *no* abortion provider. There is clearly a sharp urban-rural cleavage in the availability of abortion services across the United States. In Canada, similarly, abortion providers are so concentrated that women seeking abortions must travel long distances or cross the border into the United States (Rosenberg 1988, 185). Moreover, Rosenberg observed that "not only is the number of hospitals where a therapeutic abortion can be obtained small compared to the number of hospitals that exist, but within provinces almost all of the abortions are being carried out at a small number of hospitals in the largest cities of the province" (Rosenberg 1988, 184). Hospital abortion providers, if anything, are more concentrated in highly urbanized areas of Canada, as comparative statistics for both countries show (table 7.6). In cities with a population of one million or more, upward of 70 percent of Canadian and American hospitals with capacity offer abortion services, but on the other hand, fewer than three in ten hospitals in Canada or the United States that provide abortion services are located in cities, towns, and villages with populations under 100,000. For all cities above that size, the majority of hospitals with the capacity do abortions in the United States, compared to two-thirds in Canada. So there is more of an urban bias to the availability of hospital-based abortion services in Canada despite its having a universal health care system.

State Resistance and *Webster*

The Supreme Court ruling in *Webster v. Reproductive Health Services* (1989) that allowed state government regulations on abortion portends a new era of state regulatory activity. A year later Guam passed a law that prohibited abortions except where the woman's life was endangered and barred information on where to obtain an abortion, and in 1991 Louisiana and Utah enacted highly restrictive abortion statutes. All three were struck down by federal courts, so there are limits to how far the states can regulate abortions despite *Webster*. A scorecard by NARAL predicted that if the Supreme Court should ever nullify *Roe,* Alabama, Louisiana, Mississippi, Missouri, Nebraska, Pennsylvania, South Carolina, Utah, West Virginia,

Table 7.6

Hospital Abortion Services in the United States and Canada by City Size, 1986* (in percent)

City Size	United States (OB-GYN)	Canada* OB-GYN	Med.-Surg.	Combined
1,000,000 or more population	73.7	71.4	37.5	59.1
500,000 to 1,000,000 population	60.7	75.0	25.0	68.8
250,000 to 500,000 population	51.2	47.8	50.0	48.3
100,000 to 250,000 population	49.3	69.2	11.1	54.3
Subtotals	56.7	65.9	29.6	57.6
Below 100,000 population	28.9	29.9	8.8	24.4
Total	34.5	35.0	12.2	28.8

Source: U.S. data tabulated from *AHA Guide,* 1986 edition (Chicago: American Hospital Association, 1987), pp. A10–A275. Canadian results tabulated from data by Statistics Canada and from *Canadian Hospital Directory* (Ottawa: Canadian Hospital Association, 1991). U.S. population data from U.S. Department of Commerce, Bureau of the Census, *Statistical Abstract of the United States, 1987* (Washington, DC: U.S. Government Printing Office, 1987), pp. 31–33. Canadian population data from *Canadian Almanac and Directory 1991* (Toronto: Copp Clark Pitman, 1991).

*Based on three measures of capacity: percent of hospitals with obstetrics-gynecology services that also do abortions; percent of hospitals with medical-surgical services that also do abortions; percent of hospitals of those with obstetrics-gynecology *or* medical-surgical services that also do abortions.

Michigan, Ohio, South Dakota, and Wisconsin likely would pass restrictive legislation. Of that group, only Mississippi and South Carolina had reformed their original antiabortion laws during the 1960s. On the other hand, NARAL speculated that, whatever the judicial outcome, California, Hawaii, Vermont, Washington, Connecticut, North Carolina, and Oregon probably would *not* tighten up their abortion laws. And of this group, only Vermont and Connecticut were *not* among the states that reformed or repealed their antiabortion laws during the 1960s (National Abortion Rights Action League 1992). In Maryland voters in a 1992 referendum supported legislation that codified *Roe v. Wade* as state law (Carney 1995); popular initiatives were used to secure abortion rights in Nevada in 1990 and in Washington State in 1991 (Hanna 1995); and in 1990 the Connecticut General Assembly passed a law legalizing all abortions before fetal viability.

It has been chronicled in chapter 1 how, beginning in 1966, the original antiabortion laws were reformed by fourteen states and repealed by four others. Of the numerous studies that attempt to explain today's variability in state abortion policies, many include a variable to measure the policy legacy of those pre-*Roe* laws. In other words, there is evidence showing that a long-term divergence of policy differentiates the eighteen states that reformed or repealed abortion laws in the 1960s from the thirty-two other states that did not act. At the time that *Roe* was decided, for example, the average abortion ratio (abortions per 1,000 live births) was highest among the four states with elective abortion laws, followed by the fourteen states with reformed laws, and was lowest among the remaining states as a group (Fung 1993, 471–72, 500).

Tatalovich and Strickland (1995) found that the pre-*Roe* state laws were more important than socioeconomic conditions in explaining the variance among states in how many hospitals with capacity actually do abortions. Exact calculations based on hospital capacity (Tatalovich and Daynes 1989, 83) reveal that, compared to the 34.5 percent of hospitals nationwide with capacity that offered abortion services, this figure rises to 49.2 percent for the eighteen pre-*Roe* liberalized states and drops to 23.9 percent for the thirty-two others. Halva-Neubauer (1993, 186–87) determined how many states enacted nineteen types of antiabortion regulations between 1973 and 1989; among the most frequent were "conscience clauses" (thirty-five states), postviability requirements or postviability standards of care (twenty-nine states), abortion funding limits (twenty-five states), and prohibitions on fetal tissue experimentation (twenty-three states). Each state averaged 6.1 antiabortion laws at some time over these fifteen years, but the mean rises to 7.8 among the subgroup of thirty-two states without pre-*Roe* liberalized abortion laws and falls to 3.1 for the eighteen other states.

Does the public support the antiabortion restrictions that Halva-Neubauer found in each state? A model devised by Goggin and Wlezien (1993, 201) indicates the answer is yes: "In those states in which abortion policy is more (less) restrictive than the public wants, the public generally is less (more) supportive of further restrictions on the availability of abortion. Ultimately, it appears that state publics are attentive and responsive to abortion policy, adjusting their preference for more policy activity in accordance with what policy-makers actually do."

State restrictions on abortion were analyzed by Strickland and Whicker (1992) according to pre-*Roe,* pre-*Webster,* and post-*Webster* time frames to assess whether public opinion or political cycles (liberalism-conservatism) best explained the pattern of state activity. They concluded:

> Political variables were not significant in the more liberal pre-*Roe* era of 1972 or during the pre-*Webster* period where state politicians were con-

> strained by the *Roe* decision, indicating that the cycle theory is less important for explaining abortion policy formation. On the other hand during the post-*Webster* era, political factors were significantly linked to abortion restrictiveness, illustrating how the dominance of conservatism may increase party differences and heighten partisan conflict over a controversial issue like abortion. (Strickland and Whicker 1992, 612)

States that more generously fund abortions for poor women are invariably included among the eighteen pre-*Roe* states. In the mid-1980s federal and state expenditures for 187,997 Medicaid abortions totaled $66,171,000, of which California and New York together accounted for 127,000 (or 74 percent) of the total (Gold and Macias 1986, 263). The thirty-five states with the most restrictive funding policies spent a mere $243,000 and provided Medicaid abortions to only 378 indigent women. The decline in federally funded abortions has been severe, going from 294,000 in 1977, before the Hyde Amendment was fully implemented, to 165 in 1990 (Gold and Daley 1991), which means that virtually all the 162,418 publicly funded abortions in 1990 were financed from state revenues. Only nineteen states reported some state-funded abortions in 1990, 99 percent occurring in thirteen states (with California and New York together accounting for 81 percent of the total).

Hansen (1993b, 247–48) coded all states according to their 1988 policies on Medicaid-funded abortions. Most liberal were nine states (including six of eighteen with pre-*Roe* laws) that funded all abortions, followed by four more states (two of which had pre-*Roe* laws) under court orders to fund all abortions, then four states that funded abortions only in cases of rape or incest, and finally the most restrictive thirty-three states, which paid only when the mother's life was endangered. On Hansen's four-point scale, all fifty states averaged 3.2, meaning that most states paid for abortions only to save the mother's life or for rape and incest, but again the average rose (to 3.5) for the subsample of thirty-two states without pre-*Roe* liberalization and fell (to 2.7) for the group of eighteen with pre-*Roe* liberalization.

Meier and McFarlane (1993) used probit analysis to predict which states fund abortions. States that are more Catholic, more conservative, and more dominated by one party are less inclined to fund abortions, though the strongest single predictor—and the only positive influence—was the relative number of residents who were members of the National Abortion Rights Action League. Thus they believe that politics is more important than socioeconomic factors: "What appears to be happening is that policy (whether or not to fund) is set in the political environment. Once policy is set, however, politics ceases to be a major direct factor; policy and need determine outputs" (Meier and McFarlane 1993, 265). The state totals for 1990 (Meier and McFarlane 1993, 250–51) confirm the above-mentioned pattern. Whereas thirty-two states funded at least one Medicaid abortion, California and New York together funded 81 percent of the total; by adding five more pre-*Roe* states (Hawaii, Maryland, North Carolina, Oregon, Washington), this grouping of seven states accounted for 91 percent of all Medicaid-funded abortions in 1990.

In sum, whether we focus on hospital abortion services or state antiabortion restrictions or the generosity of Medicaid funding for abortions, there is a pattern showing that many, but not necessarily all, of the eighteen states that reformed or repealed their antiabortion laws prior to the 1973 landmark ruling have continued to this day with a more tolerant policy agenda as compared to the other thirty-two states whose criminal codes did not anticipate the advent of legal abortions.

Apart from the state-by-state and regional variations in access to abortion services is the question, perhaps more fundamental, of why the mainstream health care community has abdicated its responsibility to comply with the law, and provide abortions. In Canada, despite the urging of the CMA, two-thirds of Canadian hospitals could not—or would not—recruit three physicians to serve on therapeutic abortion committees. In the United States, it has been observed how the free market saved *Roe v. Wade* by not limiting abortions to hospitals, thus enabling a primary network of clinic providers to emerge (Rosenberg 1991). The clinics also freed the medical establishment from having to undertake a professionally unattractive service. Thus, says Rosenberg (1991, 198), "the Court's structural inability to change institutions, as demonstrated by . . . hospital abortions, and the unlikeliness of Congress requiring it for abortion, suggests that without clinics the Court's decisions would have been frustrated."

Although surveys indicate that most physicians (and specifically obstetricians-gynecologists) approve legalized abortion, and given that only 650 antiabortion MDs belong to the American Association of Pro-Life Obstetricians and Gynecologists (Gross 1991), it seems that the vast majority of doctors would prefer not to get involved. The abortion trade is apparently becoming a marginalized medical practice with little, if any, professional esteem attached but with plenty of risks and social stigma. A 1985 poll by the American College of Obstetricians and Gynecologists, based on 4,000 respondents (out of its 29,000 members), showed that 84 percent believed abortion should be legal and available, yet only a third of those doctors favoring abortions actually performed them—and those that did performed very few (96 percent did fewer than twenty-six a month). "The term 'abortionist' still has a very heavy stigma," says Dr. Curtis E. Harris, who heads the American Academy of Medical Ethics, adding: "I don't think physicians are any different from society at large. Many feel that abortions should be provided for rape, incest, the life of the mother or severe fetal malformation. Physicians act out of the same social conscience that we all do" (quoted in Kolata 1990, 1, 11).

A 1991 study by the National Abortion Federation found that only 12 percent (a 50 percent decline since 1985) of hospital training programs routinely include abortion training; 50 percent make such training optional; and 38 percent do not offer any abortion training (Belkin 1993). The scarcity of doctors has gotten so bad that the National Abortion Federation, joined by the American College of Obstetricians and Gynecologists, recommended training nurses and physician assistants to do abortions (Wolinsky 1991). "Unless drastic changes are made, American women will lose the right to abortion, and the Supreme Court won't be the cause. . . . The reason will be that physicians either can't or won't perform this essential service," noted NAF executive director Barbara Radford (quoted in Wolinsky 1991). In mid-1993 Planned Parenthood of New York began plans to offer abortion training at some of its family planning clinics (Belkin 1993). And in 1995 the Liaison Committee on Medical Education, which evaluates and accredits the nation's 126 medical schools, indicated that future residents in obstetrics and gynecology will be required to learn abortion procedures, although universities with objections to abortion would not be required to directly provide that training. Thus most medical schools affiliated with the Roman Catholic Church, such as the Stricht School of Medicine at Loyola University in Chicago (which does not teach abortion procedures), would not be affected by the new guidelines.

Provincial Reaction to *Morgentaler*

In the aftermath of *Morgentaler* (1988) there were efforts by provinces, with two especially noteworthy, to curb abortions through funding limits, although both were defeated in litigation (Dunsmuir 1991, 17–20). In March 1988 the British Columbia cabinet passed a regulation under the Medical Service Act to make abortions an uninsured service unless performed in a hospital and when a significant threat existed to the woman's life. The British Columbia Civil Liberties Association sued, and the regulation was invalidated on technical grounds by the British Columbia Supreme Court. Its chief justice took "judicial notice of the fact that, if there is to be a lawful abortion, such a procedure requires medical services." Therefore

> the legislature did not authorize the Cabinet by regulation to provide that services rendered by a medical practitioner that are medically required are to be considered as services that are not medically required. (Dunsmuir 1991, 17)

The Court took issue with the cabinet position that abortion was not a medically required service and therefore was not insured, though, on the other hand, the Court also implied that the cabinet could have declared that abortion was not an insured service despite it being a medically necessary service.

But the funding issue is a complicated one. Says Brodie (1994, 134): "Perhaps most disconcerting is the potential for provincial governments, whether because of pro-life sentiments or cost-cutting initiatives, to remove abortion from national health insurance, or attempt to carve a regulatory distinction between 'non-therapeutic' and 'therapeutic' abortions—the 'wanted' and the 'needed.' " As late as September 1995 the Progressive Conservative government of Alberta announced plans to fund only "medically necessary" abortions rather than abortion on demand, but within weeks that objective was abandoned because of resistance from organized medicine. The College of Physicians and Surgeons and the Alberta Medical Association did not want to make any changes in current policy, which placed the abortion decision in the hands of the patient and her physician.

In June 1989 the Nova Scotia legislature passed the Act to Restrict Privatization of Medical Services, which restricted certain medical procedures to hospitals. One restricted procedure was abortion. The act stated that medical services performed contrary to the law were not reimbursable by the provincial health program, and fines of $10,000 to $50,000 were levied against those persons who violated the statute. Although this law applied to a range of medical procedures, "it was widely considered that the timing of the legislation was influenced by Dr. Morgentaler's public announcements that he intended to establish an abortion clinic in Halifax" (Dunsmuir 1991, 18). The Canadian Abortion Rights Action League (CARAL) brought suit on the grounds that this action was beyond the jurisdiction of a province, violating Sections 7, 15, and 28 of the 1982 Canadian Charter of Rights and Freedoms.[*]

On October 13, 1989, the Nova Scotia Trial Division held that CARAL

---

[*]Section 7 reads: "Everyone has the right to life, liberty and security of the person and the right not to be derived thereof except in accordance with the principles of fundamental justice."

Section 15 reads: "(1) Every individual is equal before and under the law and has the right to the equal protection and equal benefit of the law without discrimination and, in particular, without discrimination based on race, national or ethnic origin, colour, religion, sex, age, or mental or physical disability.

(2) Subsection (1) does not preclude any law, program or activity that has as its object the amelioration of conditions of disadvantaged individuals or groups including those that are disadvantaged because of race, national or ethnic origin, color, religion, sex, age, or mental or physical disability."

Section 28 reads: "Notwithstanding anything in this Charter, the rights and freedoms referred to in it are guaranteed equally to male and female persons."

did not have standing, and the Court of Appeal upheld that ruling in March 1990. On October 26 Dr. Morgentaler announced at a press conference that he had performed seven abortions that day, and the next day he was charged with seven counts of performing unlawful abortions contrary to the so-called Medical Services Act. Because Morgentaler announced that he planned to do more abortions, the authorities asked for an injunction restraining him from any more violations of that statute.

On November 6, 1989, the injunction was granted. Justice Richard, of the Supreme Court Trial Division, assessed the argument that the Nova Scotia legislation had violated the 1988 *Morgentaler* ruling and stated:

> One must not lose sight of the fact that *Morgentaler 1988* was a constitutional challenge of a section of the *Criminal Code*. The present application concerns a provincial statute purportedly regulating the manner in which certain medical services can be administered within the province. There was no question raised as to the constitutional competence of the legislature of Nova Scotia to regulate matters respecting the delivery of health care services. (quoted in Dunsmuir 1991, 19)

He issued the injunction because no evidence indicated that a private abortion clinic was needed for the health of the citizens or that there was a compelling need not otherwise being met. He felt that provincial law ought not be violated, and his ruling was upheld by the Nova Scotia Court of Appeal in March 1990.

In Morgentaler's trial on charges before the provincial court on October 19, 1990, Judge Joseph Kennedy held that the Medical Services Act and regulations made pursuant to it were, in fact, criminal law and thus beyond the jurisdiction of the province. He also found that the purpose of this legislation was primarily to restrict abortions, and although Judge Kennedy felt that Nova Scotia had genuine concerns about privatization of medical services, he believed them incidental to the paramount purpose of preventing freestanding abortion clinics. Given the grounding of his opinion, Kennedy did not address the question of whether the law violated sections of the Canadian Charter.

On July 5, 1991, the Nova Scotia Court of Appeal affirmed the Kennedy ruling, holding that the act could have been a valid exercise of provincial authority, or "in pith and substance . . . an exercise of the exclusive provincial jurisdiction in relation to hospitals or in the unassigned field of health," but its review of the provincial legislative debates confirmed that the main objective was to prevent Dr. Morgentaler from operating a private abortion clinic in Nova Scotia. The subsequent decision by the Supreme Court of Canada in *R. v. Morgentaler* (1993), upholding the Nova Scotia Court of

Appeal ruling that invalidated the provincial ban on freestanding abortion clinics, signaled that the high court would not allow provincial authorities to discourage the establishment of non-hospital-based abortion facilities.

But that decision did not wholly answer the question about provincial discretion in the funding of abortions. Two years later yet another lawsuit was brought by Dr. Morgentaler against the Liberal government of Prince Edward Island, based on its 1988 policy on abortion funding. The Prince Edward Island authorities would fund only abortions performed in hospitals where a special board deemed the procedure to be medically necessary, but because all physicians on Prince Edward Island had refused to perform any abortions, women had to find abortion services on the mainland. If the pregnancy was terminated in a hospital, the physicians' fees were covered, but the patient had to pay those expenses if the abortion was performed in a private clinic. In 1993 Morgentaler sued, and in 1995 the Prince Edward Island Supreme Court agreed with him, declaring that policy illegal. "It is not apparently based on a health consideration," ruled Justice David Jenkins. "It does not appear directed towards any legitimate objective of controlling cost" (quoted in MacAndrew 1995, 58). This lawsuit was the latest success story for Morgentaler, who had previously won similar court challenges in Newfoundland, New Brunswick, and Manitoba as well as Nova Scotia. Morgentaler acted to "highlight the fact that Prince Edward Island is the only province in Canada where women have absolutely no recourse. They have to go outside the province. I wanted to apply enough pressure so the province would have to fund those services completely" (quoted in MacAndrew 1995, 58).

The existence of freestanding abortion clinics has prompted pro-life activists to apply direct-action tactics against those facilities. British Columbia reacted by enacting the Access to Abortion Services Act, which provided a fifty-meter protest-free zone around clinics and the homes of physicians who perform abortions. In December 1995 its restrictions were challenged by Maurice Lewis, the first person arrested for violating the law, with Lewis's attorney arguing that the legislation violated his client's freedom of religion and freedom of speech under the Charter of Rights and Freedoms.

In another twist, abortion clinics have complicated the regulatory relationship between Ottawa and provincial authorities. In Ontario and British Columbia freestanding abortion clinics obtain full funding from those provinces under the Canada Health Act, and by accepting those reimbursements, the clinics there do not charge user fees. However, in Quebec and elsewhere, there has emerged a dispute over whether provinces are violating the Canada Health Act by allowing their abortion clinics to charge fees. Quebec is a case in point, because authorities only partially reimbursed clinics for the cost of abortions. In Newfoundland, Nova Scotia, and Alberta only doctors' fees were covered for clinic abortions, so the clinics there required patients to pay a user fee, while in Manitoba and New Brunswick patients were not reimbursed, since those provinces funded neither the physicians' fees nor the clinic fees; the result is that a patient's cost for an abortion can range up to $400 during the first trimester. In this showdown the federal minister of health imposed an October 15, 1995, deadline for provinces to comply with the Canada Health Act; otherwise the amount of clinic revenues from patients would be deducted from the federal transfer payments to those provinces.

Summary

Despite the status of abortion as a constitutional right in the United States and its availability as a medical service under the Canadian health care system (though legally health care is not an entitlement in Canada akin to Social Security pensions in the United States; see Dossetor 1994), in both nations there is tremendous variation in abortion services. The fact that most established health care providers—hospitals—do not provide abortion services must suggest that, beneath the legal niceties, abortions are deemed a marginalized area of health care, one that should be avoided. The cultural stigma attached to abortions must be even greater in Canada, otherwise how else can we explain the lack of services despite the publicized efforts of organized medicine to gain a liberalized statute in 1969 and to prevent recriminalization in 1990? In the United States the growth of specialized abortion clinics offered an alternative delivery system, and a similar development has been taking place in Canada since 1988.

At base, despite structural differences in the political regimes and health care systems, abortion implementation has followed similar lines of development in both countries over the past two decades. It is noteworthy that, generally speaking, the American states that liberalized or repealed their abortion laws before *Roe* have continued to support more access to abortion services, while in Canada Quebec, Ontario, and British Columbia had complied more fully with the 1969 abortion reforms and today represent the most liberal provinces in terms of access to abortion services. To anticipate policy developments in the aftermath of *Webster* and *Morgentaler,* one is tempted to conclude that the past is prologue to the extent that those regional and state or provincial variations in the abortion service delivery system will continue unabated.

On the other hand, litigation to provoke judicial intervention may achieve for Canadian women nearly universal access to publicly funded abortion services, something which seems beyond the pale in the United States. If freestanding abortion clinics cannot be prohibited, if abortions are defined as a medically necessary procedure under the Canada Health Act, if provincial authorities cannot refuse to fund abortions under their health care insurance schemes, and if abortion clinics ultimately are denied the privilege of charging user fees, then abortions may develop into an entitlement through judicial decree and administrative edict—without affirmative action by Parliament.

Conclusion

Social Convergence
and Institutional Divergence

How Close Are the Parallels?

This analysis was driven by thirteen systemic, process, and abortion-specific hypotheses. At the outset let me summarize the findings in reverse order, going from microlevel hypotheses to macrolevel hypotheses, and proceed with a more thorough explanation. Below I indicate for each hypothesis whether, based on the evidence, it is accepted or rejected, unless the record is so mixed that a definitive judgment cannot be made.

Hypothesis	Proposition	Accept or Reject
A1	Rights-based jurisprudence politicizes abortion conflict in the United States	X
A2	Scope of "social" conflict over abortion greater in the United States	X
A3	Direct-action tactics more common among United States pro-lifers	X
A4	More "moralistic" debate in the United States due to postmaterialist conflicts	X
P1	Governments equivocate in promoting moral agendas	?
P2	Legislative voting on moral conflicts will be unwhipped	X
P3	Backbenchers assume leadership roles on moral issues	X

P4	Moral conflicts fracture unity of legislative majority party	?
P5	Single-issue groups predominate over moral conflicts	X
S1	Policymaking by legislature is more consensual than by court	X
S2	Less institutional scope of conflict in parliamentary regime	X
S3	More decentralized federalism allows more policy variability	X
S4	Collectivist political ethos yields more support for public policy	X

What this rendering suggests is that the macrolevel expectations about how unified and parliamentary regimes differ from the uniquely American separation-of-powers system do not operate uniformly with respect to moral conflicts, certainly not abortion. There is more reliability to the hypotheses that define how the legislative process in parliamentary systems deals with volatile issues of morality, and some of those expectations have applicability to the United States Congress, indisputably the most autonomous legislative body in the world. The abortion-specific propositions seem generally valid, and all indicate that Canada would experience less conflict over abortion than the United States. In other words, there looks to be a trade-off between the systemic and the abortion-specific hypotheses, which implies that abortion as a moral controversy has unique properties that derive from sociopolitical dynamics and *not* from regime attributes.

Abortion-Specific

Hypothesis A1 involves the terms of the abortion debate, not just in the judicial arena but also in the legislature (chapters 2 and 3). Of relevance is the contrast between the agitation leading to abortion reforms in both countries (chapter 1) during the 1960s as compared to what followed in the wake of *Roe v. Wade*, since the U.S. Supreme Court abandoned the medical rhetoric of the reformers and embraced the language of rights. In Canada, then as well as later, rights rhetoric was entirely irrelevant in the legislative arena and, regarding *Morgentaler* (1988), nearly as irrelevant in the judicial arena. Organized medicine clearly was the most influential force in shifting the debate against Bill C-43 in the Canadian Senate, which is why feminist scholarship makes the argument that "no rights were granted to Canadian women amidst the clash of meanings in the Senate" (Brodie, Gavigan, and Jenson 1992, 116). Even though women's groups had the force of numbers, feminist rhetoric did not carry the day. What doomed C-43 was the power of medical rhetoric, showing the illogic of the government position that physicians cannot be trusted to rely upon their medical judgment even though abortion was deemed a medical procedure.

Thus Bill C-43 was defeated by an essentially conservative political force—doctors—which is why feminists believe that Canada made no advance on incorporating abortion into a rhetoric of rights. In the United States medicalized rhetoric once dominated the abortion debate, but today a rights rhetoric is the language of discourse among pro-choice advocates, with women's groups more influential than ever. However, transforming the terms of the debate has failed to secure the constitutional right of abortion and arguably has undercut support for access to abortion services because they have been stigmatized as illegitimate. There is a lesson to be learned about the survival of abortion in Canada without constitutional rights and its near demise in the United States despite its being called a right. As Brodie, Gavigan, and Jenson explain this feminist dilemma in assessing the impact of *Morgentaler* (1988) for Canadian women:

> The victory was also contradictory in that the Court reinforced the notion that abortion is a medical matter. Contradictions abound in this maintenance of a medicalized conception of abortion. On the one hand, Canadian feminists and pro-choice activists have articulated a long-standing critique of the implications of denoting of abortion as a medical or therapeutic matter. Yet, on the other hand, in very important and paradoxical ways the continued denotation of abortion as a *health* matter has been significant in the Canadian context. Health care in Canada has come to be regarded as a social right, enshrined in a comprehensive and fully funded health care system based upon principles of accessibility and universality. (Brodie, Gavigan, and Jenson 1992, 127)

If abortion as a health service was perceived to be an "entitlement" in Canada (though not legally), the definition of abortion as a personal liberty in the United States made it vulnerable on the exact same grounds. First, according to Brodie (1994), "the idea of personal choice carried with it an implicit message that 'non-therapeutic' abortions were consumer items, something one chose according to personal preference. While the state might be responsible for providing funding for a poor woman whose life was at risk, it was not obliged to fund a consumer preference. Second, pro-choice advocates were unable to show that the withdrawal of state funding was a threat to women's right to privacy. This right no more required the state to fund abortions than the right to bear arms obliged it to make guns freely available."

Hypothesis A2, about the scope of social conflict, can be assessed based on the discussion of public opinion, organized interests (chapter 4), and electoral behavior (chapter 5). The contour of public attitudes toward abortion is centrist and almost exactly the same in both these societies, so the contagion of conflict cannot be attributed to a polarized public opinion. Abortion is a marginal influence, at best, on how the American *electorate* chooses between presidential candidates, and in Canada abortion was essentially a nonissue in the 1988 and 1993 national elections. So irrelevant was abortion that scholarly analyses of the Canadian elections give it no attention at all, whereas American political scientists continually look for its electoral impact simply because we assume that any issue that has been around so long on the political landscape *ought* to be influential with the voters.

Rather, societal conflict is due to polarization among organized interests. In terms of the number, type, and variety of interest-groups mobilized by the abortion debate, in both countries the pro-choice coalition is exactly that. But the question here is whether the boundaries of this organizational conflict are greater in the United States than Canada. Other research suggests that the scope of social conflict in Canada would be less pronounced than the mobilization of interest groups in the United States. A study of environmentalists led Pierce, Steger, Steel, and Lovrich (1992, 188) to conclude that the Canadian political culture "actually may serve to suppress a recognition of the need and legitimacy of that sort of distinct political communication activity on the part of interest groups," whereas the American political culture "leads to more frequent group involvement as an instrument to satisfy individual needs or influence, information, and belongingness." Likely so, if submitting friend-of-the-court briefs and giving legislative testimony are any barometer.

Webster galvanized the pro-choice forces just as *Roe* was the catalyst for the pro-life movement. The 78 amicus briefs filed in that case were a record for the U.S. Supreme Court. Previously the largest outpouring of amicus briefs had occurred when the Court debated "reverse discrimination" in *Regents of the University of California v. Bakke* (1978), when 117 organizations cosponsored those briefs (O'Neill 1985). The number in *Webster* was three times greater (381), of which 83 percent represented the pro-choice position. In Canada, though the *Morgentaler* ruling had the potential to undo the 1969 restrictions on reproductive freedom, *no* organizations filed as interveners in that case. The *Tremblay* litigation got six organizations (three pro-life and three pro-choice) plus the attorneys general of Quebec and of Canada to file as interveners, and three groups (two pro-life and one pro-choice) did so in the *Borowski* case.

In the United States, between 1973 and 1988 there were twenty-three abortion hearings before congressional committees and eighteen Supreme Court cases. Those opportunities to influence abortion policy caused 67 pro-life and 139 pro-choice groups to testify, while 156 pro-life and 465 pro-choice organizations filed amicus briefs. All told, "on *both* sides of the abortion dispute . . . a total of 621 *different* organizations . . . presented at least one testimony or *amicus* brief since 1973" (Tatalovich and Daynes 1993, 47). In Canada, the stakes were high when Parliament considered recriminalizing abortion in 1990, yet on that occasion, before Bill C-43 was debated in the House of Commons, twenty-two pro-life and thirty-five pro-choice groups testified before a parliamentary committee.

When a bomb ripped through Dr. Morgentaler's Toronto abortion clinic on May 18, 1992, breaking the quietude of the Canadian abortion debate, "there arose a new and, for many, a more troubling question: Did the clinic bombing represent a further Americanization of Canadian society?" (Morton 1992, 316). As CARAL president Kit Holmwood was quoted as saying, "This happening in Canada? I don't believe it" (quoted in Morton 1992, 316). Professor F.L. Morton (1992, 316) believes that the Canadian polity is changing, and he sees a linkage between this event and the Charter: "It was ironic that these re-awakened fears of Americanization occurred in the context of the Morgentaler Clinic and the Supreme Court's Charter ruling that allowed it to operate."

If the Canadian politics of "rights" is breeding a moral zealotry of the U.S. variety, it remains qualitatively and quantitatively different from that found in the United States. This is the conclusion for Hypothesis A3. The Morgentaler Clinic bombing was a first for Canada; contrast it with the American record of mayhem:

Since 1977 there have been more than 1,500 violent acts at abortion clinics nationwide. These include 37 bombings, 87 cases of arson, 178 death threats, 31 burglaries, 91 assaults, 300 bomb threats, 567 incidents of vandalism, and 2 kidnappings. There have been 525 clinic blockades and 31,230 arrests of protesters at abortion clinics. The cost of such blockades to city and county law enforcement officials between 1988 and 1993 totaled more than $3 million. Between 1992 and May 1994, the cost to abortion clinics of noxious chemical vandalism (use of tear gas and butyric acid) at clinics was $853,050. (Segers 1995a, 233)

Add to this listing the murder of five people during 1993–94, including Drs. Gunn, Tiller, and Britton.

Hypothesis A4 conceptualizes moral conflict as an outgrowth of social development into the postmaterialist age. Inglehart (1990) posited a "cultural shift" in Western civilization that would displace the historical class division over economic resources and redistribution of wealth between the left and right to a new cleavage between the materialists, who share traditional social values, and the postmaterialists, who operate at a higher level of self-actualization. According to Inglehart:

> Materialist/Postmaterialist values seem to be part of a broader syndrome of orientations involving motivation to work, political outlook, attitudes toward the environment and nuclear power, the role of religion in people's lives, the likelihood of getting married or having children, an attitude toward the role of women, homosexuality, divorce, abortion, and numerous other topics. (Inglehart 1990, 423)

Gross economic statistics indicate that Canada generally has experienced higher inflation, more unemployment, and lower per capita national income than the United States; moreover, one would think that economic uncertainty has increased in Canada insofar as economic growth declined sharply from an average 4.6 percent annually between during 1970 and 1980 to 2.8 percent between 1980 and 1992; compare this to the stable growth rate of 2.7 percent in both of those periods for the United States (World Bank 1994, 165). To that extent, presumably materialistic values would be stronger in Canada than in the United States.

A more immediate consideration is that Canadian elections since 1974 have been dominated by economic issues—fiscal policy and especially trade relations—or constitutional questions about the relationship between provincial authority and the central government (in the case of Quebec). Abortion, by all accounts, is a nonissue there, whereas abortion has surfaced or been exploited as a campaign issue in every U.S. presidential election since 1972. Taking 1988 as an illustration, while NAFTA was literally the only issue in Canada, it was barely mentioned by presidential candidates George Bush or Michael Dukakis, who proceeded to argue about a host of social issues—abortion, gun control, crime, teacher-led recitations of the Piedge of Allegiance, and school prayer. More than any presidential election in recent memory, the 1988 campaign focused on the social agenda, though underlying the entire contest were the themes of general prosperity, peace, and the popularity of the incumbent president. To say that campaign rhetoric and party platforms in the Unites States included references to abortion, but did not do so in Canada, does not mean that Americans were any more inclined to single-issue vote on that particular subject. In fact they were not. But one would think that a debate over abortion would emerge in the Canadian campaigns unless—as hypothesis A4 indicates—Canada is essentially more preoccupied with materialistic concerns, while the advent of postmaterialism in the United States helped fuel a very contentious, moralistic debate that symbolized abortion as either murder or a right.

Process

Information to evaluate hypotheses P1 through P4 is given in chapter 3, on Congress and Parliament. Do governments equivocate and avoid promoting a moral agenda (P1)? Tatalovich and Daynes (1988, 216) predicted that "presidents generally do not exert decisive leadership to change social regulatory policy although they may make symbolic gestures." Even during the Reagan and Bush years, most pro-life legislation that Congress enacted *originated* in Congress. Reagan's activities—speaking before pro-life meetings, making speeches, his call for a constitutional amendment to protect the unborn—were more symbolic than otherwise, and observers generally agree that the Reagan tenure, especially his first term, was dominated by economic and fiscal policy at the expense of his social agenda. The need for such pro-choice legislation as FACE and repeal of the gag rule on abortion counseling by agencies that receive family planning grants was recognized by abortion proponents in Congress before Clinton came on the political scene.

In Canada the record is mixed. The Trudeau government proposed wholesale reform of laws governing moral behavior, including abortion, so that 1960s legislative initiative seems to be exceptional. While the Mulroney government eventually introduced Bill C-43, the way in which that was accomplished can hardly be called heroic leadership. In May 1988 the Mulroney government authored a three-pronged measure to get the sense of the House on abortion, which, according to Brodie, Gavigan, and Jenson (1992, 67) "was unprecedented in the annals of Canadian parliamentary democracy." Had any one option been approved by the MPs, then presumably it would have been introduced as a government bill to recriminalize abortion. But the effort failed, so the government tried again in July, with one proposal, but that was rejected on a roll call. Then came Bill C-43 in 1990. "Mulroney formed a caucus committee composed of both pro-life and pro-choice MPs and ordered them to reach a consensus" (Morton 1992, 290). This time, however, floor amendments were allowed, though obviously Mulroney had hoped that his partisans in the House of Commons would stick with the original proposal. They did, barely, but then the Senate defeated the measure on an unprecedented tie vote. The Mulroney government capitulated and announced that it would make no more attempts to enact an abortion law (Morton 1992, 292). This approach to abortion legislation by Mulroney was very different from the Trudeau tactic, and hardly indicative of how governments in parliamentary regimes formulate their economic or social-welfare legislative agendas.

The Canadian experience with legislative voting on moral issues such as abortion is consistent with that of the British Parliament—namely, that government protects its political standing by not making those roll calls a test of party loyalty. Thus they are typically unwhipped (P2). The Mulroney government allowed freedom of conscience to prevail during the parliamentary deliberations in 1988 and 1990, and during debate over the 1969 reforms the Progressive Conservatives "suspended party discipline and allowed a free vote," whereas the Liberal "Prime Minister [Trudeau] had never approved a free vote, yet party leaders claimed that no Liberals were being forced to vote against their conscience" (Morton 1992, 24). While the formality of a free vote does not exist in the United States Congress, arguably *all* roll calls are undisciplined, given our weak congressional party leadership.

Hypothesis P3 suggests that backbenchers will assume leadership roles on moral issues, not the legislative leadership. Generally this statement is true. It is the very nature of parliamentary government that frontbenchers do not offer amendments on the floor in opposition to legislation backed by their government. Joe Borowski, the ardent pro-life spokesman, had been minister of transport as well as minister of public works under Manitoba's NDP premier Ed Schreyer during the late 1960s, but he eventually resigned from the cabinet rather than stop being outspoken on pro-life matters. Nor should the rank-and-file membership act in a fashion contrary to the wishes of their government, but they did with impunity on Motion 36 (1988) and Bill C-43. On these two occasions twenty-seven MPs offered amendments; Progressive Conservatives accounted for twenty-two, of which twenty were pro-life proposals. In the United States pro-life activism in the House of Representatives is personified by Congressman Henry J. Hyde (R-Illinois), who was not the minority leader or the minority whip. The sponsors of pro-life legislation in the 100th Congress were the rank and file, and disproportionately backbenchers from the Republican side. Neither the majority leader nor the majority whip was among the 49 Democratic sponsors of pro-life bills, although the minority leader and minority whip were counted among the much larger number (122) of Republican sponsors.

According to hypothesis P4, moral conflicts tend to fracture the unity of the majority party in the legislature, which is most relevant to the U.S. Congress. But different moral issues will fracture the legislative parties along different lines. Since religion is the most important crosscutting cleavage on the abortion issue—given that on domestic social-welfare legislation, historically most Catholics belonged to the party of the left but have conservative views on abortion—hypothesis P4 has special application when Liberals in Canada and Democrats in the United States are in the legislative majority. Research on legislative voting in the House of Representatives, the U.S. Senate, and the Canadian House of Commons shows a religious dimension. Catholic legislators are more antiabortion in their voting than non-Catholics. For Republicans, religion and partisanship mutually enforce conservative voting on abortion, but for the majority Democrats, religion and party are incompatible. Catholic Democrats may not bring pro-life bills onto the floor of Congress, but when forced to vote on such measures, they generally support their church rather than their party.

In parliamentary regimes one way to express nonsupport for the majority party without jeopardizing its political status is for dissenting backbenchers to simply abstain. On the free vote of May 9, 1969, authorized by the Trudeau government, which would have deleted the abortion provision from the omnibus reform bill, 56 percent of Progressive Conservatives (the opposition), 44 percent of Liberals, and 27 percent of New Democrats did not vote. As Morton (1992, 26–27) suggests: "In a classic display of political cowardice, sixty-eight of the 155 Liberal Members of Parliament somehow managed to be absent from Parliament when the vote was taken." In 1990 the Progressive Conservatives were the majority when free votes were taken on Bill C-43. Of the eleven motions defeated on the floor, ten were pro-life to varying degrees and they garnered support from between 3 percent and 21 percent of the Progressive Conservatives, while the majority (ranging from 54 percent to 71 percent) supported the government by rejecting them. But nonvoters among Progressive Conservatives comprised 23 percent to 32 percent of their membership. Liberal MPs who did not vote on the ten pro-life amendments to Bill C-43 (ranging from 42 percent to 55 percent) far exceeded the number who voted for or against the motions (Tatalovich, Overby, and Studlar 1993).

So hypothesis P4 seems valid, but with a caveat. An exception would occur, as recalled by the 1964 debate over a new Canadian flag (Smith 1975, 112–23), when the economic cleavage that divides parties of the left from parties of the right overlies emotive-symbolic or social regulatory issues. That situation would lessen intraparty disunity, and in the Canadian case the flag dispute forced Progressive Conservative MPs from Quebec to desert their party's leadership and vote with the Liberal government.

Finally, consider hypothesis P5 on moral conflicts as a single-issue phenomenon, which is largely true (chapter 4). Pro-lifers are organized as the National Right to Life Committee in the United States and as the Alliance for Life in Canada, but in the United States the pro-life lobby is more dominated by a variety of single-issue groups—the older variety, which focused on litigation and lobbying, and a newer type (Operation Rescue), which specializes in direct action. On the pro-choice side are NARAL and its Canadian analogue, CARAL, but, on the other hand, apparently single-issue groups are more prominent within the pro-choice coalition of Canada than in the United States.

Systemic

Material directly relevant to the consensus-building assumptions of S1 are found in chapters 1 and 5. Part of the answer is that there was no political fallout in Canada after the 1969 reformed abortion law was enacted until the *Morgentaler* (1988) ruling forced the issue back onto the legislative agenda, and then only briefly. Attempts in 1988 and 1990 to formulate a new abortion policy failed, and since then there has been a de facto political resolution of the dispute. Had Parliament gone the route of the U.S. Congress, with annual attempts to rewrite the Criminal Code covering abortion, then clearly an entirely different political scenario would have developed. In the United States the ability of eighteen state legislatures to rewrite their abortion laws did not prompt any sustained pro-life activities, probably because physicians, if not organized medicine, led the lobbying effort, there were small Catholic concentrations in those (mainly) southern states, at that time the religious right was not mobilized, and southern states were more elitist than most.

Critics of the 1973 Supreme Court ruling, such as Glendon (1989; 1987), argue that judicial decrees are not the optimal way to generate a political consensus, which is a mainstay of the legislative process, but the situations in Canada and the United States in 1973 were not analogous. The Canadian Parliament enacted fairly restrictive abortion reforms compared to other Western democracies, whereas the U.S. Supreme Court decreed the most permissive policy of any nation outside the Eastern Bloc. My speculation was that a backlash might have been avoided if the high court had pursued a narrower strategy of nullifying "vague" state laws and built upon its precedent in *United States v. Vuitch* (1971).

An aspect of consensus-building (S1) is bipartisanship or *nonpartisanship,* which means that controversies are not transformed into political conflicts. This is exactly what happened in Canada. Although a minor party—the NDP—formally endorsed the pro-choice position, neither the Progressive Conservatives nor the Liberals took any stand, instead maintaining a position of neutrality or ambiguity on abortion. The Canadian electorate is no more divided by their abortion attitudes than are Americans, yet in the United States we have witnessed the Republican and Democratic parties taking polarized positions on this issue since 1980, with no end in sight. The conclusion seems inevitable that the partisan conflict over abortion in the United States is driven by political elites, who have made a conscious decision to exploit the issue for some political advantage (activating single-issue voters or fund-raising), whereas the Canadian political establishment has refused to do so.

Laws are not implemented by the legislative branch; with respect to abortion, the key decision makers are physicians and especially hospitals. If the law is truly majestic, then people should be compliant regardless of whether an elected Parliament or an unelected Supreme Court lays it down. We know that is not the case, which is why compliance studies are an outgrowth of the judicial process, whereas law-enforcement activities flow from the lawmaking process. Various enactments by the U.S. Congress were designed to prevent or limit the implementation of *Roe*, but obviously Parliament, after the fact, did not move to sabotage the 1969 Criminal Code on abortion. So while the connection between legislative consensus building and administrative implementation is more indirect, there should be some relationship insofar as a legislative body is popularly elected and supposedly reflects the general will. What escapes rational explanation, if this reasoning is tenable, is why the reformed 1969 abortion law was not implemented more fully, at least to the extent of more hospitals establishing therapeutic abortion committees as the law required. Whether or not there was an unmet demand for abortions in Canada only begs the real question of why there were so few suppliers of abortion services when every indication was that Canadian doctors were the key pressure group in gaining parliamentary action.

Hypothesis S2 can be assessed based on information in chapters 2, 3, 5 and 6. The institutional (as opposed to the social) scope of conflict (see Goggin 1993, 1–15; Smith and Bobic 1990) refers to the number and variety of governmental branches and agencies that become embroiled in a conflict. Since a parliamentary regime integrates the executive and legislative branches around the government's legislative agenda, the reformed abortion measure introduced by Prime Minister Trudeau was enacted with minimal opposition, and six years later the Supreme Court of Canada, in its first *Morgentaler* ruling (1976), upheld both the Criminal Code and parliamentary supremacy. The second *Morgentaler* ruling (1988) did invalidate the 1969 law but in a way deferential to Parliament. Some provinces tried to exert their authority over medical services to deny benefits for abortions, but, so far at least, all attempts have been rebuffed by the courts. This stable relationship among the two legislative and judicial branches in Canada and between the national and provincial governments stands in sharp contrast with the ongoing battle in the United States between the judiciary and the popularly elected branches—even between the White House and Congress during periods of "divided" party rule—and which implicates various state governments (such as those of Pennsylvania and Missouri) seemingly bent on repealing the right to abortion.

Most telling, however, is the bureaucratic experience in these countries.

Presidents Reagan and Bush politicized the permanent government that oversees abortion policy: foreign aid and United Nations programs, grants to family planning agencies, appointments to cabinet and subcabinet positions, and (dis)approval of the abortifacient RU-486. It was not always this way. Medicaid under Presidents Nixon and Ford was funding nearly 300,000 abortions yearly for poor women, and the practice likely would have continued had Congress not passed the Hyde Amendment to limit such monies for abortion. For his part, President Clinton reversed some administrative restrictions inherited from his immediate GOP predecessors, with thanks from pro-choice advocates. Nor did Congress refrain from micromanaging agencies to prevent abortion advocacy—the U.S. Civil Rights Commission and the Legal Services Corporation. Certainly with respect to abortion the ideal of a neutral-competent bureaucracy (Heclo 1975) has given way to politicization (Moe 1985; Nathan 1983). Such seems not to be the case in Canada, and the best illustration was the continued pro-choice advocacy of the quasi-governmental Canadian Advisory Council on the Status of Women under Liberal and Progressive Conservative rule.

The longitudinal and cross-sectional statistics on implementation (chapter 7) are relevant to assessing two systemic hypotheses: S3, involving federalism, and S4, reflecting political culture. S3 suggests that the decentralizing influence of Canadian federalism would allow more geographical variability in abortion providers as compared to the United States. Since the regional distribution of abortion services shows marked similarities between the United States and Canada, it would be too close a call to conclude that federalism yields less uniformity among the regions or provinces of Canada relative to our regions or states. On both counts the parallels are more striking than any differences.

For S4 to be validated, the expectation is (1) more rapid implementation by Canadian hospitals than by U.S. hospitals in the period immediately following the 1969 or 1973 policy change, (2) greater uniformity between public and private hospitals and between highly urban and less urban areas in Canada, and (3) implementation by a larger percentage of Canadian hospitals as compared to U.S. hospitals. Stated differently, it was assumed that a more collectivist and deferential political ethos in Canada, when coupled with its universal health care system, would yield faster and more complete implementation of abortion policy and more uniformity across hospitals—public and private, urban and rural. Both governmental and private-sector hospitals in Canada should show greater compliance with the legal policy on abortion than their equivalent facilities in the United States. Certainly we presume that government-controlled hospitals (since there are proportionally more in Canada) would be more deferential to political authority in a so-called collectivist society.

There has been a long-term decline in the number of hospitals with capacity that perform abortions in Canada and especially in the United States, and only recently have clinics begun to provide a significant percentage of abortions in Canada. In the United States clinics accounted for the majority of abortions as early as 1974. The evidence shows, however, that Canadian hospitals operated by governmental authorities were *less* likely to implement the new policy on abortion than those in the United States, whereas nongovernmental and not-for-profit hospitals were *more* likely to do so in Canada. So the Rosenberg (1991) thesis that market forces allowed clinics to meet the demand for abortion services in the United States seems to have some applicability to private-sector hospitals in Canada as well. While the urban bias in the location of hospital abortion providers was even greater in Canada than in the United States, the percentage of hospitals in smaller communities that failed to implement a legalized abortion policy was similar in both nations. Also recall that the overall percentage of hospitals with obstetrics-gynecology capacity to perform abortions that actually did so was essentially the same in both countries. So hypothesis S4 is rejected.

Two broad conclusions seem warranted from this study. First and foremost, as Mildred Schwartz (1981) rightly observed, the differences between Canada and the United States are sufficiently great for us to believe that governmental institutions and the party systems that undergird them affect how regimes handle moral conflicts. The Canadian parliamentary system, with its strongly disciplined parties, was able to neutralize the abortion controversy, whereas the American separation-of-powers system, with its loosely organized parties, gave expression to its explosive qualities.

But neutralizing the controversy does not mean that it becomes value-free, nor does it suggest that the future of Canadian politics will be as sanguine as its past. Parliamentary institutions may not be able to contain socially divisive issues if the trend toward "Americanization" of the Canadian judiciary is not arrested (see Morton 1992, 315–20). What resulted from *Morgentaler* (1988) and the Senate rejection of Bill C-43 (1990) is a situation whereby Canada today has *no* abortion law whatsoever; moreover, this result was accomplished by two nonelected institutions that are not directly accountable to the Canadian citizenry. The restrictive legal regime of 1969 has been replaced with arguably the most permissive abortion policy of any Western democracy (see table 2.1). Viewed from this larger perspective, 1988 may be a mark of transition, when the judicially active Supreme Court of Canada began sliding into an era of judicial activism akin to that which has characterized the U.S. Supreme Court.

Second, moral conflicts are polarizing conflicts, and even though Canada has avoided the debilitating political turmoil that surrounds the abortion controversy in the United States, abortion seems to be a unique kind of issue that tests the underlying normative cohesion of any society. The debate over abortion brought forth the same kind of pro-life counterarguments in Canada as were experienced in the United States—abortion is killing the unborn—and they were expressed in both societies by Catholics and fundamentalist Protestants. When Seymour Martin Lipset and others take note of the communal nature of Canadian society, as opposed to the libertarian strain of American society, undoubtedly they are thinking more about collective economic goods—the welfare state—than about moral conflicts. In Canada there is widespread support for universal access to health care, including among medical practitioners. On the other hand, for most citizens a moral conflict may provoke nothing more than an expression of belief, whereas abortion is a deliberate act that requires physicians to reconcile the necessity for abortion against a competing value—the protection of life. And rather than face that situation, what seems to be happening in Canada as well as in the United States is that most physicians—despite their supportive views on abortion—have chosen to avoid the moral dilemma by simply not getting involved in the delivery of abortion services.

So formal institutions matter, to answer the question posed by Weaver and Rockman (1993), and this comparative analysis of moral policy adds a theoretical and empirical dimension to the emerging literature on "new institutionalism" in American and cross-cultural political studies (Steinmo, Thelen, and Longstreth 1992; Powell and DiMaggio 1991; March and Olsen 1989). As to the next step, these findings beg researchers to focus their energies on determining whether the Canadian experience is analogous to how European parliamentary systems coped with the abortion controversy. The degree to which that proposition is validated would tell us, at least with respect to abortion, whether the United States is the *only* outlier among Western democracies.

Appendix

Regression Models of Three Vote Clusters on Bill C-43

Variables	Vote Clusters[*]		
	Cluster I		
	b	SE	t
Religion	0.3852	.1388	2.775[b]
Party	0.4621	.0863	5.354[a]
Cabinet	0.4858	.1778	−2.732[b]
Ethnic	−0.0005	.0005	0.979
Constant	1.1097	.1504	7.378[a]
Adj. R^2 = .160			
	Cluster II		
	b	SE	t
Religion	3.0050	.7579	3.965[a]
Party	0.1145	.4711	0.243
Cabinet	−4.5548	.9706	4.693[a]
Ethnic	−0.0051	.0012	4.287[a]
Constant	8.8515	.8210	10.781[a]
Adj. R^2 = .144			
	Cluster III		
	b	SE	t
Religion	−0.9178	.2150	−4.269[a]
Party	3.3377	.1336	24.977[a]
Cabinet	0.8891	.2753	−3.230[a]
Ethnic	0.0013	.0003	−3.882[a]
Constant	2.2125	.2329	9.500[a]
Adj. R^2 = .750			

Source: E. Marvin Overby, Raymond Tatalovich, and Donley T. Studlar, "Free Voting on Abortion in the Canadian House of Commons" (unpublished manuscript, 1995).

[*]Cluster I includes Introduction and first reading; Cluster II includes motions 5, 10, 12, 13, 14, 16, 17A, 17B, and 19; Cluster III includes second reading, motion 24, report stage, and third reading. Also indicated is statistical significance at (a) .001 or (b) .01 levels.

References

Aberbach, Joel D., and Bert A. Rockman. 1995. "The Political Views of U.S. Senior Federal Executives, 1970–92." *Journal of Politics* 57: 838–52.

Abortion Report. 1992. "Canada: Health Ministers Ask for RU-486." July 22.

Abramowitz, Alan I. 1995. "It's Abortion, Stupid: Policy Voting in the 1992 Presidential Election." *Journal of Politics* 57: 176–86.

Action. 1987. Bulletin from the National Action Committee on the Status of Women. February. Toronto.

Action Bulletin Action. 1985. National Action Committee on the Status of Women. October 17. Toronto.

Action Now! 1995a. Monthly newsletter from the National Action Committee on the Status of Women. April-May. Toronto.

———. 1995b. Monthly newsletter from the National Action Committee on the Status of Women. March. Toronto.

———. 1991. Monthly newsletter from the National Action Committee on the Status of Women. April. Toronto.

Adams, Greg. 1992. "Abortion: Evidence of an Issue Evolution?" Paper presented at the annual meeting of the Midwest Political Science Association, Chicago.

Agar, Herbert. 1950. *The Price of Union.* Boston: Houghton Mifflin.

Albritton, Robert B., and Matthew E. Wetstein. 1991. "Determinants of Abortion Use in the American States." Paper presented at the annual meeting of the Midwest Political Science Association, Chicago.

American Bar Association. 1992a. *Report to the House of Delegates* (August). National Association of Women Lawyers, National Conference of Women's Bar Associations, and the Following Members of the House of Delegates (Resolution on Abortion Rights). Chicago: American Bar Association Library.

———. 1992b. *Annual Report* (August). Chicago: American Bar Association Library.

———. 1990a. *Report to the House of Delegates* (February). Section of Individual Rights and Responsibilities, Section of Criminal Justice, American Bar Association Commission on Women in the Profession, Beverly Hills Bar Association, National Association of Women Lawyers (Resolution on Abortion Rights). Chicago: American Bar Association Library.

———. 1990b. *Annual Report* (February). Chicago: American Bar Association Library.

———. 1990c. *Annual Report* (August). Chicago: American Bar Association Library.

————. 1978. *Annual Report* (August). Chicago: American Bar Association Library.

————. 1976a. *Report to the House of Delegates* (August). Law Student Division Recommendation (Resolution on *Roe v. Wade*). Chicago: American Bar Association Library.

————. 1976b. *Annual Report* (August). Chicago: American Bar Association Library.

American Law Institute. 1959. *Model Penal Code*. Tentative draft no. 9.

American Life Lobby. 1980. *Planned Parenthood and the Christian Family*. Pamphlet.

Apple, R.W. Jr. 1989. "Limits on Abortion Seem Less Likely." *New York Times*, September 29.

Baker, Ross, Laurily Epstein, and Rodney Forth. 1981. "Matters of Life and Death: Social, Political and Religious Correlates of Attitudes on Abortion." *American Politics Quarterly* 9: 89–102.

Barringer, Felicity. 1989. "U.S. Appeals Panel Backs Clinics on Right to Counsel on Abortion." *New York Times*, May 10.

Bashevkin, Sylvia. 1994. "Confronting Neo-conservatism: Anglo-American Women's Movements Under Thatcher, Reagan and Mulroney." *International Political Science Review* 15:275–96.

————. 1989. "Free Trade and Canadian Feminism: The Case of the National Action Committee on the Status of Women." *Canadian Public Policy* 15:363–73.

Bates, Jerome E., and Edward S. Zawadski. 1964. *Criminal Abortion*. Springfield, IL: Charles C. Thomas.

Belkin, Lisa. 1993. "Planned Parenthood Starting to Train Doctors in Abortion." *New York Times*, June 19.

Berke, Richard L. 1991. "Panel Backs Bush Nominee for Attorney General." *New York Times*, November 16.

Biskupic, Joan. 1989. "Abortion Protagonists Gird for Crucial Court Test." *Congressional Quarterly Weekly Report*, April 8, 753–58.

Blake, Judith. 1977. "The Supreme Court's Abortion Decisions and Public Opinion in the United States." *Population and Development Review* 3:45–62.

————. 1973. "Elective Abortion and Our Reluctant Citizenry: Research on Public Opinion in the United States." In *The Abortion Experience*, edited by Howard J. Osofsky and Joy D. Osofsky, pp. 447–67. New York: Harper and Row.

————. 1971. "Abortion and Public Opinion: The 1960–1970 Decade." *Science* 171:540–49.

Blake, Judith, and Jorge H. Del Pinal. 1981. "Negativism, Equivocation, and Wobbly Assent: Public 'Support' for the Prochoice Platform on Abortion." *Demography* 3:309–20.

Boffey, Philip M. 1988a. "White House Backs Away from Ban on Fetal Tissue Research." *New York Times*, September 10.

————. 1988b. "Aides at White House Draft Ban on Use of Fetal Tissue." *New York Times*, September 9.

Bolce, Louis. 1988. "Abortion and Presidential Elections: The Impact of Public Perceptions of Party and Candidate Positions." *Presidential Studies Quarterly* 18:815–29.

Bond, Jon R., and Richard Fleisher. 1990. *The President in the Legislative Arena*. Chicago: University of Chicago Press.

Bond, Jon R., and Charles A. Johnson. 1982. "Implementing a Permissive Policy: Hospital Abortion Services After Roe v. Wade." *American Journal of Political Science* 26(1):1–24.

Boyd, Monica, and Deirdre Gillieson. 1975. "Canadian Attitudes on Abortion: Results of the Gallup Polls." *Canadian Studies in Population* 2.

Boyd, Gerald M. 1988. "Bush Team Battles Foes of Abortion over Cabinet Job." *New York Times*, December 21.

Brady, D., and E.P. Schwartz. 1995. "Ideology and Interests in Congressional Voting: The Politics of Abortion in the U.S. Senate." *Public Choice,* July, 25–48.

Brady, David W., and Kathleen Kemp. 1976. "The Supreme Court's Abortion Rulings and Social Change." *Social Science Quarterly* 57:535–46.

Breckenridge, Joan. 1995. "The Last Gasp?" *Globe and Mail* (Toronto), January 28.

Brodie, Janine. 1994. "Health Versus Rights: Comparative Perspectives on Abortion Policy in Canada and the United States." In *Power and Decision: The Social Control of Reproduction,* edited by Gita Sen and Rachel Snow, pp. 123–46. Boston, MA: Harvard School of Public Health.

Brodie, Janine, Shelley A.M. Gavigan, and Jane Jenson. 1992. *The Politics of Abortion.* Toronto: Oxford University Press.

Brody, Jane E. 1995. "Abortion Method Using Two Drugs Gains in a Study." *New York Times,* August 31.

Bromhead, Peter. 1956. *Private Members Bills in the British Parliament.* London: Routledge.

Brooks, Stephen. 1989. *Public Policy in Canada: An Introduction.* Toronto: McClelland and Stewart.

Brown, Barry. 1995. "Conservatives Add Abortion to Platform." *Buffalo News,* July 4.

Brown-John, C. Lloyd. 1989. "Reagan's 'New Federalism': Is There a Canadian Version?" Paper presented at the annual meeting of the American Political Science Association, Atlanta.

Brozan, Nadine. 1989. "Ban Upheld on Funds to Abortion Advisers." *New York Times,* November 3.

Buutap, Nguyenphuc. 1979. "Legislation, Public Opinion, and the Press: An Interrelationship Reflected in the *New York Times* Reporting of the Abortion Issue." Ph.D. dissertation, University of Chicago.

Byfield, Virginia, with Lori Cohen, Patrick McManus, and Rene Mauthe. 1988. "Assessing the Abortion Factor." *Western Report* (Alberta), November 14.

Byrnes, Timothy A. 1991. *Catholic Bishops in American Politics.* Princeton, NJ: Princeton University Press.

Campbell, Robert M., and Leslie A. Pal. 1989. *The Real Worlds of Canadian Politics.* Peterborough: Broadview Press.

Canadian Advisory Council on the Status of Women. 1992–1993. *Annual Report.* Ottawa.

———. 1990–1991. *Annual Report.* Ottawa.

———. 1989–1990. *Annual Report.* Ottawa.

———. 1988–1989. *Annual Report.* Ottawa.

———. 1987–1988. *Annual Report.* Ottawa.

Canadian Bar Association. 1966. *The 1966 Yearbook of the Canadian Bar Association and the Minutes of Proceedings of Its Forty-Eighth Annual Meeting.* Ottawa: National Printers Limited.

———. 1965. *The 1965 Yearbook of the Canadian Bar Association and the Minutes of Proceedings of Its Forty-Seventh Annual Meeting.* Ottawa: National Printers Limited.

———. 1963. *The 1963 Yearbook of the Canadian Bar Association and the Minutes of Proceedings of Its Forty-Fifth Annual Meeting.* Ottawa: National Printers Limited.

Canadian Medical Association. 1971. *Proceedings of the One Hundred and Fourth Annual Meeting of the Canadian Medical Association, Including the Transactions of the General Council.* Ottawa: Canadian Medical Association Archives.

———. 1967. *Transactions of the General Council at the One Hundredth Annual Meeting of the Canadian Medical Association.* Ottawa: Canadian Medical Association Archives.

————. 1966. *Transactions of the Ninety-Ninth Annual Meeting of the Canadian Medical Association.* Ottawa: Canadian Medical Association Archives.

————. 1965. *Transactions of the Ninety-Eighth Annual Meeting of the Canadian Medical Association.* Ottawa: Canadian Medical Association Archives.

Canadian Medical Association Journal. 1988. "CMA Policy Summary: Induced Abortion." Vol. 139, 1176A.

Caplan, Lincoln. 1987. *The Tenth Justice: The Solicitor General and the Rule of Law.* New York: Knopf.

Carney, Eliza Newlin. 1995. "Maryland: A Law Codifying *Roe v. Wade.*" In *Abortion Politics in American States,* edited by Mary C. Segers and Timothy A. Byrnes, pp. 51–68. Armonk, NY: M.E. Sharpe.

Chandler, Marthe A., Elizabeth Adell Cook, Ted G. Jelen, and Clyde Wilcox. 1994. "Abortion in the United States and Canada: A Comparative Study of Public Opinion." In *Abortion Politics in the United States and Canada,* edited by Ted G. Jelen and Marthe A. Chandler, pp. 131–43. Westport, CT: Praeger.

Chressanthis, George A., Kathie S. Gilbert, and Paul W. Grimes. 1991. "Ideology, Constituent Interests, and Senatorial Voting: The Case of Abortion." *Social Science Quarterly* 72:588–600.

Christian Century. 1985. "Abortion in Canada: A New Phase in the Conflict." October 16, 923–26.

Christianity Today. 1976. "Is Abortion a Catholic Issue?" January 16, 29.

Clarke, Harold D., Lawrence LeDuc, Jane Jenson, and Jon H. Pammett. 1991. *Absent Mandate: Interpreting Change in Canadian Elections.* Toronto: Gage Educational Publishing.

Clines, Francis X. 1995. "Clinton's Choice for Top Doctor Is Rebuffed by a Vote in Senate." *New York Times,* June 23.

Clymer, Adam. 1991. "Bill to Let Clinics Discuss Abortion Is Vetoed by Bush." *New York Times,* November 20.

————. 1982. "Poll Hints Democrats Could Make Key Gains in the House Elections." *New York Times,* September 22.

Cohan, Alvin. 1986. "Abortion as a Marginal Issue: The Use of Peripheral Mechanisms in Britain and the United States." In *The New Politics of Abortion,* edited by Joni Levenduski and Joyce Outshoorn, pp. 27–48. London: Sage.

Cohodas, Nadine. 1981. "Bipartisan Support: Lawyers Begin Effort to Save Legal Services Corporation." *Congressional Quarterly Weekly Report,* March 21, 529.

————. 1980. "Legal Services Corporation Authorization Bill in Senate Passed After Abortion Fight." *Congressional Quarterly Weekly Report,* June 21, 1767.

Coleman, William D., and Grace Skogstad. 1991. *Policy Communities and Public Policy in Canada.* Mississauga, Canada: Copp Clark Pitman.

Committee on the Operation of the Abortion Law. 1977. *Report of the Committee on the Operation of the Abortion Law.* Ottawa, Canada: Ministry of Supply and Services.

Congressional Quarterly Almanac. 1989. "Abortion: Litmus Test for Nominees?" 305.

————. 1976. "Veto of Labor-HEW Funds Bill Overridden," 790–804.

————. 1973. "Legal Services Program Transfer Stalled," 581–85.

Congressional Quarterly Weekly Report. 1980. "Hyde Amendment Reviewed: Supreme Court Considering Cases Challenging Congress' Curbs on Abortion Funding." April 19, 1038.

Congressional Record. 1988. "RU 486—The Death Pill." Extension of Remarks, Robert K. Dornan (R-California), 100th Cong., 2nd sess., June 14, E1972.

————. 1978. "Remarks by Congressman David C. Treen." 95th Cong., 2nd sess., September 6, 28089–91.

Cook, Elizabeth Adell, Ted G. Jelen, and Clyde Wilcox. 1994a. "Issue Voting in Gubernatorial Elections: Abortion and Post-Webster Politics." *Journal of Politics* 56:187–99.

———. 1994b. "Issue Voting in U.S. Senate Elections: The Abortion Issue in 1990." *Congress and the Presidency* 21: 99–112.

———. 1992. *Between Two Absolutes: Public Opinion and the Politics of Abortion.* Boulder, CO: Westview Press.

Cook, Elizabeth Adell, Frederick Hartwig, and Clyde Wilcox. 1992. "The Abortion Issue Down Ticket: The Virginia Lieutenant Governor's Race of 1989." *Women and Politics* 12(4): 5–17.

Couzinet, Beatrice, M.D., et al. 1986. "Termination of Early Pregnancy by the Progesterone Antagonistic RU 486 (Mifepristone)." *New England Journal of Medicine,* December 18:1565–70.

Craig, Barbara Hinkson, and David M. O'Brien. 1993. *Abortion and American Politics.* Chatham, NJ: Chatham House Publishers.

Cuneo, Michael W. 1989. *Catholics Against the Church: Anti-Abortion Protest in Toronto, 1969–1985.* Toronto: University of Toronto Press.

Czarnowski, Gabriele. 1994. "Abortion as Political Conflict in the Unified Germany." *Parliamentary Affairs* 47:252–67.

Darney, Philip D., Uta Landy, Sara MacPherson, and Richard L. Sweet. 1987. "Abortion Training in U.S. Obstetrics and Gynecology Residency Programs." *Family Planning Perspectives,* July-August, 158–62.

Day, Phillip, Greg Heaton, Mike Byfield, and Mark Stevenson. 1988. "The Abortion Cauldron Boils Over." *Western Report* (Alberta), August 1.

Daynes, Byron W., and Raymond Tatalovich. 1992. "Presidential Politics and Abortion, 1972–1988." *Presidential Studies Quarterly* 22:545–61.

de Valk, Alphonse. 1982. "Understandable for Mistaken: Law, Morality and the Catholic Church in Canada, 1966–1969," *Canadian Catholic Historical Association, Study Sessions* 49.

———. 1974. *Morality and Law in Canadian Politics: The Abortion Controversy.* Montreal: Palm.

Dickens, Bernard. 1979. *Medico-Legal Aspects of Family Law.* Toronto: Butterworths.

Doctors for Repeal of the Abortion Law. 1975. *Survey of Hospital Abortion Committees in Canada.* Ottawa: Library of Parliament.

Dossetor, John B. 1994. "The Right to Health Care in Canada." *Bioethics Bulletin,* October, 10–11.

Dunsmuir, Mollie. 1991. "Abortion: Constitutional and Legal Developments." Ottawa: Library of Parliament, Research Branch, Law and Government Division (Current Issue Review, 89-10E), revised 3 September 1991.

Durant, Robert F. 1992. *The Administrative Presidency Revisited: Public Lands, the BLM, and the Reagan Revolution.* Albany, NY: State University of New York Press.

Dworkin, Ronald. 1993. *Life's Dominion: An Argument About Abortion, Euthanasia, and Individual Freedom.* New York: Alfred A. Knopf.

Eccles, Mary E. 1978. "Abortion: How Members Voted in 1977." *Congressional Quarterly Weekly Report,* February 4, 259.

Ely, John Hart. 1973. "The Wages of Crying Wolf: A Comment on *Roe v. Wade.*" *Yale Law Journal* 82:920–949.

Facts on File World News Digest. 1988. "Party Leaders Debate." October 28, 795G3.

———. 1975. "CMA Scores Lang on Abortion." January 18, 28B1.

Family Planning Perspectives. 1985a. "Little or No Change in Attitudes on Abortion; Clinic Bombings Are Universally Condemned." March-April, 76–78.

————. 1985b. "ACOG Poll: Ob-Gyns' Support for Abortion Unchanged Since 1971." November-December, 275.

Federalist Society for Law and Public Policy Studies. 1994. *The American Bar Association in Law and Social Policy: What Role?* Washington, DC: Federalist Society for Law and Public Policy Studies.

Field, Marilyn J. 1979. "Determinants of Abortion Policy in Developed Nations." *Policy Studies Journal* 7:771–81.

Finkbine, Sherri. 1967. "The Lesser of Two Evils." In *The Case for Legalized Abortion Now,* edited by Alan F. Guttmacher. Berkeley, CA: Diablo.

Flanagan, Scott C. 1987. "Changing Values in Industrial Societies Revisited: Towards a Resolution of the Values Debate."*American Political Science Review* 81:1303–19.

Franks, C.E.S. 1987. *The Parliament of Canada.* Toronto: University of Toronto Press.

Fraser, Laura. 1988. "Pill Politics." *Mother Jones,* June, 30–33, 44.

Frendreis, John P., and Raymond Tatalovich. 1994. *The Modern Presidency and Economic Policy.* Itasca, IL: Peacock Publishers.

Fried, Amy. 1988. "Abortion Politics as Symbolic Politics: An Investigation into Belief Systems." *Social Science Quarterly* 69:137–54.

Friendly, Henry J. 1978. "The Courts and Social Policy: Substance and Procedure." *University of Miami Law Review* 33(1): 21–42.

Fung, Archon. 1993. "Making Rights Real: *Roe*'s Impact on Abortion Access." *Politics and Society* 21:465–504.

Gallup Opinion Index. 1978. April: 25–29.

Gallup Poll Monthly. 1993a. No. 331 (April):35–43.

————. 1993b. No. 330 (March):25–26.

Gallup Report. 1989. No. 281 (February):16–23.

————. 1983. No. 215 (August):18.

————. 1982. No. 206 (November):19.

————. 1981a. No. 190 (July):18–22.

————. 1981b. No. 191 (August):52.

————. 1979. No. 166 (May):21.

————. 1975. No. 121 (July):12.

Gans, Herbert. 1988. *Middle-American Individualism.* New York: Free Press.

Garreau, Joel. 1981. *The Nine Nations of North America.* Boston: Houghton Mifflin.

George, B. James, Jr. 1973. "The Evolving Law on Abortion." In *Abortion, Society, and the Law,* edited by David F. Walbert and J. Douglas Butler, pp. 3–32. Cleveland, OH: Case Western Reserve University Press.

Gibbins, Roger. 1982. *Regional Politics in Canada and the United States.* Toronto: Butterworths.

Gillespie, Michael W., Elisabeth M. Ten Vergert, and Johannes Kingma. 1988. "Secular Trends in Abortion Attitudes: 1975–1980–1985." *Journal of Psychology* 122:323–41.

Ginsburg, Ruth Bader. 1992. "Speaking in a Judicial Voice." *New York University Law Review* 67:1185–1209.

————. 1985. "Some Thoughts on Autonomy and Equality in Relation to *Roe v. Wade*." *North Carolina Law Review* 63:375–86.

Girvin, Brian. 1994. "Moral Politics and the Irish Abortion Referendums, 1992." *Parliamentary Affairs* 47:203–21.

Githens, Marianne, and Dorothy McBride Stetson, eds. 1996. *Abortion Politics: Public Policy in Cross-Cultural Perspective.* New York: Routledge.

Glendon, Mary Ann. 1989. "A Beau Mentir Qui Vient De Loin: The 1988 Canadian

Abortion Decision in Comparative Perspective." *Northwestern University Law Review* 83(3): 569–91.

———. 1987. *Abortion and Divorce in Western Law.* Cambridge, MA: Harvard University Press.

Gober, Patricia. 1994. "Why Abortion Rates Vary: A Geographical Examination of the Supply of and Demand for Abortion Services in the United States in 1988." *Annals of the Association of American Geographers* 84:230–50.

Goggin, Malcolm L. 1993. "Introduction: A Framework for Understanding the New Politics of Abortion." In *Understanding the New Politics of Abortion,* edited by Malcolm L. Goggin, pp. 1–18. Newbury Park, CA: Sage Publications.

Goggin, Malcolm L., and Christopher Wlezien. 1993. "Abortion Opinion and Policy in the American States." In *Understanding the New Politics of Abortion,* edited by Malcolm L. Goggin, pp. 190–202. Newbury Park, CA: Sage Publications.

Gold, Rachel Benson, and D. Daley. 1991. "Public Funding of Contraceptive, Sterilization, and Abortion Services, Fiscal Year 1990." *Family Planning Perspectives,* September-October, 204–11.

Gold, Rachel Benson, and Jennifer Macias. 1986. "Public Funding of Contraceptive, Sterilization, and Abortion Services, 1985." *Family Planning Perspectives,* November-December, 259–64.

Granberg, Donald. 1987. "The Abortion Issue in the 1984 Elections." *Family Planning Perspectives,* March-April, 59–62.

———. 1985. "The United States Senate Votes to Uphold *Roe* Versus *Wade.*" *Population Research and Policy Review* 4:115–31.

———. 1981. "The Abortion Activists." *Family Planning Perspectives,* July-August, 157–63.

Granberg, Donald, and James Burlison. 1983. "The Abortion Issue in the 1980 Elections." *Family Planning Perspectives,* September-October, 231–38.

Gray, Jerry. 1995. "Anti-Abortion Group Uses Transcript of 1978 Hearing to Attack Surgeon General Nominee." *New York Times,* February 7.

Greenhouse, Linda. 1994a. "Abortion Clinics Upheld by Court on Rackets Suits." *New York Times,* January 25.

———. 1994b. "High Court Backs Limits on Protest at Abortion Clinic." *New York Times,* July 1.

———. 1993a. "High Court Rules 1871 Klan Act Cannot Stop Abortion Blockades." *New York Times,* January 14.

———. 1993b. "On Privacy and Equality." *New York Times,* June 16.

———. 1987. "Abortion Counseling." *New York Times,* August 1.

Greschner, Donna. 1990. "Abortion and Democracy for Women: A Critique of *Tremblay v. Daigle.*" *McGill Law Journal* 35:633–69.

Grescoe, Audrey. 1980. "Rebirth of the Abortion Furore." *Maclean's,* June 2, 46–47.

Gross, Jane. 1991. "Opposing Abortion, More Doctors Seek an Ethical Balance." *New York Times,* September 8.

Guth, James L., Lyman A. Kellstedt, Corwin E. Smidt, and John C. Green. 1994. "Cut from the Whole Cloth: Antiabortion Mobilization Among Religious Activists." In *Abortion Politics in the United States and Canada,* edited by Ted G. Jelen and Marthe A. Chandler, pp. 107–30. Westport, CT: Praeger.

Halva-Neubauer, Glen. 1993. "The States After *Roe:* No 'Paper Tigers.' " In *Understanding the New Politics of Abortion,* edited by Malcolm L. Goggin, pp. 167–89. Newbury Park, CA: Sage Publications.

Hanna, Mary T. 1995. "Washington: Abortion Policymaking Through Initiative." In

Abortion Politics in American States, edited by Mary C. Segers and Timothy A. Byrnes, pp. 152–67. Armonk, NY: M.E. Sharpe.

Hansen, Susan B. 1993a. "What Didn't Happen: The Implementation of the *Casey* Abortion Decision in Pennsylvania." *Comparative State Politics* 14:9–18.

———. 1993b. "Differences in Public Policies Toward Abortion: Electoral and Policy Context." In *Understanding the New Politics of Abortion,* edited by Malcolm L. Goggin, pp. 222–48. Newbury Park, CA: Sage Publications.

———. 1980. "State Implementation of Supreme Court Decisions: Abortion Rates Since *Roe v. Wade.*" *Journal of Politics* 42:372–95.

Hartnagel, Timothy F., James J. Creechan, and Robert A. Silverman. 1985. "Public Opinion and the Legalization of Abortion." *Canadian Review of Sociology and Anthropology* 22:411–30. .

Hebert, Monique, and Mollie Dunsmuir. 1989. "Abortion: Legal Aspects." Ottawa: Library of Parliament, Research Branch, Law and Government Division (Current Issue Review), revised September 18.

Heclo, Hugh. 1977. *A Government of Strangers: Executive Politics in Washington.* Washington, DC: Brookings Institution.

———. 1975. "OMB and the Presidency—The Problem of 'Neutral Competence.' " *The Public Interest* 38:80–98.

Henshaw, Stanley K. 1994. "Abortion Services Under National Health Insurance: The Examples of England and France." *Family Planning Perspectives,* March-April, 87–89.

Henshaw, Stanley K., and Jennifer Van Vort. 1994. "Abortion Services in the United States, 1991 and 1992." *Family Planning Perspectives,* May-June, 100–6.

Herbers, John. 1984. "Abortion Issue Threatens to Become Profoundly Divisive." *New York Times,* October 14.

Hershey, Marjorie Randon, and Darrell M. West. 1983. "Single-Issue Politics: Prolife Groups and the 1980 Senate Campaign." In *Interest Group Politics,* edited by Allan J. Cigler and Burdett A. Loomis, pp. 31–59. Washington, DC: CQ Press.

Hibbing, John R., and David Marsh. 1987. "Accounting for the Voting Patterns of British MPs on Free Votes." *Legislative Studies Quarterly* 12:275–97.

Hill, Paul J. 1993. "Who Killed the Innocent—Michael Griffin or Dr. David Gunn?" *Life Advocate,* August, 41.

Hilts, Philip J. 1995. "Abortion Pill Issue Creates a Quandary." *New York Times,* March 1.

———. 1993. "Door May Be Open for Abortion Pill to Be Sold in U.S." *New York Times,* February 25.

———. 1992a. "Justices Refuse to Order Return of Abortion Pill." *New York Times,* July 18.

———. 1992b. "Judge Overturns Federal Seizure of Abortion Pill." *New York Times,* July 15.

———. 1991. "Anguish Over Medical First: Tissue From Fetus to Fetus." *New York Times,* April 16.

———. 1990. "Cleveland Cardiologist Selected for a Top Federal Research Post." *New York Times,* September 9.

———. 1989. "Ideological Tests Are Ruled Out in Filling U.S. Science Jobs." *New York Times,* October 30.

Hindell, Keith, and Madeleine Simms. 1971. *Abortion Law Reformed.* London: Peter Owen.

Hinds, Michael deCourcy. 1994. "Federal Court Rejects a Challenge to Pennsylvania's Abortion Law." *New York Times,* January 1.

Hodgetts, J.E. 1973. *The Canadian Public Service: A Physiology of Government, 1867–1970.* Toronto: University of Toronto Press.

Holland, Kenneth M. 1991. *Judicial Activism in a Comparative Perspective.* New York: St. Martin's Press.

House of Commons. 1990. *Minutes of Proceedings and Evidence of the Legislative Committee on Bill C-43.* Issue 3, appendix C-43/1; issue 4, appendix C-43/4; issue 5, appendix C-43/6; issue 11, appendices C-43/21, C-43/22, C-43/23.

Howell, Susan E., and Robert T. Sims. 1993. "Abortion Attitudes and the Louisiana Governor's Election." *American Politics Quarterly* 21:54–64.

Inglehart, Ronald. 1990. *Culture Shift in Advanced Industrial Society.* Princeton, NJ: Princeton University Press.

Jackson, Robert J., and Michael M. Atkinson. 1980. *The Canadian Legislative Sytstem.* 2nd ed. Toronto: Macmillan.

Jackson, Robert J., and Doreen Jackson. 1994. *Politics in Canada.* Scarborough, Ontario: Prentice Hall Canada.

Jaffe, Frederick S., Barbara L. Lindheim, and Philip R. Lee. 1981. *Abortion Politics: Private Morality and Public Policy.* New York: McGraw-Hill.

Jain, Sagar C., and Laurel Gooch. 1972. *Georgia Abortion Act 1968: A Study in Legislative Process.* Chapel Hill: School of Public Health, University of North Carolina at Chapel Hill.

Jain, Sagar C., and Steven Hughes. 1968. *California Abortion Act 1967: A Study in Legislative Process.* Chapel Hill: Carolina Population Center, University of North Carolina at Chapel Hill.

Jain, Sagar C., and Steven W. Sinding. 1972. *North Carolina Abortion Law 1967: A Study of Legislative Process.* Chapel Hill: Caroline Population Center, University of North Carolina at Chapel Hill.

Janigan, Mary. 1988. "Abortion." *Maclean's,* February 8, 10.

Janigan, Mary, Hilary Mackenzie, Marc Clark, and Ross Laver. 1988. "Shirting the Issue: The Abortion Question Dogs the Candidates." *Maclean's,* October 17, 16.

Jasper, James M., and Dorothy Nelkin. 1992. *The Animal Rights Crusade: The Growth of a Moral Protest.* New York: Free Press.

Jelen, Ted G. 1994. "Conclusion: The Future of the Abortion Debate." In *Abortion Politics in the United States and Canada: Studies in Public Opinion,* edited by Ted G. Jelen and Marthe A. Chandler, pp. 185–93. Westport, CT: Praeger.

Jelen, Ted G., and Marthe A. Chandler, eds. 1994. *Abortion Politics in the United States and Canada: Studies in Public Opinion.* Westport, CT: Praeger.

Johnson, Charles A., and Jon R. Bond. 1982. "Policy Implementation and Responsiveness in Nongovernmental Institutions: Hospital Abortion Services After *Roe v. Wade.*" *Western Political Quarterly* 35:385–405.

———. 1980. "Coercive and Noncoercive Abortion Deterrence Policies: A Comparative State Analysis." *Law and Politics Quarterly,* January, 106–28.

Johnston, David. 1993. "Attorney General Weighs Greater Federal Role in Abortion Rights." *New York Times,* March 13.

———. 1994a. "F.B.I. Undertakes Conspiracy Inquiry in Clinic Violence." *New York Times,* August 4.

———. 1994b. "Federal Agents Sent to Protect Abortion Clinics." *New York Times,* August 2.

Jones, Elisie F., and Charles F. Westoff. 1973. "Changes in Attitudes Toward Abortions: With Emphasis upon the National Fertility Study Data." In *The Abortion Experience,* edited by Howard J. Osofsky and Joy D. Osofsky, pp. 468–81. New York: Harper and Row.

Kamen, Al. 1989. "Cannon on the Left, Cannon on the Right: Forceful Solicitor General Sparked Dissent that Still Rages." *Washington Post,* January 19.

Kay, Barry J., Ronald D. Lambert, Steven D. Brown, and James E. Curtis. 1991. "Single-Issue Interest Groups and the Canadian Electorate: The Case of Abortion in 1988." *Journal of Canadian Studies* 26:142–54.

Kemp, Kathleen A., Robert A. Carp, and David W. Brady. 1978. "The Supreme Court and Social Change: The Case of Abortion." *Western Political Quarterly* 31:19–31.

Kolata, Gina. 1990. "Under Pressures and Stigma, More Doctors Shun Abortion." *New York Times,* January 8.

———. 1989. "More U.S. Curbs Urged in the Use of Fetal Tissue." *New York Times,* November 19.

———. 1988. "Any Sale in U.S. of Abortion Pill Still Years Away." *New York Times,* October 30.

Koop, C. Everett, and Francis A. Schaeffer. 1983. *Whatever Happened to the Human Race.* Wheaton, IL: Crossway Books

Kornberg, Allan, and Harold D. Clarke. 1992. *Citizens and Community: Political Support in a Representative Democracy.* New York: Cambridge University Press.

Lacayo, Richard. 1989. "Whose Life Is It?" *Time,* May 1, 21.

Lader, Lawrence. 1966. *Abortion.* Indianapolis, IN: Bobbs-Merrill.

Leary, Warren E. 1992. "Bush to Set Up Fetal Tissue Bank with Restrictions over Abortion." *New York Times,* May 20.

———. 1988. "Panel Supports Research Uses of Fetal Tissue." *New York Times,* September 17.

Leavy, Zad, and Jerome M. Kummer. 1962. "Criminal Abortion: Human Hardship and Unyielding Laws." *Southern California Law Review* 35:123–48.

Léger, Huguette, and Judy Rebick. 1993. *The NAC Voters' Guide, 1993.* National Action Committee on the Status of Women. Hull, Quebec: Voyageur Publishing.

Legge, Jerome S. Jr. 1987. "Abortion as a Policy Issue: Attitudes of the Mass Public." *Women and Politics* 7:63–82.

———. 1983. "The Determinants of Attitudes Toward Abortion in the American Electorate." *Western Political Quarterly* 36:479–90.

Lewin, Tamar. 1990. "With Thin Staff and Thick Debt, Anti-Abortion Group Faces Struggle." *New York Times,* June 11.

———. 1988a. "Reagan Signs Measure Barring Sale of Fetal Organs." *New York Times,* November 6.

———. 1988b. "U.S. Abortion Rule Is Upheld by Judge." *New York Times,* July 2.

———. 1988c. "Groups Challenging Abortion Rules." *New York Times,* February 2.

Lewis, Neil A. 1995. "White House Seeks to Blunt New Questions on Nominee." *New York Times,* February 26.

Lipset, Seymour Martin. 1990. *Continental Divide: The Values and Institutions of the United States and Canada.* New York: Routledge.

———. 1963. *Political Man: The Social Bases of Politics.* Garden City, NY: Anchor Books.

Littlewood, Thomas B. 1977. *The Politics of Population Control.* Notre Dame: University of Notre Dame Press.

Lovenduski, Joni, and Joyce Outshoorn, eds. 1986. *The New Politics of Abortion.* London: Sage.

Lowi, Theodore J. 1964. "American Business, Public Policy, Case Studies, and Political Theory." *World Politics* 16:677–715.

Lucas, Roy. 1968. "Federal Constitutional Limitations on the Enforcement and Administration of State Abortion Statutes." *North Carolina Law Review* 46:730–78.

Luker, Kristin. 1984. *Abortion and the Politics of Motherhood.* Berkeley: University of California Press.

MacAndrew, Barbara. 1995. "A Victory for Choice." *Maclean's,* February 13, 58.

McCormick, E.P. 1975. *Attitudes Toward Abortion.* Lexington, MA: Lexington Books.

McDaniel, Susan A. 1985. "Implementation of Abortion Policy in Canada as a Women's Issue." *Atlantis,* spring, 74–82.

McIntosh, William Alex, and Jon P. Alston. 1977. "Acceptance of Abortion Among White Catholics and Protestants, 1962 and 1975." *Journal for the Scientific Study of Religion* 16:295–303.

McIntosh, William Alex, Letitia T. Alston, and Jon P. Alston. 1979. "The Differential Impact of Religious Attendance on Attitudes Toward Abortion." *Review of Religious Research* 20:195–213.

Maclean's. 1994. "Abortion Pill Offered." February 28, 33.

March, James, and Johan Olsen. 1989. *Rediscovering Institutions: The Organizational Basis of Politics.* New York: Free Press.

Marcus, Ruth, and Joe Pichirallo. 1985. "Intensive Investigation Led to Clinic Bombing Arrests." *Washington Post,* January 21.

Marmor, Theodore R. 1991. "Canada's Health Care System: A Model for the United States,?" *Current History* 90:422–27.

Marsh, David, and Joanna Chambers. 1981. *Abortion Politics.* London: Junction Books.

Marsh, David, and Melvyn Read. 1988. *Private Members Bills.* London: Cambridge University Press.

Maxwell, Carol J. 1994. " 'Where's the Land of Happy?' Individual Meaning and Collective Antiabortion Activism." In *Abortion Politics in the United States and Canada,* edited by Ted G. Jelen and Marthe A. Chandler, pp. 89–106. Westport, CT: Praeger.

Medical Tribune. 1966. "Law on Abortion in California Target of Revision Campaign." December 12, 1, 24.

———. 1964. "Social, Economic Basis for Abortion Upheld." October 31–November 1, 21–22.

Meier, Kenneth J., and Deborah R. McFarlane. 1993. "Abortion Politics and Abortion Funding Policy." In *Understanding the New Politics of Abortion,* edited by Malcolm L. Goggin, pp. 249–67. Newbury Park, CA: Sage Publications.

Merelman, Richard M. 1991. *Partial Visions: Culture and Politics in Britain, Canada, and the United States.* Madison: University of Wisconsin Press.

Meyer, David S., and Suzanne Staggenborg. 1995. "Countermovement Dynamics in Federal Systems: A Comparison of Abortion Politics in Canada and the United States." Paper presented at the annual meeting of the American Political Science Association, Chicago.

Mezey, Susan Gluck. 1983. "Civil Law and Common Law Traditions: Judicial Review and Legislative Supremacy in West Germany and Canada." *International and Comparative Law Quarterly* 32:689–707.

Mezey, Susan Gluck, Raymond Tatalovich, and Michael Walsh. 1994. "Keeping Abortion Clinics Open: The Importance of *Ragsdale v. Turnock* in the Post-*Casey* Era." *Policy Studies Review* 13:111–26.

Millns, Susan, and Brian Thompson. 1994. "Constructing British Abortion Law: The Role of the Legislature, the Judiciary, and European Institutions." *Parliamentary Affairs* 47:190–202.

Modern Medicine. 1967. "Abortion: The Doctor's Dilemma." April 24, 12–14, 16, 22, 26, 30, 32.

Moe, Terry M. 1985. "The Politicized Presidency." In *The New Direction in American Politics,* edited by John E. Chubb and Paul K. Peterson, pp. 235–71. Washington, DC: Brookings Institution.

Mohr, James C. 1978. *Abortion in America: The Origins and Evolution of National Policy, 1800–1900.* New York: Oxford University Press.

Monroe, Kristen R., Michael C. Barton, and Ute Klingemann. 1991. "Altruism and the Theory of Rational Action." In *The Economic Approach to Politics,* edited by Kristen Renwick Monroe, pp. 317–52. New York: HarperCollins.

Mooney, Christopher A., and Mei-Hsien Lee. 1995. "Legislating Morality in the American States: The Case of Pre-Roe Abortion Regulation Reform." *American Journal of Political Science* 39:599–627.

Morton, F.L. 1992. *Morgentaler v. Borowski: Abortion, the Charter, and the Courts.* Toronto: McClelland and Stewart.

Morton, F.L., and Rainer Knopff. 1992. "The Supreme Court as the Vanguard of the Intelligentsia: The Charter Movement as Postmaterialist Politics." *In Canadian Constitutionalism, 1791–1991,* edited by Janet Ajzenstat, pp. 57–80. Ottawa: Canadian Study of Parliament Group.

Moyser, George. 1979. "Voting Patterns on 'Moral' Isssues in the British House of Commons, 1964–1969." Paper presented at the Conference on Power and Religion, London School of Economics, October.

Muldoon, Maureen. 1991. *The Abortion Debate in the United States and Canada.* New York: Garland Publishing.

Nathan, Richard P. 1983. *The Administrative Presidency.* New York: John Wiley.

———. 1975. *The Plot That Failed: Nixon and the Administrative Presidency.* New York: John Wiley.

The Nation. 1968. "Humane Doctors, Inhumane Law." February 26, 261.

National Abortion Rights Action League. 1992. *Who Decides? A State-by-State Review of Abortion Rights.* 3rd ed. Washington, DC: NARAL Foundation.

National Advisory Council on the Status of Women. 1983–1984. *Annual Report.* Ottawa.

———. 1976–1977. *Annual Report.* Ottawa.

———. 1975–1976. *Annual Report.* Ottawa.

Nevitte, Neil, William P. Brandon, and Lori Davis. 1993. "The American Abortion Controversy: Lessons from Cross-National Evidence." *Politics and the Life Sciences* 12:19–30.

Newsweek. 1989a. "Abortion and the Churches." July 24, 45–46.

———. 1989b. "The Future of Abortion." July 17, 15.

———. 1966a. "Test Case." June 6, 58.

———. 1966b. "The Abortion Epidemic." November 14, 92.

New York Times. 1994. "Canadian Abortion Clinics Under Guard After Shooting." November 10.

———. 1992a. "Compare and Contrast: Quotes From the Platforms." August 16.

———. 1992b. "Presbyterian Church Moderates Policy Favoring Abortion Rights." June 10.

———. 1990. "AMA Supports Testing of French Abortion Pill." June 29.

———. 1974a. "Catholic Conference Is Sued as Lobbyist." May 21.

———. 1974b. "Court Rejects Suit Asserting Catholics Lobby on Abortion." May 25.

———. 1965. "A New Abortion Law." February 13.

Oliver, C. 1983. "Abortions Under Attack." *Canadian Forum* 62:37, 42.

Olson, Mancur Jr. 1969. *The Logic of Collective Action: Public Goods and the Theory of Groups.* New York: Schocken Books.

O'Neil, Maureen, and Sharon Sutherland. 1996. "The Machinery of Women's Policy: Implementing the RCSW." In *Women and the Canadian State,* edited by Carolyn Andrew and Sanda Rodgers. Montreal: McGill-Queens Press.

O'Neill, Timothy J. 1985. *Bakke and the Politics of Equality: Friends and Foes in the Classroom of Litigation.* Middletown, CT: Wesleyan University Press.

Oreskes, Michael. 1988. "Delegates Conservative, Poll Shows." *New York Times,* August 14.

Overby, E. Marvin, Raymond Tatalovich, and Donley T. Studlar. 1995. "Free Voting on Abortion in the Canadian House of Commons." Unpublished manuscript.

Pagel, Stacey. 1989. "Key House Votes on Abortion." *Congressional Quarterly Weekly Report,* August 5, 2021.

Pal, Leslie A. 1991. "How Ottawa Dithers: The Conservatives and Abortion Policy." In *How Ottawa Spends: The Politics of Fragmentation, 1991–92,* edited by Frances Abele, pp. 269–306. Ottawa: Carleton University Press.

———. 1987. *Public Policy Analysis: An Introduction.* Toronto: Methuen.

Pear, Robert. 1994. "States Rebelling at Federal Order to Cover Abortion." *New York Times,* January 5.

———. 1988a. "U.S. Suspends Plan to Cut Off Funds for Abortion Ties." *New York Times,* March 4.

———. 1988b. "Rule on Abortion Counseling Is Blocked." *New York Times,* February 17.

———. 1987a. "Profile: Nabers Cabanias; 'The Last Job a Normal Person Would Want.' " *New York Times,* September 16.

———. 1987b. "U.S. Issues Limits on Abortion Aid by Family Clinics." *New York Times,* August 30.

———. 1987c. "U.S. Aide Fights Abortion Policy Ouster." *New York Times,* July 4.

Peltzman, Sam. 1984. "Constituent Interest and Congressional Voting." *Journal of Law and Economics* 27:181–210.

Peterson, Larry R., and Armand L. Mauss. 1976. "Religion and the 'Right to Life': Correlates of Opposition to Abortion." *Sociological Analysis* 37:243–254.

Phillips, Susan D. 1991. "Meaning and Structure in Social Movements: Mapping the Network of National Canadian Women's Organizations." *Canadian Journal of Political Science* 24:755–82.

Pierce, John C., Mary Ann E. Steger, Brent S. Steel, and Nicholas P. Lovrich. 1992. *Citizens, Political Communication, and Interest Groups.* New York: Praeger.

Plissner, Martin, and Warren J. Mitofsky. 1988. "The Making of the Delegates, 1968–1988." *Public Opinion,* September-October, 45–46.

Pomeroy, Richard, and Lynn C. Landman. 1973. "American Public Opinion and Abortion in the Early Seventies." In *The Abortion Experience,* edited by Howard J. Osofsky and Joy D. Osofsky, pp. 482–95. New York: Harper and Row.

Pomper, Gerald M. 1992. "The Presidential Election." In *The Election of 1992,* edited by Gerald M. Pomper, pp. 132–56. Chatham, NJ: Chatham House Publishers.

Potts, Malcolm, Peter Diggory, and John Peel. 1977. *Abortion.* Cambridge: Cambridge University Press.

Powell, Walter, and Paul DiMaggio, eds. 1991. *Institutionalism in Organizational Analysis.* Chicago: University of Chicago Press.

Presthus, Robert. 1973. *Elite Accommodation in Canadian Politics.* Toronto: Cambridge University Press.

Purdum, Todd S. 1996. "President Vetoes Measure Banning Type of Abortion." *New York Times,* April 11.

Pym, Bridget. 1974. *Pressure Groups and the Permissive Society.* Newton Abbot, Canada: David and Charles.

Read, Melvyn, David Marsh, and David Richards. 1994. "Why Did They Do It? Voting on Homosexuality and Capital Punishment in the House of Commons." *Parliamentary Affairs* 47:374–86.

Religious Coalition for Abortion Rights. 1978. "Sponsors and Members." Pamphlet.

Report by the Comptroller General of the United States. 1982. *Restrictions on Abortion and Lobbying Activities in Family Planning Programs Need Clarification.* GAO/HRD-82-106. September 24. Washington, DC: U.S. Government Printing Office.

Rich, Spencer. 1987. "Thomas R. Burke: Tough Talking Administrator a Target for HHS Critics." *Washington Post,* April 6.

Richards, Peter. 1970. *Parliament and Conscience.* London: Allen and Unwin.

Ridgeway, James. 1963. "One Million Abortions." *The New Republic,* February 9, 14.

Riker, William H. 1964. *Federalism: Origin, Operation, Significance.* Boston: Little, Brown.

Roberts, Steven V. 1987. "U.S. Proposes Curb on Clinics Giving Abortion Advice." *New York Times,* July 31.

Roemer, Ruth. 1971. "Abortion Law Reform and Repeal: Legislative and Judicial Developments." In *Abortion and the Unwanted Child,* edited by Carl Reiterman, pp. 39–58. New York: Springer.

Rosenberg, Gerald N. 1991. *The Hollow Hope: Can Courts Bring About Social Change?* Chicago: University of Chicago Press.

Rosenberg, M.W. 1988. "Linking the Geographical, the Medical, and the Political in Analyzing Health Care Delivery Systems." *Social Science and Medicine* 26(1):179–86.

Rossi, Alice. 1967. "Public Views on Abortion." In *The Case for Legalized Abortion Now,* edited by Alan F. Guttmacher. Berkeley: Diablo.

Rovner, Julie. 1989. "Abortion Continues to Shape Hill Plans, Bush Policies." *Congressional Quarterly Weekly Report,* November 4, 2953–54.

Rubin, Eva R. 1987. *Abortion, Politics, and the Courts.* New York: Greenwood Press.

Samar, Vincent J. 1991. *The Right to Privacy: Gays, Lesbians, and the Constitution.* Philadelphia, PA: Temple University Press.

Sarvis, Betty, and Hyman Rodman. 1973. *The Abortion Controversy.* New York: Columbia University Press.

Savoie, Donald J. 1994. *Thatcher, Reagan, Mulroney: In Search of a New Bureaucracy.* Pittsburgh, PA: University of Pittsburgh Press.

Schwartz, Mildred. 1981. "Politics and Moral Causes in Canada and the United States." *Comparative Social Research* 4:65–90.

Scientific American. 1986. "Medicine: RU 486." December 29, 81.

Seelye, Katharine Q. 1994. "Accord Opens Way for Abortion Pill in U.S. in 2 Years." *New York Times,* May 17.

Segers, Mary C. 1995a. "The Pro-Choice Movement Post-*Casey:* Preserving Access." In *Abortion Politics in American States,* edited by Mary C. Segers and Timothy A. Byrnes, pp. 225–245. Armonk, NY: M.E. Sharpe.

———. 1995b. "The Catholic Church as a Political Actor." In *Perspectives on the Politics of Abortion,* edited by Ted G. Jelen, pp. 87–113. Westport, CT: Praeger.

Segers, Mary C., and Timothy A. Byrnes. 1995. *Abortion Politics in American States.* Armonk, NY: M.E. Sharpe.

Shils, Edward A. 1956. *The Torment of Secrecy.* Glencoe, IL: Free Press.

Silverberg, Helene. 1990. "The Abortion Debate and the American Welfare State." Paper presented at the annual meeting of the American Political Science Association, San Francisco.

Simpson, John H. 1994. "The Structure of Attitudes Toward Body Issues in the American and Canadian Population: An Elementary Analysis." In *Abortion Politics in the United States and Canada,* edited by Ted. G. Jelen and Marthe A. Chandler, pp. 145–60. Westport, CT: Praeger.

Skelton, George. 1989. "Most Americans Consider Abortion Immoral." *Los Angeles Times,* March 19.

Skerry, Peter. 1978. "The Class Conflict Over Abortion." *Public Interest.* 52:69–84.

Smith, T. Alexander. 1975. *The Comparative Policy Process.* Santa Barbara, CA: Clio Press.

Smith, T. Alexander, and Michael P. Bobic. 1990. "Testing Comparative Policy Theory: Lowian Analysis, Schattschneider's Shadow, and Independent Variables." Unpublished manuscript.

Smothers, Ronald. 1994. "Anti-Abortion Violence Rises Slightly, Study Finds." *New York Times,* December 22.

Spitzer, Robert J. 1987. *The Right to Life Movement and Third Party Politics.* New York: Greenwood Press.

Staggenborg, Suzanne. 1986. "Coalition Work in the Pro-Choice Movement: Organizational and Environmental Opportunities and Obstacles." *Social Problems* 33 (5):374–90.

Star, Jack. 1965. "Growing Tragedy of Illegal Abortion." *Look,* October 19, 149, 153, 155.

State Bar of Texas. 1990. *Recommendation* (Resolution on Abortion Neutrality). August. Chicago, IL: American Bar Association Library.

Statistics Canada. 1991. "Therapeutic Abortions 1990." *Health Reports* 3, no. 4 (supplement 9).

Statues of Canada. 1988. 37 Eliz. 2, vol. 14.

———. 1989–1990. 38–39 Eliz. 2.

Steinmo, Sven, Kathleen Thelen, and Frank Longstreth, eds. 1992. *Structuring Politics: Historical Institutionalism in Comparative Analysis.* New York: Cambridge University Press.

Stewart, Barbara. 1989. "Prison Looms for Pro-lifers." *Alberta Report,* October 2, 46–48.

Strickland, Ruth Ann, and Marcia Lynn Whicker. 1992. "Political and Socio-Economic Indicators of State Restrictiveness Toward Abortion." *Policy Studies Journal* 20:598–617.

———. 1986. "Banning Abortion: An Analysis of Senate Votes on a Bimodal Issue." *Women and Politics* 6(1):41–56.

Sutherland, Sharon L. 1995a. "The Problem of Dirty Hands in Politics: Peace in the Vegetable Trade." *Canadian Journal of Political Science* 28:479–507.

———. 1995b. "Executives and Public Administration in Canada, Mexico, and the United States." Paper presented at the Conference on Political Systems of North America: Conflicts and Convergences, National Autonomous University of Mexico, Mexico City, May 17–19.

Tatalovich, Raymond. 1988. "Abortion: Prochoice Versus Prolife." In *Social Regulatory Policy: Moral Controversies in American Politics,* edited by Raymond Tatalovich and Byron W. Daynes, pp. 177–209. Boulder, CO: Westview Press.

———. 1971. "After Medicare: Political Determinants of Social Change in the American Medical Association." Ph.D. dissertation, University of Chicago.

Tatalovich, Raymond, and Byron W. Daynes. 1993. "The Lowi Paradigm, Moral Conflict, and Coalition-Building: Pro-Choice Versus Pro-Life." *Women and Politics* 13(1):39–66.

———. 1989. "The Geographical Distribution of U.S. Hospitals with Abortion Facilities." *Family Planning Perspectives,* March-April, 81–84.

———. Eds. 1988. *Social Regulatory Policy: Moral Controversies in American Politics.* Boulder, CO: Westview Press.

————. 1981a. *The Politics of Abortion.* New York: Praeger.

————. 1981b. "The Trauma of Abortion Politics." *Commonweal* 108:644–49.

Tatalovich, Raymond, L. Marvin Overby, and Donley T. Studlar. 1993. "Patterns of Abortion Voting in the Canadian House of Commons." Paper presented at the annual meeting of the Canadian Political Science Association, Ottawa.

Tatalovich, Raymond, and David Schier. 1993. "The Persistence of Ideological Voting on Abortion Legislation in the House of Representatives, 1973–1988." *American Politics Quarterly* 21:125–39.

Tatalovich, Raymond, and Ruth Ann Strickland. 1995. "Supply and Demand: Delivery Systems, *Roe v. Wade,* and Abortion Rates." Unpublished manuscript.

Tatalovich, Raymond, and Donley T. Studlar. 1995. "Abortion Policy Implementation in Canada and the United States." *American Review of Canadian Studies* (summer-autumn): 203–17.

Tedrow, Lucky M., and E.R. Mahoney. 1979. "Trends in Attitudes Toward Abortion: 1972–1976." *Public Opinion Quarterly,* summer, 181–89.

Thorne, Susan. 1990. "Private Member's Bill: Success Stories in Canada's Parliament." *The New Federation,* February-March, 21–23.

Time. 1989. "The Battle Over Abortion." July 17, 63.

————. 1967. "The Desperate Dilemma of Abortion." October 13, 33.

Tofani, Loretta. 1985. "Justice Dept. Limits Role in Abortion Harassment." *Washington Post,* April 4.

Tolchin, Martin. 1989. "Koop's Stand on Abortion's Effect Surprises Friends and Foes Alike." *New York Times,* January 11.

Toner, Robin. 1993. "Clinton Orders Reversal of Abortion Restrictions Left by Reagan and Bush." *New York Times,* January 23.

————. 1988. "Probable Appointee Assures Lawmakers on Abortion Views." *New York Times,* December 22.

Tremblay, Manon. 1991. "La Question de l'avortement au Parlement canadien: de l'importance due genre dans l'orientation des debats." *Canadian Journal of Women and the Law* 4(2):459–76.

Tushnet, Mark. 1989. "Rights: An Essay in Informal Political Theory." *Politics and Society* 17: 403–51.

United Nations Development Programme. 1994. *Human Development Report, 1994.* New York: Oxford University Press.

Uslander, Eric M., and Ronald E. Weber. 1980. "Public Support for Pro-Choice Abortion Policies in the Nation and States: Changes and Stability after the *Roe* and *Doe* Decisions." In *The Law and Politics of Abortion,* edited by Carl E. Schneider and Maris A. Vinovskis, pp. 206–23. Lexington, MA: Lexington Books.

Van Loon, Richard J., and Michael S. Whittington. 1971. *The Canadian Political System: Environment, Structure, and Process.* Toronto: McGraw-Hill.

Vickers, J., P. Rankin, and C. Appelle. 1993. *Politics as if Women Mattered: A Political Analysis of the National Action Committee on the Status of Women.* Toronto: University of Toronto Press.

Vinovskis, Maris A. 1980a. "The Politics of Abortion in the House of Representatives in 1976." In *The Law and Politics of Abortion,* edited by Carl E. Schneider and Maris A. Vinovskis, pp. 224–61. Lexington, MA: Lexington Books.

————. 1980b. "Abortion and the Presidential Election of 1976: A Multivariate Analysis of Voting Behavior." In *The Law and Politics of Abortion,* edited by Carl E. Schneider and Maris A. Vinovskis, pp. 184–205. Lexington, MA: Lexington Books.

Walls, Sharon. 1982. "Abortion Law and Improved Abortion Services." Unpublished manuscript. Ottawa: Victoria Caucus of Women and the Law.

Washington Post. 1985. "Editorial: The Bombing Arrests." January 22.

Wattier, Mark J., Byron W. Daynes, and Raymond Tatalovich. 1997. "Abortion Attitudes, Gender, and Candidate Choice in Presidential Elections: 1972 to 1992." *Women and Politics* 17(1).

Wattier, Mark J., and Raymond Tatalovich. 1995. "Senate Voting on Abortion Legislation Over Two Decades: Testing a Reconstructed Partisanship Variable." *American Review of Politics* 16:167–83.

Weaver, R. Kent, and Bert A. Rockman, eds. 1993. *Do Institutions Matter?* Washington, DC: Brookings Institution.

Weil, Martin, and Victoria Churchville. 1985. "Bombing Suspect Denies Charges." *Washington Post,* January 21.

Wetstein, Matthew E. 1996. *Abortion Rates in the United States.* Albany, NY: State University of New York Press.

Wickens, Barbara, with Nora Underwood. 1988. "Abortion Warfare." *Maclean's,* November 7, 51.

Wilcox, Clyde. 1995. "The Sources and Consequences of Public Attitudes Toward Abortion." In *Perspectives on the Politics of Abortion,* edited by Ted G. Jelen, pp. 55–86. Westport, CT: Praeger.

———. 1989. "Political Action Committees and Abortion: A Longitudinal Analysis." *Women and Politics* 9(1):1–19.

Wills, Garry. 1989. " 'Save the Babies.' " *Time,* May 1, 26–28.

Wilson, Woodrow. 1887. "The Study of Administration." *Political Science Quarterly* 2:197–222.

Wines, Michael. 1993. "Elders Confirmed as Surgeon General." *New York Times,* September 8.

———. 1989. "Justice Dept. Lawyers Assail Anti-Abortion Effort." *New York Times,* March 26.

Witt, Elder. 1986a. "Private Choices Are Shielded: Court Renews Abortion Rights, Strikes 'Baby Doe' Regulations." *Congressional Quarterly Weekly Report,* June 14, 1334.

———. 1986b. "Record Number of Advisory Briefs: Reagan Crusade Before Court Unprecedented in Intensity." *Congressional Quarterly Weekly Report,* March 15, 616–18.

———. 1985. "Reagan vs. Court: A Continuing Crusade." *Congressional Quarterly Weekly Report,* July 20, 1463.

Wolinsky, Howard. 1991. "Doctor Lag Limits Access to Abortion, Groups Say." *Chicago Sun-Times,* May 1.

Wolpert, Robin, and Gerald N. Rosenberg. 1990. "The Least Dangerous Branch: Market Forces and the Implementation of *Roe.*" Paper presented at the annual meeting of the American Political Science Association, San Francisco.

World Bank. 1994. *World Development Report, 1994.* New York: Oxford University Press.

Cases

Beal v. Doe, 432 U.S. 438 (1977).

Belotti v. Baird, 428 U.S. 132 (1976).

Belotti v. Baird, 443 U.S. 622 (1979).

Benten v. Kessler, 112 S.Ct. 2929 (1992).

Bigelow v. Virginia, 421 U.S. 809 (1975).

Borowski v. Canada (Attorney General), [1989] 1 S.C.R. 342 (S.C.C.).

Bowers v. Hardwick, 478 U.S. 186 (1986).

Boyd v. United States, 116 U.S. 616 (1886).
Bray v. Alexandria Women's Health Clinic, 506 U.S. 263 (1993).
Brown v. Board of Education, 347 U.S. 483 (1954).
Carey v. Population Services International, 431 U.S. 678 (1977).
City of Akron v. Akron Center for Reproductive Health, 462 U.S. 416 (1983).
Colautti v. Franklin, 439 U.S. 379 (1979).
Connecticut v. Menillo, 423 U.S. 9 (1975).
Doe v. Bolton, 410 U.S. 179 (1973).
Eisenstadt v. Baird, 405 U.S. 438 (1972).
Griswold v. Connecticut, 381 U.S. 479 (1965).
Grove City College v. Bell, 104 S.Ct. 1211 (1984).
Harris v. McRae, 448 U.S. 297 (1980).
H.L. v. Matheson, 450 U.S. 398 (1981).
Hodgson v. Minnesota, 497 U.S. 417 (1990).
Katz v. United States, 389 U.S. 347 (1967).
Loving v. Virginia, 388 U.S. 1 (1967).
McCready (1909) 14 C.C.C. 481.
Madsen v. Women's Health Center, 114 S. Ct. 2516 (1994).
Maher v. Roe, 432 U.S. 464 (1977).
Meyer v. Nebraska, 262 U.S. 390 (1923).
Morgentaler v. The Queen, [1988] 1 S.C.R. 30 (S.C.C.).
National Organization for Women v. Scheidler, 510 U.S. 249 (1994).
Ohio v. Akron Center for Reproductive Health, 497 U.S. 502 (1990).
People v. Belous, 71 Cal. 2d 954, 458 P. 2d 194 (1969).
Pierce v. Society of Sisters, 268 U.S. 510 (1925).
Planned Parenthood Association of Kansas City v. Ashcroft, 462 U.S. 476 (1983).
Planned Parenthood of Central Missouri v. Danforth, 428 U.S. 552 (1976).
Planned Parenthood of Southeastern Pennsylvania v. Casey, 505 U.S. 833 (1992).
Poelker v. Doe, 432 U.S. 59 (1977).
Prince v. Massachusetts, 321 U.S. 158 (1994).
R. v. Bourne, [1939] 1 K.B. 687.
R. v. Morgentaler, (1975) 53 D.L.R. (3d) 203.
R. v. Morgentaler, 85 C.C.C. (3d) 118 (1993).
R. v. Newton and Stungo [1958] Crim. L.R. 469.
Regents of the University of California v. Bakke, 98 S.Ct. 3140 (1978).
Roe v. Wade, 410 U.S. 113 (1973).
Rust v. Sullivan, 111 S.Ct. 1759 (1990).
Simopoulos v. Virginia, 462 U.S. 506 (1983).
Skinner v. Oklahoma, 316 U.S. 535 (1942).
Stanley v. Georgia, 394 U.S. 557 (1969).
Terry v. Ohio, 392 U.S. 1 (1968).
Thornburgh v. American College of Obstetricians and Gynecologists, 476 U.S. 747 (1986).
Tremblay v. Daigle, [1989] 2 S.C.R. 530 (S.C.C.).
United States v. Vuitch, 402 U.S. 62 (1971).
Webster v. Reproductive Health Services, 492 U.S. 490 (1989).
Williams v. Zbaraz, 448 U.S. 358 (1980).
Zbaraz v. Hartigan, 108 S.Ct. 479 (1987).

Index

Raymond Tatalovich (Ph.D., University of Chicago) is a professor of political science at Loyola University of Chicago, where he specializes in American politics and the study of moral conflicts in public policy. Among his most recent publications are *Nativism Reborn: The Official English Language Movement and the American States* (1995) and *The Modern Presidency and Economic Policy* (1994). Dr. Tatalovich is a member of both the American Political Science Association and the Canadian Political Science Association.

DATE DUE